The Second Battle of the Marne

MICHAEL S. NEIBERG

THE SECOND BATTLE OF THE MARNE

Twentieth-Century Battles

Spencer C. Tucker, editor

This famous propaganda poster shows a soldier who has "twice held and vanquished on the Marne" urging his civilian peers to keep up their morale for the final victory. Library of Congress.

THE
SECOND BATTLE
OF
THE MARNE

MICHAEL S. NEIBERG

INDIANA UNIVERSITY PRESS

BLOOMINGTON AND INDIANAPOLIS

This book is a publication of

Indiana University Press
601 North Morton Street
Bloomington, IN 47404-3797 USA

http://iupress.indiana.edu

Telephone orders	800-842-6796
Fax orders	812-855-7931
Orders by e-mail	iuporder@indiana.edu

Manufactured in the United States of America

Library of Congress Cataloging-in-Publication Data

Neiberg, Michael S.
The Second Battle of the Marne / Michael S. Neiberg.
    p. cm. — (Twentieth-century battles)
Includes bibliographical references and index.
ISBN-13: 978-0-253-35146-3 (cloth)
1. Marne, 2nd Battle of the, France, 1918. I. Title.
D545.M35N45 2008
940.4'34—dc22
                                                    2007043237

1 2 3 4 5 13 12 11 10 09 08

CONTENTS

MAPS

ACKNOWLEDGMENTS

THEY SAY BREAKFAST is the most important meal of the day, and it certainly was for this project. At the 2006 Society for Military History Conference in Manhattan, Kansas, I had the good fortune to sit next to Spencer Tucker at a breakfast hosted by ABC-CLIO. Spence and I had worked together on a few ABC-CLIO projects, so it seemed natural for me to go. I almost slept through it, and if I had, this book might never have been written. Over coffee and a buffet breakfast, Spence began talking to me about his Twentieth-Century Battles series, one volume of which (H. P. Willmott's book on Leyte Gulf) had won a prize at that year's meeting. Spence asked me if I thought any World War I battles needed to be included in the series. I answered that the Second Battle of the Marne was, in my view, the most important twentieth-century battle about which there was no scholarly monograph. Before my coffee cup was empty, Spence had talked me into writing this book. I thank him and Indiana University Press editor Robert Sloan for their support in getting this project started.

I am also grateful first and foremost to my Southern Miss comrade in arms, Andrew Wiest, for reading these chapters, providing me with excellent criticism, and helping me to improve both my scholarship and my darts game. Bill Astore and John Grenier, close friends, excellent historians, and wonderful editors, also read the manuscript and helped me to fine-tune my ideas. Several World War I scholars, most notably Mark Grotelueschen, Dennis Showalter, Gary Sheffield, Bill Philpott, Martin Alexander, and Jennifer Keene, all graciously listened to ideas and offered their suggestions. I'd like to single out two other people for special assistance in this project. David Zabecki went far out of his way to help me sharpen some finer points about the German side, without which this book might have become too one-sided. Robert "Bo" Bruce and I spent almost a week together on the Second Marne, Meuse-Argonne, Champagne, and Verdun battlefields, and I benefited enormously from our discussions. Walking the ground is always key to understanding a battle, and walking it with a friend who is also an expert is irreplaceable. Any errors that remain in this book are mine, not theirs. All translations from the French are also mine.

It is my great fortune to have so many friends and colleagues upon whom I can call for advice and help. Partha Mazumdar, who has now been one of my closest friends for more than twenty-five years, provided tremendous hospitality during a research trip to London. I would also like to thank the late Elliott Pood, Kyle Zelner, and Kevin Dougherty for making Southern Miss a first-rate place to think about the problems of military history. Christian Pinnen graciously offered me photographs taken by his grandfather, and David Barber took time from his busy schedule to prepare maps. Thanks also go to Stephen Sloan, who helped me track down an oral history, and Shelia Smith, without whom I could never accomplish all the tasks I am assigned here at Southern Miss. Edward Brady and Tony Urbanik provided research assistance that made this project possible. I would also like to thank the staff of the Military History Institute in Carlisle, Pennsylvania, especially Michael Lynch, Louise Arnold-Friend, David Keough, and Isabel Manske. As always, the staffs of the Imperial War Museum, the British Library, and the Liddell Hart Centre provided the excellent services to which researchers have become accustomed. I would like to single out Christopher Hunt at the Imperial War Museum for help above and beyond the call of duty. My last two visits to the Liddell Hart Centre have coincided with a broken air conditioner during a heat wave and a flood in the building. In case it's me, I promise to stay away for a little while.

A few words in the acknowledgments will never be able to thank my wife, Barbara, and my two daughters, Claire and Maya, for all that they do to make my life and work so rewarding. Although I doubt she will remember it, Claire was on the Second Marne battlefields with me in 2003. Her cheerful presence stood at a marked contrast to the events of 1918, and in her own way she helped me to understand the motivations of the men who fought there. I dedicate this book to my two daughters, for making my life happy enough that I can think about something as ugly as war.

THE SECOND BATTLE OF THE MARNE

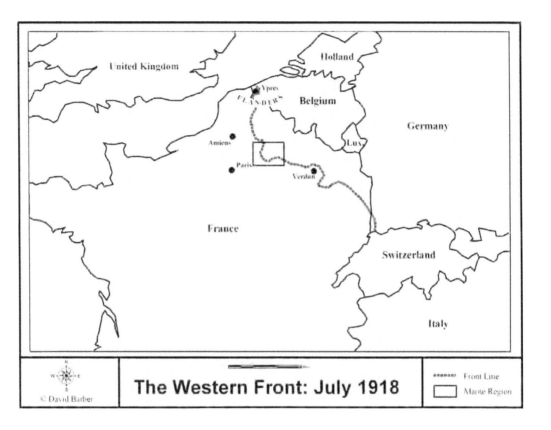

The Western Front: July 1918

© David Barber

Front Line
Marne Region

INTRODUCTION:
THE TWO MARNES

[Allied Supreme Commander General Ferdinand] Foch was in
the best of spirits. He told me that after three hours' bombardment, the Enemy had attacked at 4am this morning on two
fronts east and west of Rheims. East of Rheims on a front of
26 miles, and west of Rheims on a front of 29 miles. A front of
16 miles about Rheims itself was not attacked. The total front
attacked seems therefore to be about 55 miles.
— Diary Entry of British Field Marshal
Sir Douglas Haig, Monday 15 July 1918

THE PICTURESQUE AND pastoral beauty of the Marne River valley belies
its violent past. Twice during the course of World War I this peaceful
region sat at the center of a massive battle. Both times, a German army
had advanced into the valley, appearing, at least to Allied eyes, to pose a
direct threat to Paris. Both times, the British and the French had faced
the problem of improvising methods for fighting coalition war in the
direst of circumstances. In 1914, the Allied coalition had held by the
narrowest of margins. In 1918, the stage was set yet again for a battle
that might decide the war. As in 1914, the British and French would
need to work together to blunt a major German offensive. Unlike 1914,
however, the Allies could draw on the strength of the new American
Expeditionary Forces, even though they remained skeptical about the
AEF's amateurishness and lack of experience. Could they work together
to defeat the Germans once again, or would the Second Battle of the
Marne mark the beginning of the final German triumph of the war?

Two of the key decision makers of 1918, Ferdinand Foch and Douglas Haig, had served on the Marne River as allies together four years
earlier. In September 1914 the Germans crossed the Marne in the final
phase of their grand opening offensive in the west. Recognizing the failure of their initial war plan, the Germans had hastily developed a plan
for a double envelopment of Allied forces in the massive theater from
the eastern approaches to Paris to the region near Verdun. The Marne
sat directly in the center of the new battle area.

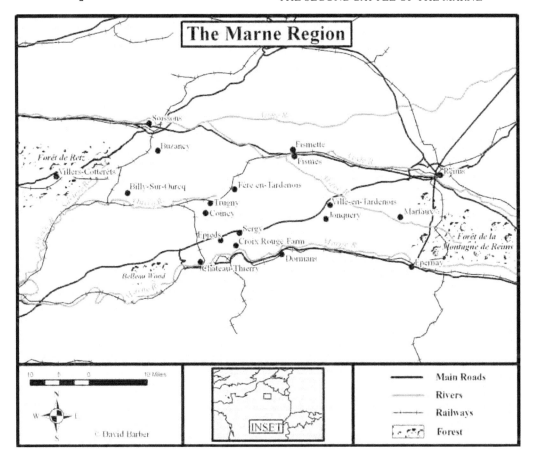

The Marne Region

As part of a larger effort to stop this German advance, Foch had been promoted and named commander of a hastily assembled French Ninth Army that he rushed into a dangerously exposed gap in the lines. He had ordered a surprise counterattack into a swamp known as the Marshes of St. Gond. The unexpected attack threw German timing off and exposed a gap between two German armies. Foch's dispatch from what later became known as the First Battle of the Marne in September 1914 read, "My center is giving way, my right is in retreat. Situation excellent. I attack." The actual orders he gave were less grandiloquent; Foch had ordered an attack because he realized that if he stayed in place, his new army would be overwhelmed, and if he retreated he would dangerously expose the flanks of the units adjacent to his. Thus, like Joshua Lawrence Chamberlain at Little Round Top in 1863, Foch realized that attacking was the best of a set of bad options. The proclamation, likely written after the battle for morale purposes, was broadcast throughout the Allied nations by public affairs officers anxious for something dramatic to publish, and it made Foch a household name across France. It also cemented his reputation as a fierce proponent of the offensive.

Haig in 1914 had been in command of the I Corps of the British Expeditionary Force (BEF). On the Marne, against rudimentary German field defenses, he had directed a charge that had disrupted German timing but failed to achieve the breakthrough that Haig still thought was possible. The failure of that charge led Haig to conclude that "the nature of the war had changed" and that the war would be long and would involve much less movement than he had originally assumed.[1] In December 1915, Haig was promoted to commander of the BEF, and, despite his bloody failures in 1916 and 1917 to deliver on repeated promises of breakthroughs of the German lines, he held on to his job.

The German commander of the 1918 Marne offensive, Crown Prince Wilhelm, had also been at the First Battle of the Marne, as commander of the German Fifth Army. His army had attacked near the French fortress city of Verdun, acting as the eastern hinge of the German army's attempt to envelop Allied forces east of Paris. Although his part of the operation failed, he had generally performed well and won the respect of German generals, many of whom had previously seen him as a spoiled and rakish playboy. After serving as one of the senior leaders at the Battle of Verdun in 1916 he had been promoted to command an army group. In 1917 he had recommended that the German civilian leadership sue for peace, believing that Germany could not win the war, but his spirits picked up in the wake of Germany's successes in the first few months of 1918. In July of that year, he led Germany's second major offensive on the Marne in four years, although most of the key strategic and operational decisions were made at German headquarters by General Erich Ludendorff.

Only the Americans were new to the Marne in 1918. They comprised a mix of prewar regular army divisions and locally based National Guard divisions, all hastily assembled for war. Inexperienced and trained under a hopelessly outdated doctrine, even the veterans were shockingly unready to fight. Jesse Hughes, a professional soldier from the American First Division, recalled his unit arriving at the front line in July with neither artillery nor gas masks. The staff officers and headquarters he found "so damned disorganized until it was a shame."[2] The Europeans who saw the American "doughboys" were virtually unanimous in their judgment that the Americans had excellent potential as soldiers, but there was much work to do before they would translate that potential into fighting power.

When the German offensive began on 15 July 1918, Foch went to his former headquarters in the small village of Mouchy le Châtel to meet with Haig. The two men had risen to great power since they had stood together on the same massive battlefield on the Marne four years earlier. As in 1914, they faced a monumental challenge, with grave and historic consequences if they failed. Despite the pressure on both of them, Haig recorded that he found Foch "in the best of spirits." An observer of the meeting might have been forgiven for wondering if Foch had taken leave of his senses, or if his habitual confidence had finally overcome reality. The offensive the two men now faced was the fifth major German operation since March; it targeted a 55-mile-long front held by Allied units that were tired and in desperate need of refitting. By the time Foch and Haig met, the German offensive had already crossed the Marne River and made penetrations of the Allied line as deep as five miles in places. Its main goals appeared to many in the Allied camp to be the critical rail junctures at Châlons and Rheims,[3] which the Germans might then use to assemble and supply forces for a move on Paris in force.

The offensive, according to Crown Prince Wilhelm, had been "an overwhelming scene." The German assault was preceded by a massive artillery barrage that included two thousand individual artillery guns. The crown prince recalled it as "a scene from the Inferno, an apocalyptic symphony of destruction." The crown prince's father, Germany's Kaiser Wilhelm II, had come to his son's headquarters to witness an expected triumph of German arms and to lead a victory procession into Rheims, the traditional coronation site of French kings.[4] The city had held out against heavy German shelling for four years, and sat as a thorn in the German side. The Rheims salient not only refused to fall to German might, it also impeded German rail communications in the area and complicated the concentration of troops and materiel. The tens of thousands of German artillery shells that had hit Rheims in the past four years might have obliterated its buildings and done serious damage to its magnificent cathedral, but the shelling had not removed the city's symbolic value to both sides. The German high command, fresh from four other successful offensives, was confident that the new

German methods would produce yet another major victory. Rumor had it that the kaiser had already counted Rheims as captured and that his staff had also prepared place cards for a celebratory dinner at the Hôtel Majestic in Paris.[5]

Nor was the serious threat to Rheims and Châlons the only concern on Foch's mind as he sat down to lunch with Haig. His American allies had officially been in the war for more than a year but had yet to translate their massive human and industrial potential into resources Foch could use to stop the series of massive German attacks. Their commander, General John J. Pershing, also showed a stubbornness and evasiveness on issues Foch considered critical. Pershing, supported by both secretary of war Newton Baker and President Woodrow Wilson, refused on principle to place his units under the command of European generals at any level. Foch agreed that for the most part American soldiers would fight better under American generals, but he believed that rules had to be bent or broken until the immediate crisis of the German offensives had passed. The Americans had agreed to increase the rate at which they sent men to Europe, but speed alone would not solve the problem. The Americans were eager, but woefully unprepared for the industrial, attritional war of 1918. Sending men to Europe faster only meant that they would arrive with even less training and less opportunity to learn the intricacies of modern war from their British and French allies.

Even as he had to look at problems to his front, Foch also had to look behind his back. In March, in the wake of the first powerful German offensive, the Allied governments had given Foch the power to coordinate the actions of the Allied armies, making him a kind of generalissimo in charge of Allied forces. The agreements empowering him were, however, left intentionally vague, and they allowed national commanders to appeal decisions they did not like to their national governments. The arrangement was far from satisfactory; Foch had the responsibility of a commander in chief, but none of the requisite authority. Foch could not give a direct order to the British, Belgian, Italian, or American armies. He could not even give a direct order to his own French army. General Henri-Philippe Pétain, a very different kind of man from Foch and one with whom Foch often disagreed, held that authority. Foch's position was difficult, to say the least.

Moreover, since he had been given his new authority, the war had not gone well for Foch and the Allies. The German Army had gained

1,200 square miles in the first two weeks of its spring offensives. German forces had come within 60 miles of Paris, close enough to begin random bombardments of the city with airplanes and massive long-range artillery pieces. The Germans brought in their 210mm "Paris Guns," with a remarkable 75-mile range. Each gun barrel by itself weighed 200 tons; each carriage and turntable weighed 500 tons more. The Germans fired 183 wildly inaccurate shells into Paris, from guns placed on railway sidings in the Marne sector, killing 256 people. Compared to the military losses of the western front, the 256 deaths in Paris seem infinitesimally small, but they were a novel and frighteningly random manifestation of violence to a city that had experienced little direct bloodshed; one shell crashed through a church on Good Friday, killing several worshippers. The shock and anger the shelling produced was thus far out of proportion to the actual damage it caused.

The casualties caused by this random German artillery shelling also seem minor in comparison to civilian casualties in later wars, but in 1918 they caused a great deal of panic. They also seemed to portend a German advance on the city. Large elements of the French government had fled Paris for the second time in the war in favor of remote Bordeaux. When the government fled, tens of thousands of Parisians, some with memories of the terrible days of the Paris Commune of 1871, fled as well. From the perspective of many people in the allied nations, the German war machine seemed to have figured out the secret to restoring mobility to warfare and appeared almost unstoppable.

The sense of panic touched Foch directly. Although he remained calm and told his wife to remain in Paris despite the government's departure and the German terror shelling, criticism of his leadership built. On June 4, French prime minister Georges Clemenceau (who had his own doubts about Foch) went to the Chamber of Deputies and gave an impassioned speech to save Foch's job from an angry group of frightened parliamentarians looking for scapegoats. Everyone who knew him knew Foch as a man of energy, confidence, and optimism, but how many more reverses could the Allies suffer without turning the blame on the commander?

In the heat and panic of the moment, few people on either side realized that the tremendous territorial gains the Germans had made had in fact placed them in a dangerous and exposed position. The territory they had gained had placed them further from their critical supply lines, and much of it had been so badly devastated that it made transportation even more difficult. Ludendorff's inability to fix definitive goals for his offensives ("We shall punch a hole," he said; "as for the rest we shall see.") further undermined their success. By May, Foch had spotted these flaws in the German offensives. All he needed was an opportunity to exploit German weaknesses, and the resources with which to strike.

The army that would have to defeat the German offensive and validate Foch's confidence was a combined force of French, British, American, and two Italian divisions. Foch would have to work through four national commanders, but without any real authority to issue orders under his own name. In the chaos of this battle, there would be no means to ensure that national divisions and brigades remained under national army and corps commanders. They would have to fight as a combined force, and find some way to overcome all of the problems that different languages, cultures, doctrines, and fighting styles entailed. As Ferdinand Foch knew, their success or failure might well determine the fate of Europe.

So why, given all of his problems, did Foch show up for his meeting with Haig in such high spirits? Because just days earlier he had taken a calculated risk, and now he knew for certain that he had been right. Although he was almost alone in his thinking, he now knew that this German offensive would be their last and that, all appearances to the contrary notwithstanding, the Allies would certainly win the war, perhaps before the year had ended.

ONE

JERUSALEM IN THE MARNE VALLEY

THE 1914 BATTLE of the Marne had immediately acquired legendary status in France and Great Britain. At the time, it was the largest battle ever fought, and involved more than 2 million men with battle lines stretching from Paris to Verdun, a distance of more than 160 miles. To the Allies, it represented the defeat of German grand designs in the west and the almost miraculous saving of Paris. The efforts of French General Joseph Gallieni to muster reinforcements and rush those men to the front in Parisian taxicabs added to the iconic nature of the "Miracle of the Marne." The Germans seemingly came so close to capturing Paris (and, presumably, to winning the war in the west in a single master stroke) that the battle has since become one of those famous "what if" moments, debated in coffee houses, pubs, beer gardens, and classrooms ever since.

Although other battles soon exceeded the Marne in terms of the numbers of men involved and the intensity of combat, the Marne always retained a sacred place in the memory and mythology of the war. The first Michelin guide to the battlefield, published in both France and Britain in 1919, described the battle as "theatrical" and compared it to the "old French traditions," including both the "suppleness of maneuver" characteristic of the Napoleonic period and the "enthusiasm" of the Revolution. It even went so far as to suggest that "the remembrance of the arresting on the soil of Gaul of the great barbarian invasions [had] inspired the Victory of the Marne."[1] The guide's capitalization of "victory" is significant, implying as it does the timeless and transcendent nature of the battle and the near sacred status of the Marne valley itself.

Even four years later, when men of the French 66th Infantry Regiment received their orders to march to Montmirail in the Marne sector, the very word "Marne" inspired them. The men remembered the Marne as having been the "tomb of [the Germans'] hopes" in 1914. The name was still to them, "This name that symbolizes all of the heroism of France defending its homes against invasion; this name that recalls the dear dead of the war's start, those who fell in repulsing the enemy in supreme effort and who wrote their names in gold letters on so many torn flags." In marching to the battlefield, the historian of the 66th compared the unit's soldiers to medieval crusaders seeing Jerusalem for the first time.[2]

Lost in the reflective glory attached to the First Battle of the Marne was the reality that, for as great a victory as the 1914 Battle of the Marne had been, it had been only a defensive success. It had also been a negative victory in the sense that the Allies had succeeded in preventing the Germans from achieving a breakthrough of their lines, but they had possessed neither the human strength nor the ammunition stocks to build on their momentum and pursue the Germans. By the time they had recovered enough of both to attack again, the Germans had entrenched on high ground. Once the so-called race to the sea had ended, the nature of the war had changed from mobility to the frustrating stasis that characterized the western front for the next three and half years. The Marne was thus a victory on an unusually large and important battlefield, but it had been an incomplete triumph that led not to victory in the war, but instead to the immobility of the trenches.

Despite the combats of 1914, the Marne River valley had escaped most of the horrors of war for nearly four years. During the race to the sea that followed the German reversal at the First Battle of the Marne, the Germans had selected high ground generally north and east of the Marne sector itself. The French held the rail junctions of Soissons at the western edge of the Marne sector and Rheims 35 miles away at its eastern edge, which allowed for consistent and reliable rail communications from Paris to the region and east to the fortifications of Verdun. The region in between Soissons and Rheims had few towns of any size, and most residents had long since fled to other parts of France, leaving an already underpopulated region even emptier.

If the Marne River valley was known for anything in the prewar years, it was undoubtedly for the world-famous eponymous export of its hinterland, champagne. Rheims and the nearby town of Epernay are world famous as rivals for the title of capital to champagne country. Each town had its own famous vineyards and family producers. The same chalky, cavernous terrain that aided in fermentation of champagne also permitted armies to marshal equipment, and even men, safely underground, making the Champagne region in some ways an ideal place to defend and, thanks to its comparative quiet, a relatively pleasant place to spend a war. British soldiers recalled buying "unheard of luxuries" from locals, such as ten-pound crocks of foie gras and all the champagne they could afford.[3]

But if the Marne Valley itself stayed relatively calm, three titanic battles raged nearby between 1915 and 1917. The bloody, but under-studied, 1915 French Champagne offensive occurred on the ground east of Rheims, gaining precious little for a tremendous sacrifice of men and munitions. The focal points of the murderous 1916 Battle of Verdun lay just 75 miles east of Rheims. A German breakthrough at Verdun would have placed Rheims and the Marne valley in a dangerously exposed spot and given it the responsibility of once again protecting the approaches to Paris, just 90 miles to the west. In 1917, French General Robert Nivelle chose the crests over the Aisne River valley 15 miles north of, and running basically parallel to, the Marne for his futile and bloody attempt to break the German lines.

Nevertheless, for all of the death and destruction that had happened nearby, the terrain of the Marne River valley remained relatively unscarred. It appeared largely as General Joseph Joffre had described it in 1914, *un joli fleuve* flowing gently through the bucolic French countryside. In 1918, one British soldier recalled the area as comprising "a pleasant well cultivated scene, unmarred by the shell holes, trenches, and barbed wire to which we had become so accustomed on the static front."[4] The Marne had almost no trench lines and, outside Soissons and Rheims, very little of the scarring of earth and crumbling of buildings caused by artillery that was so characteristic of front-line areas. An American soldier who arrived just hours before the German offensive began had time to write home that he was camping in "one of the prettiest places in France."[5]

The Marne sector certainly was picturesque, especially when compared to the moonscapes that Verdun, the Somme, and Ypres had become. The charm of the landscape also formed many of the area's key military features. The region was shaped by its five rivers, from north to south the Aisne, the Vesle, the Ardre, the Ourcq, and the Marne. All of them ran west to east except the Ardre, which ran northwest into the Vesle. To Americans accustomed to thinking of the Mississippi, the Ohio, and the Missouri when they thought of rivers, these five French rivers hardly merited the name. The historian of the American 4th Division noted that many of that unit's officers crossed the Ourcq without even taking notice of it. Others had reported "that they had passed a creek but were unable to find a river."[6]

But if the Ourcq and Vesle did not compare with the Mississippi, they could still provide important advantages to a determined defender. Their river banks rose as high as 200 meters; those above the Aisne, as Nivelle had cause to rue, rose even higher. The marshy ground around the rivers, moreover, made the movement of tanks, artillery, and other heavy equipment very difficult. The rivers themselves served, if not quite as brakes on large-scale movement, then at least as speed bumps. The Vesle River, according to one observer in 1918, "is not much to look at; a narrow, muddy, snake-like, sluggish-flowing stream winding through a partly wooded valley with more or less steeply inclining ridges on both sides. As a river, it little deserves the name, but as an obstacle to the passage of our troops, it proved more valuable to the Germans than a hundred dozen tons of barbed wire."[7] Even smaller streams and creeks had to be taken seriously. The Savières, a small creek southwest of Soissons that ran north to south, was "fordable everywhere" and did not present "an obstacle in itself," but the men of the French 48th Infantry Division still had to account for a valley 250 to 350 meters wide that was so marshy as to present "a very difficult crossing" for men, horses, and equipment alike.[8]

The Marne region also featured thick forests "plutonian in [their] darkness."[9] The two largest were the Forêt de la Montagne de Rheims south of Rheims and the Forêt de Villers-Cotterêts (also called the Forêt de Retz) southwest of Soissons. Everywhere in the region one could find wooded ravines and thick forests "through which roads proceeded like tunnels through gloom."[10] One British general, a veteran of the western front, had to call on a different part of the world to describe a small forest known as the Bois du Petit Champ: "I have never seen anything which more resembled the Burma jungles than that wood."[11] General Sir Alexander Godley also used the word "jungle" to describe the woods he saw in the eastern half of the Marne sector.[12]

The relative peace of the region's war experience had also allowed those farmers who chose to stay to continue to grow their crops. Tall grain fields, mostly corn and wheat, provided what General John Pershing later called "excellent cover" for infantry and machine gunners.[13] The historian of the West Yorkshire Regiment agreed, recalling the Marne region's "gently undulating corn land with the crops ripe for cutting and of sufficient height to afford excellent cover for attacking or defending troops." Even relative novices could see that this battle would be, as the West Yorks realized, "of a kind vastly different from anything they had previously gone through."[14] Trench warfare, the seemingly enduring condition of the First World War soldier's life, would not characterize this battle.

But trench warfare was all most of the men in the French, British, and German armies on the Marne knew. Their commanders might have remembered the fluid combat on this same ground four years earlier, but few of the men in the ranks were likely to have had that experience. The unprecedented casualty rates of First World War battles had taken a tremendous toll on the youth of Europe. Large and small battles merged together to create a world for soldiers that did not always allow for an easy bifurcation into periods of fighting and periods of rest. French veteran Jean-Norton Cru recalled "monotonous recurrence of days almost identical in their activity or their uneventfulness, the repetition of the same anguish under bombardment and the same anguish before the attack, the reduplication of the same periods of calm when joyous unconcern is powerless to still the same unvoiced grief at the thought of sudden death on some ever-threatening morrow."[15] The young men who formed the armies on the Marne had become older than their years and survivors of a baptism by fire theretofore unknown in human history.

The Hour of the Great Revenge:
The French Army on the Marne

Of all the armies on the Marne in 1918, the French army had both suffered the most and come the furthest since 1914. Unlike the Germans, the British, or the Americans, the French had for four years faced the task of repelling an invader from their home soil. The reality of the "true reign of terror"[16] put in place by the Germans in Belgium and

occupied France, embellished by creative Allied journalists, helped
to keep France dedicated to the Herculean (or perhaps more appropriately, Sisyphean) task of fighting an offensive war in an age where
defensive weapons dominated. The resulting long casualty lists were at
once inevitable and unproductive to the larger goal of liberation.

The tremendous battlefield losses suffered by the French army were
also a function of an antediluvian French military system that needed
redesigning, root and branch. Although it had many important thinkers and was second to none in élan and spirit, the French army that
fought on the Marne in 1914 was a relic of an earlier age. The French
army's famous red pants and bright képis constituted "the most irratio-
nal uniform ever known." Both heavy and brightly colored, the French
uniform was at once "a target and a burden" to the men who wore it,
slowing them down and making them stand out against the earth tones
in which they fought.[17]

Nor were French weapons much better suited to modern war than
French uniforms. Expecting a fast-moving war of pursuit, the French
had based their doctrine around the mobile and rapid-firing 75mm field
artillery piece. France had almost no heavy artillery at all at the outset
of the war, in part because there was little prestige, and few chances for
advancement, for officers working with a weapons system too heavy to
advance in glory with the infantry.[18] Expected to move forward with the
infantry to provide covering fire for troops on the move, the 75mm was
too light for the work demanded of it in 1914. Many units, moreover,
soon ran short of shells, or had far too many anti-personnel shrapnel
shells and far too few of the high-explosive shells needed to destroy
enemy field defenses.

Firing a relatively light shell on a flat trajectory, the 75mm soon
proved to have limited utility in the defensive conditions of 1915. During the trench war that ensued, French artillerists had to adapt the
75mm's battlefield role, and it always remained the most numerous
artillery piece in the French arsenal. Nevertheless, it was rarely used
in the pursuit role many had envisioned for it. The bayonet, the classic weapon of the French Revolutionary wars, was also at the center of
French doctrine, and, even more than the 75mm, it proved to be of little
use in trench warfare. Jean-Norton Cru called the army's faith in the
bayonet "the most inexcusable of staff illusions," and another veteran
recalled his comrades using their bayonets only "to cut meat or sharpen
their pencils."[19]

The French doctrine that led to the reliance on the 75mm and the bayonet was perhaps the fundamental flaw in the French system. French generals in 1914 held to a belief in the *offensive à outrance*[20] that was not quite as dim-witted as has often been caricatured, but was nonetheless nearly suicidal when matched against the battlefield conditions of 1914. The theory, expounded by officers such as Louis de Grandmaison and Foch, was more complex and elaborate than many scholars appreciate. It presumed that France's material inferiority relative to Germany made a long war of attrition unwinnable. It also presumed that France should not rely upon Russia or Britain to make unlimited commitments on France's behalf and, finally, that the attacking side could throw its enemy's plans off schedule and could benefit economically by living off of the enemy's land.

The theory had much to recommend it, as long as the guiding assumptions called for planning a short war. Preaching as it did the moral superiority of French national character to German, an offensive doctrine also held tremendous appeal in an era of nationalist revival. Unfortunately, attired and equipped as they were, French soldiers in 1914 had almost no chance of converting the theory into practice. French generals, on average older and in less physically fit condition than their German counterparts, had been so thoroughly indoctrinated into the offensive mindset that it took them much longer than it should have to adjust to new realities.[21] They also failed as a group to understand how to use aviation, artillery, and other arms to support their infantry; nor, as a group, could they be classified as innovators or deep military thinkers.[22] Foch, it should be noted, was a clear exception, and that might help to explain his rise to senior command in the wake of the war's early disasters.[23]

Given the reality of the German invasion of France, any French general in 1914 who wished to hold on to his job had to advocate attacking, but in the war's early months many did so haphazardly and recklessly, leading to thousands of unnecessary casualties. One study of the war's early campaigns noted that French divisions usually made the same mistakes, because their prewar training had been uniformly insufficient: they failed to reconnoiter the battlefield; failed to protect their lines by securing flanks; maintained weak liaisons with adjoining units; and made "absurdly imprudent attacks, unsupported by artillery fire."[24] The French army that fought on the Marne in 1914 looked and acted much more like the one that fought the Prussians in 1870 or the one that had fought imperial wars in Indochina and Africa than should have been the case.

Not so the French army that fought on the Marne in 1918. The red trousers and brightly colored cloth headgear of 1914 quickly disappeared in favor of uniforms of a bluish gray color, known to the men as "cigar smoke blue," and metal helmets based on the model of those worn by firefighters. Commanders went as well. Some, like Grandmaison, were killed leading men on the field of battle. Others, including two of France's five army commanders, ten corps commanders, and thirty-eight division commanders, were relieved of their jobs before 1914 was over, and usually replaced by younger and more capable officers. The dismissed officers were disproportionately older men, political appointees, and men who had not passed through the French *École Supérieur de Guerre.*

Recent studies by American historian Robert Doughty and French historian Michel Goya both underscore this lack of preparedness for modern war, but both equally credit the French army for its rapid learning process. Even after just one month, the French army had made critical adjustments that helped them win the First Battle of the Marne. The Germans, notes Goya, were "excellent professors," forcing the French to learn how to use terrain, support their actions with artillery fire, and coordinate their actions with nearby units.[25] That they did so despite a flawed doctrine and the loss of thousands of officers and NCOs in the war's first weeks speaks volumes about how quickly the French army improved.

French industry, despite losing its most valuable resource areas to the German occupation, performed truly amazing feats to supply French soldiers with new weapons. By the time of the Second Battle of the Marne, each French division had nine 75mm artillery batteries and one 155mm group under its direct command. A powerful reserve of artillery pieces (5,933 field and 5,355 heavy guns) stood by at the discretion of higher headquarters. Each French corps had at its disposal between four and six air squadrons; the French air force then numbered 770 airplanes. The French also had a massive fleet of tanks, including 540 light and 240 medium tanks, available to fight on the Marne in 1918.[26] At the conclusion of hostilities, France had 3,187 Renault FT-17 tanks in service.[27]

These reforms came at an almost unimaginable human cost. Although one thinks of Verdun and the disastrous Nivelle Offensive as the emblematic campaigns of the French war effort, France suffered more than half of its casualties before the end of 1915, when the process of reform was still in its adolescence, if not still in its infancy. Another 20 percent of France's total war casualties came in 1916, mostly at Verdun and on the Somme. By the time of the German offensive in July 1918 the French had already suffered 80 percent of all of the casualties they would suffer during the war, although no one knew that at the time.[28]

Remarkably enough, the morale of the French army held. The "acts of collective indiscipline" that followed the Nivelle Offensive seem in retrospect to be not only exceptional to the war's larger patterns, but also a reasonable response to the incompetent leadership and murderous tactics of the French high command during the offensive itself. As Leonard Smith, the incident's most eloquent historian, notes, the soldiers involved in those incidents almost never threatened violence against their officers, made the decision themselves to return to the trenches, and were careful never to place the French army in a position where the Germans might be able to take advantage.[29] Thus he and his co-authors conclude that "paradoxically, the French Army mutinies of 1917 became one of the Great War's most extraordinary exercises in patriotism," because they forced the French high command to rethink its operations, its tactics, even its handling of its own men.[30]

Indeed, there is plenty of evidence to show that by 1918 the French army's morale was not only high, but perhaps higher than it had been at any point since the outbreak of the war. To argue that the French army's morale in the latter months of the war was higher than many scholars have appreciated is not simultaneously an argument that French soldiers were not tired of the war and anxious for the return of peace. Nor is it inconsistent with arguing that French soldiers had real grievances with both their leaders and the French military system more generally. Nevertheless, one should not read too much into the Nivelle mutinies, if mutinies they were. The renewed German offensives in 1918, and their initial surprising successes, had created a sense of crisis that bound French soldiers together and gave them new reasons to fight even harder. They also provoked a sense of "shame and humiliation" in soldiers unable to prevent more civilian suffering and the abandonment of the capital.[31] Thus 1918 witnessed a rise in morale, even if it was *faute de mieux*. To cite one statistic among many, in 1918 only 0.88 percent of French conscripts refused to answer the call to serve, the lowest figure for any year of the war, and down significantly from 2.59 percent in

1915.[32] In short, the French, soldier and civilian alike, had little choice but to endure the horrors of the war because the alternatives (defeat, occupation, humiliation, and a possible rerun of the Paris Commune) were too horrifying to contemplate.

Still, the war took a terrible toll on French soldiers. Compared to the new Americans and even to the veteran British, French soldiers looked disheveled, tired, and worn. Despite Pétain's rather more lenient treatment of French soldiers (compared to that of his predecessors) and reforms to the French supply system, French soldiers still received less pay, less leave, and less frequent changes of uniform than their allies. Their grubby, unshaven appearance led to their ubiquitous nickname *poilu*, or "hairy one." Even more revealing is that the French word *poil* was more often used to describe the hair of animals than that of men.

Testimony from both foreign observers and French soldiers themselves supports the conclusion that the French army was far from fought out in 1918. The French soldier may have looked less kempt and less polished than his counterparts, but looks could be deceiving. British soldiers, who had plenty of cause to speak ill of an ally with whom there had been significant tensions, uniformly praised the *poilus* they met on the Marne. A veteran of the Argyll and Seaforth Highlanders recalled the French soldiers on the Marne as "active and useful," especially when compared to the "lousy looking mob" he saw in the two Italian divisions.[33] John Clarke MacDermott agreed, noting that "my general impression of these Frenchmen was that they were first-class troops, steady and reliable."[34] The official history of the 51st (Highland) Division agreed, noting "what magnificent men they are, and what a false impression of them is obtained from the odd and rather bedraggled French soldiers that were occasionally seen on leave in the zone of the British armies."[35] To cite one more example, the history of the 15th (Scottish) Division remembers the French soldiers on the Marne in 1918 as "big, stalwart men" and "an inspiring spectacle." Their commanding officer was "the very type an artist would select as a perfect soldier."[36]

The French soldiers were, of course, fighting to defend their own land against a hated invader, so it should not come as a surprise that their morale and motivation was high. Still, it has become almost axiomatic in the English-language literature to argue that the French army was worn out by the summer of 1918 and played clearly secondary roles in the fighting that ended the war.[37] How much of this impression is due to the ignominious collapse of the French army in 1940 is a question for another study, but it is clear that historians, especially in the English-speaking world, have badly misunderstood the morale of the French army in 1918.

This lacuna is both unfortunate and misleading. In quantitative terms, the French army dominated the Allied effort. In May 1918 the French army held 72 percent of the western front. By the time of the German Marne offensive, the French had 103 divisions, compared to 56 British divisions and 17 (double-strength) American divisions on the western front.[38]

Moreover, by 1918 there were few, if any, lasting signs of the 1917 morale crisis that had struck in the wake of the Nivelle Offensive. French soldiers themselves no longer spoke of disillusion, but of the need to see the war to a successful conclusion. To be sure, most of them were sick of the war and fed up with the hypocrisy and dislocations that the war produced. But by the time of the Marne, they sensed that the war was at its decisive point. The men of the 74th Regiment marched toward the Marne understanding that the time had come to stop the Germans or lose the war, and they were determined to do the former. One unit *journal de marche* noted, "We all know that the Boches cannot pass. Confidence! The hour of the great revenge is upon us."[39] Even well-known leftist "anti-war" writers such as Henri Barbusse, author of the best-selling French book to come out of the war, "never advocated anything but the most ferocious prosecution of the national struggle," although the left generally hoped that the war would produce a favorable environment for the spread of international socialism.[40]

Assessing the French home front is more complicated. French industry was producing 261,000 artillery shells and more than 6 million cartridges per day despite the loss of 50 percent of French coal, 64 percent of iron, and 58 percent of steel production to German occupation. The truly amazing accomplishments of French industry say much about the willingness of French civilians (especially the trade unions) to make major sacrifices for the war effort. To be sure, strikes were a common feature of the French home front, but even the leaders of those strikes were careful to state that they were not "defeatist" and that they would not allow their actions to give the Germans an advantage. Most strikes, therefore, lasted only a few days and caused only minor disruptions to production timetables.[41]

British and American soldiers noted generally warm receptions from French people, even if the cities and towns themselves were sad and dour places owing to the absence of young men. One British soldier noted being greeted with flowers, food, and wine on his unit's trip toward the Marne.[42] Nor was he alone in depicting scenes more reminiscent of the ecstatic early days of 1914 than of the more somber days of spring and summer, 1918. John Clarke MacDermott noted that civilians at a suburban Paris train station threw flowers at the men of his unit and sent them off with hearty "expressions of goodwill." He noted that French civilians were "rather elated" at the growing sense that "the tide of the war was about to change," an impression that the appearance of large numbers of British and American soldiers could only have increased. The random arrival of two German shells during the departure festivities undoubtedly underscored how important the presence of these Allied soldiers was to the future of Paris and France.[43]

The French countryside struck most visitors as much sadder than even the depopulated towns and cities. Soldiers noticed that "back in village streets there are many solemn women and girls all in deep mourning. There is no celebrating."[44] Negative, even defeatist, talk was more common in the countryside, populated as it was with thousands of refugees. One American officer noted that "French peasants had become extremely despondent, and openly told the [American] soldiers that their entrance into the war would merely prolong it for four or five years. They declared they were ready to make peace even at the German's terms." Still, it is hard to know what exactly to make of the comment from the same observer that "This attitude was not evidenced by the more intelligent French people," except to say that defeatism was likely most common among those who had already lost what little they had.[45]

While war weariness was an understandable consequence of four years of deadly combat for uncertain gains, France remained committed to winning. The French saw that a "German victory would be a defeat for all of humanity" and "almost unanimously interpreted the Great War as a struggle of civilization against barbarism."[46] That they vocally and demonstrably expressed their dissatisfaction with the war's prosecution says more about their desire to see the war fought more efficiently than it does their desires to see it end at any cost. France in the summer of 1918 knew that it sat at a turning point in its history, and it stood ready to "faire face" to meet it.

Great Britain's Fourth Army

The British sent four divisions to fight at the Marne. They represented each of the four armies that Great Britain used to fight the Great
War. The first was the original British Expeditionary Force (BEF), a
100,000-man force of professional volunteers. Britain was the only European great power that did not have conscription; thus the men of the
BEF were long-service men who quickly developed a reputation for cool
discipline and excellent marksmanship. Most of the enlisted men (what
the British called the other ranks) were urban and had been through
at least one bout of unemployment before enlisting. A disproportionate
number were from Ireland and Scotland, and their educational and
health levels were often significantly below those of their peers.

    The majority of their officers, by contrast, were public school edu-
cated and from comfortable, often quite privileged, backgrounds. In
1913, only 2 percent of the British officer corps had been promoted
from the ranks. It was, as historian Gary Sheffield has argued, an army
recruited from the bottom and led from the top. It functioned because
of its high degree of training and because the army closely replicated
the patterns of deference found in British society more generally. Officers saw themselves as representatives of an elite who were performing
public service in exchange for the privilege into which they had been
born. They were expected to lead their men, often through a highly
structured system wherein many officers did not know their soldiers'
first names and did not care to do so because of the disruption to good
order and discipline that informality might create.[47]

    This army, a product of Victorian and Edwardian mores, marched
off to war in 1914 with ideas that might be called quaint, if they had
not had such deadly consequences. One popular (and almost surely
apocryphal) tale from Belgium in 1914 has a British officer asking a
subordinate why his unit had been outflanked. The subordinate replied that he had left one flank unguarded because he expected that
the Germans would not advance over private property. True or not, the
story lives on because it holds a grain of truth about the psychological
and material shortcomings in the BEF. The British were little better
prepared for the realities of modern warfare than were their French
allies. Focused on a doctrine that emphasized mobility and counting
on individual marksmanship to win battles, the BEF fought well and

fought hard, but suffered terribly in the face of the much larger and better-equipped German forces.

The battles of 1914 destroyed the old BEF, forcing the British to hastily cobble together their second army, made up of BEF survivors, rushed transfers of Indian soldiers, and 268,000 "Saturday afternoon soldiers" of the prewar Territorials. Regarded in the prewar years primarily as a home defense force, the Territorials were under no obligation go overseas, but almost all volunteered to do so.[48] This second British army fought the battle of Neuve Chapelle in 1915 and generally performed well, temporarily breaking the German lines there. Two of the Territorial divisions, the Highland and the Second West Riding, later fought on the Marne as the 51st (Highland) and 62nd (West Riding) divisions.

The British high command decided to reassign the Indian troops away from the western front in 1915, in part to make way for Britain's third army of the war, the famous Kitchener, or New, Armies. Formed from local communities and guaranteeing men the right to serve with their pals for the duration of the war, these units had intense connections to communities large and small. The 15th (Scottish) and 34th divisions that fought on the Marne were products of this period. The 15th included battalions such as the Seaforth Highlanders, raised in Ft. George, and the Gordon Highlanders, raised in Aberdeen. The 34th included the Northumberland Fusiliers, raised among the Tyneside Irish in Newcastle, and the Highland Light Infantry, from Glasgow.

Few of the men who joined these "pals" battalions had had any sustained connection to the military before 1914. Most had never even fired a rifle. The men of the New Armies had much to learn, little time, and few experienced veterans around to train them.[49] Still, they formed quickly, underwent rudimentary training, and shipped off to France to meet the emergency of the western front. The 15th, for example, formed in September 1914 out of men who had volunteered in the original rush to the colors, and was in France by January 1915. The 34th underwent an equally brief training period, forming in August 1915 and landing in France by January 1916.

Three of the four divisions that fought at the Second Battle of the Marne also fought on the Somme, soon to be known as the baptism of fire for the New Armies. The 15th fought at Pozières and Flers-Courcelette, although it was mercifully spared the horrors of the Somme's first day, 1 July 1916, which remains the bloodiest single day in the history of the British army. The 34th was not so lucky, and it suffered heavily in attacks on La Boiselle. The 51st won a reputation for excellence at the Somme, but it, too, suffered huge losses.[50] The 62nd was the only one of the four British divisions that later fought on the Marne to escape the killing fields of the Somme.

All four divisions had to accept replacements from Britain's fourth army, the one that finally represented Britain's acceptance of conscription. The realization that Britain would need to compel military service was a tough one for the British, and conscription was never extended to Ireland for fear of a violent Irish backlash. Officially introduced in January 1916 to unmarried men aged 18 to 41, it did not permit men to select the unit they entered, although some preference was given to men who volunteered to join the Royal Navy.[51] In September, following the heavy losses on the Somme, conscription was extended to married men as well.

Although it failed to produce the numbers of men the government had sought, the draft, and the voluntarism it concomitantly inspired, meant important changes to the nature of British units. Conscription produced a renewed rush of volunteers who preferred to go into the army on their terms rather than be branded as men who answered the call of king and country only unwillingly. Perhaps most importantly at the small unit level, conscription meant the end of the tight local networks that had sustained the New Armies. By 1918 only 10 percent of the men in the West Yorkshire battalions of the 62nd Division had any personal links to West Yorkshire.[52]

The repeated forming and reforming of the British army meant fundamental changes to the nature of leadership. The officer corps alone grew from about 9,000 in the BEF of 1914 to 164,255 by the end of the war, significantly larger than the entire BEF had been in 1914. With such rapid growth, it was impossible to keep the same social backgrounds in the officer corps except at the most senior levels. Whereas 41 percent of Boer War officers had been educated at the "top ten" British public schools, the comparative figure for World War I was only 13 percent. The British army, which had traditionally resisted promoting from the ranks, had no choice but to do so. These "temporary gentlemen" came largely from the middle class and had shown some particular aptitude for soldiering while serving in the ranks.[53]

Despite the promotion involved with taking a commission, many men were reluctant to do so. The same chasm in social backgrounds that had served as a foundation in British officer-man relations also made it hard for many men to imagine joining the officer corps. During the war the chasm was less class-based than rank-based, but it was real all the same. One of the characters in Frederic Manning's highly autobiographical masterpiece of the war, Corporal Bourne, was offered a commission, but saw "officers, NCOs, the military police, and brass-hats as the natural enemies of deserving men like myself." He much preferred to remain in the ranks where the men "all muck in together," although Bourne eventually took the commission.[54] The tremendous casualty rates of junior officers, expected to lead from the front, was another important disincentive to taking a commission.

The need for more officers came amidst a personnel emergency that threatened to undermine Britain's role in the war. Late in 1917 the War Office revised its estimate of personnel shortfalls from 80,000 men to 256,000 men over the coming year. Some officers on Haig's staff feared that the real shortcoming might be closer to 450,000 men. In early 1918, the British considered cannibalizing fifteen divisions to bring under-strength divisions up to their full allotment, but decided instead to reduce the number of battalions in fifty-eight of its divisions from twelve to nine. Then in the spring came Germany's hammer-blow offensives, causing greater concern about British manpower and forcing the British to add more than 500,000 men to the ranks. These men came from drafts as well as reassignments of men previously assigned to Palestine, Italy, and other fronts.

By the summer of 1918, British manpower problems were real and of great concern to the Allied governments. The British continued to exempt more than 2 million military-aged men in "starred" occupations deemed crucial to the prosecution of the economic war. They also needed men for the Royal Navy to keep lines of supply and communication open and the blockade of Germany effective. In April, the War Office extended conscription to men aged 41 to 50, though few such men actually served in the front lines. Instead, the British reorganized. In May, ten British divisions were officially deemed "exhausted," with some companies down to 50 men as opposed to their ideal strength of 225. Foch noted as late as the middle of July that the British manpower situation was "extremely precarious."[55]

The quantity of British manpower was only one concern. By July 1918 British recruits and draftees were notable for their youth (many were 17 years old) and their "slight physique." The British army, in the words of one of its most highly regarded historians, was "scraping the bottom of the manpower barrel."[56] Great Britain's ability to lean heavily on the excellent soldiers from the Dominion forces of Canada, Australia, New Zealand, and South Africa helped to ease the crisis, but it could not solve it.

The British units that fought at the Second Battle of the Marne were thus a mixture of the surviving experienced men from Britain's first three armies and rough, poorly trained replacements from the draft army. Many men were tired from the heavy combat since March. One field artillerist noted that his battery had had just one two-week period out of the line from January 1917 to July 1918, and that had been spent training in new methods.[57]

But if some men were tired veterans, others were complete novices. The official historian of the 34th Division noted that the majority of its men in July 1918 had never seen action before.[58] The 34th was typical of many British units, having fought and suffered heavily in April in the defense of Kemmel. It had been so badly bloodied that it had been withdrawn from the front to be reorganized. Its artillery had suffered so heavily that it had been designated unfit for action, and its remaining personnel sent to train Americans. The 34th had only been reorganized and returned to the line with new personnel in late June, far earlier than would have been the case if not for the emergency caused by the repeated German successes.

The 51st (Highland) Division had a similar tale. It had been in the thick of the fighting since the German offensives had begun in March. Hit hard by German gas attacks in March, it fought desperate rearguard actions that cost the division 4,900 casualties in March alone. In April the division was moved to a sector that the British thought would be quieter, but was instead directly in the path of the second German offensive. The month therefore meant more fighting and 2,500 more casualties instead of an expected rest.

Tired though they were, the British, too, had undergone a critical reformation of their war-fighting skills. Now known by the ubiquitous title "the learning curve," the British from 1914 to 1918 transformed from a small, imperial defense force to an army of 1,166,395 officers and men, well supported by sophisticated artillery, aviation, and armor. The British had been at the forefront of technological advancement as well, introducing the tank, the box respirator as a defense against gas, the deoxygenated flamethrower, the Livens projector for firing gas shells, and the Mills bomb for trench warfare, to name just a few. The

British also led the way in complex techniques such as sound-ranging and flash-spotting methods for locating enemy artillery and resupply of ground units by air.

These methods came together at the Battle of Le Hamel on 4 July 1918. There the British Fourth Army, led by the Australian Corps under General John Monash, used gas and more than sixty tanks to take a key German position by surprise with amazingly light casualties. Aviators had carefully marked the position of enemy guns, which gas shells then neutralized. Using gas for such missions allowed for a much greater margin of error and had the additional advantage of not chewing up the ground over which the infantry and tanks would need to advance. The battle also showed, on a small scale, the ability of the various armies to work together within a British command structure. The Australians advanced with several companies of Americans and were supported by artillery fire from French batteries. Although none of the units from Le Hamel fought on the Marne, the "textbook" success at that battle showed the very real progress the British army had made since landing on the continent in 1914 wearing soft caps and relying on rifles.[59]

The technical progress of the British army made it a first-class force, but its numerical weakness combined with uncertainty surrounding Germany's next possible move worried its commander. Accordingly, Haig wrote that during the meeting on July 15, "I put my case strongly to Foch why I was averse to moving my reserves from my front." Haig insisted that the divisions be put in such a position that they could be returned to his command "*at once* in case the British front was threatened," and he further insisted on having his views placed in writing for the official record, but he also saw the wisdom in Foch's plan.[60] As Foch recalled it in his memoirs, Haig finally "yielded to my arguments" and ordered the 15th (Scottish) and 34th divisions to join the 51st (Highland) and the 62nd (West Riding) divisions, which were then already en route.[61] The British army, although very different from the BEF of 1914, would thus fight on the Marne again.

MARCHING TOWARD THE MARNE

IN 1914 AND 1915, few generals expected the trenches to become a fixed condition of war. As a means of prosecuting war, trench warfare suited neither side particularly well. The Allies knew that they would have to restore mobility to the battlefield if they hoped to force the Germans out of the parts of France and Belgium that they occupied; sitting in trenches would not accomplish that essential prerequisite of victory. Allied generals thus faced what came to seem like an insoluble dilemma: attacking was extremely costly, but only attacking could force the Germans out of the excellent defensive positions they had selected and developed since the "race to the sea" of 1914.

The Germans may have had the luxury of choosing their ground and waiting for the Allies to attack, but trench warfare did not suit their needs, either. For decades, German war planning had presumed as an article of faith that the worst-case scenario involved fighting a war on multiple static fronts while simultaneously facing a British naval blockade. To make matters worse, the Germans were fettered to an Austro-Hungarian ally that had performed abysmally in the 1914 and 1915 campaigns, absorbing needed German resources and requiring German rescue from several disastrous operations. Not for nothing did several senior German officers claim that because of the alliance with Austria, Germany was "shackled to a corpse."[1]

German planning had centered on defeating one opponent quickly in order to be able to redirect resources against the other. Few Germans expected a quick victory against the Russians, given Russia's vast expanses of land and seemingly inexhaustible pools of manpower. Thus the focus in German planning on defeating France first, despite the risks of bringing Britain into the war by doing so. In any case, the Germans expected to win the war before the British could effectively deploy either their army or their navy. France, German planners believed, might collapse upon the fall of Paris, although several generations of German general staff officers doubted that the German army could cause the fall of Paris in the six weeks the staff had predicted. Memories of the long, difficult siege of Paris in 1871 still lingered in the minds of many senior German officers.

Nevertheless, if Paris would be difficult to seize in six weeks, Moscow would be absolutely impossible to seize in so short a time. Nor did Moscow's seizure necessarily guarantee victory, as the capture of Paris presumably would. The Napoleonic experience haunted those German planners with a sense of history. Thus German planners gambled everything on a six-week victory over the French, the Belgians, and whatever resistance the British could mass. A rapid defeat of the Allies in the west, moreover, would allow German diplomats to write peace terms that would neutralize the Royal Navy and negate its chances to put an effective blockade in place. The German failure on the Marne in 1914, however, made it impossible for Germany to defeat France and Britain on the unrealistically rapid timetable called for in prewar German planning. The gamble had failed.

The Marne setback stood in contrast to several titanic German victories in the east, holding out the tantalizing prospect of bringing the Russians to a quick and favorable peace. Doing so would free up tens of thousands of German and Austrian soldiers to go to other fronts. The Germans soon discovered that they could soundly defeat larger Russian armies almost at will. Unfortunately, even lopsided battlefield victories had virtually no impact on German fortunes in the larger war. In the war's opening weeks, the Germans destroyed two entire Russian field armies at the battles of Tannenberg and the Masurian Lakes, but were no closer to concluding the war on favorable terms.[2] As they had done against Napoleon, and would do to a future generation of German soldiers, the Russians took enormous casualties, but they fell back, simplifying their supply system while complicating their enemy's. They soon reformed their lines farther east, replaced their losses with seemingly endless drafts of Russian peasants, and lived to fight another day.

The Russians took a severe beating from the Germans in the first few months, but they recovered effectively enough to wake the Germans from their dreams of an easy victory. Tannenberg especially had been so elegantly and deftly planned that the Germans soon developed (and with considerable hubris believed wholly in) a myth of their strategic genius. But even if they had possessed such genius, it could not compensate for Russia's mass. Russia had 1.4 million men in uniform at the outbreak of the war, meaning that even after the enormous losses at Tannenberg and the Masurian Lakes the Russians could still count on well over a million men. To these the Russians added 5.1 million conscripts in 1914, more than 5.6 million conscripts in 1915, and 3 million more in 1916.[3] To be sure, the Russians had monumental problems in organizing, training, equipping, and leading these men, but, with help from Britain and France, Russia was able to stay in the war until 1917.

Even if the Germans could find a way to eliminate the Russian front, the stasis of the western front still represented an expensive investment of scarce resources for little gain. The two-front dilemma haunted senior German commanders, most of whom knew that Germany's odds of winning the war diminished the longer the war raged. At different points of the war both General Helmuth von Moltke, who commanded German forces in the war's opening phase, and his successor, General Erich von Falkenhayn, came to the conclusion that Germany could not win the war.[4] An entire generation of German military teaching on the extreme dangers of a two-front war added to the gloom. But for Germany to extricate itself from the dilemma meant making a compromise peace with one or more of its opponents. Even if one of the allies could be induced to sign a separate peace, the price would undoubtedly involve ceding territory Germany had conquered during the course of the war. German generals and diplomats alike were loath to even consider such a step as long as they still held hundreds of square miles of enemy territory.

Consequently, from 1914 to 1917 German strategy jumped back and forth between seeking a decision in the east and in the west. Even on the western front, the German high command seemed unable to determine whether France or Great Britain represented the more important target.

In any event, the stalemate of the western front presented a challenge for the Germans that was every bit as real as it was for the Allies. The former needed to gain time, while the latter needed to gain land.

As I have argued elsewhere, the great tragedy of so many First World War battles was that they often produced just enough success to convince their planners to try again.[5] Even operations that historians now look back upon as bloody disasters often appeared to contemporaries as lessons (albeit costly ones) on the road to finding an eventual solution to the problem of trench warfare. Douglas Haig, for example, recognized that the Battle of Loos in September 1915 had been a failure owing to the inability of the British to concentrate reserves, but he still told secretary of state for war Lord Kitchener that he had not entirely given up hope "to make this the turning point in the war," although he was at the same time "annoyed at the lost opportunity" to do so at Loos.[6] The key point is that at this stage of the war senior commanders were still thinking in terms of refining methods in the hopes of finding a combination that would work rather than admitting that the new style of war made offensives too costly to be sustained for long even when they produced positive operational results.

Breaking the trench stalemate required new systems, new weapons, and new thinking. The old methods took time to disappear, but disappear they did. French General Marie Émile Fayolle, one of the war's fastest learners, noted in his diary in January 1915 that *offensive à outrance* was still alive and well in some sectors of the French Army. "We are senselessly bleeding some admirable troops to death. . . . I believe that an epileptic who ran around everywhere crying 'Attack! Attack!' would be lauded as a great man."[7] Still, the bloody failures that accompanied repeated charges annealed the French high command and led to a more systematic attempt to find solutions to the problem of trench warfare.

Once *offensive à outrance* had been finally discredited, the armies of the western front sought to win the new war of positions through four grand approaches. These approaches often overlapped one another; thus it would be inaccurate to describe them as phases or stages of the war. They could also work together in combination and be supported by the same people. Thus it is more appropriate to think of them as methodologies or coincident evolutions than as paradigms or radical revolutions in thought and action that replaced the one that had come before.

Following on the belief that the early battles of the war had been near-run things, one conclusion generals drew was that the war could be won with mass. More men, more guns, and more shells would allow basically sound planning to succeed in the future where it had failed in the past. More men would provide the missing reserves that Haig believed had been all that he had lacked at Loos and at Neuve Chapelle in 1915. More guns firing more shells would eradicate German defenses, while at the same time compensate for the relatively low skill level of new soldiers. Artillery conquers, Foch grew fond of saying, infantry occupies. Given the relative power discrepancy between artillery shells and bayonets, there was much wisdom in this oft-repeated maxim. Pétain was even more laconic, stating, "Le feu tue" (firepower kills).

Having more men and more shells also allowed the armies to experiment. Artillerists in particular came up with a dizzying variety of ways to use their weapons. Rolling barrages preceded infantry by 100 yards or less to provide cover and protection from enemy fire; deception barrages lured the enemy into giving away the positions of its guns so they could be pinpointed and destroyed; hurricane barrages concentrated fire in a given space to open holes for infantry; and box barrages protected men engaged in trench raids. Poison gas also saw the development of new methods, including the firing of irritants to make men remove their gas masks, followed quickly by asphyxiants to incapacitate or kill them.

The allure of a seemingly cheap victory won with mass helps to explain much of the furor in Britain over the so-called shell scandal of 1915. The implication, pushed by BEF commander Sir John French through the influential military correspondent for the London *Times*, Charles Repington, was that but for a lack of munitions, the British would have achieved great successes in 1915. This conclusion remains spurious, but it placed the blame for the failures of the year comfortably away from the army itself, while at the same time holding out hope that once British industry corrected the munitions problem, victory was sure to follow. The scandal reached such proportions that it became the single largest factor leading to the creation of a new coalition government in Britain while, it should be noted, also undermining the War Office's confidence in John French's leadership. Not everyone in Whitehall was as convinced as Sir John that the problem lay with the munitions supply.

The French offensives in Champagne in 1915 and British operations on the Somme in 1916 show most clearly attempts to win by mass.

The former concentrated 155,000 infantrymen, 8,000 cavalrymen, and 879 artillery pieces along a narrow front of just five kilometers. Once the massive weight of shell had done the seeming inevitable and cracked the German lines, twenty-six divisions of reserves would fan out to the left and right to "attack the still-intact German defenses from the rear." Given this astonishing concentration of men and materiel, the French could be forgiven for being confident. When the offensive gained only three square kilometers for 43,000 men dead, wounded, and missing, its commander could do little except release a rather perfunctory statement praising the "offensive capacity, warrior spirit, spirit of sacrifice, and devotion to country" shown by his men. He could not, however, explain why they had not succeeded.[8]

The British offensive on the Somme is the most famous case of trying to win by mass. Unsure of how much sophistication they could expect from relatively untrained volunteers, British generals planned to win the battle with a massive weight of shell that would clear the ground of enemy opposition. Some British generals, including Haig, hoped for a mass breakthrough. Others, including Henry Rawlinson, hoped that inexperienced British soldiers would at the very least be able to capture key positions in the German lines, dig in on high ground, and meet an expected German counterattack on favorable terms. In order to support its 400,000 men, the British Fourth Army assembled 100,000 horses, 1,100 field guns, 182 heavy guns, and 245 howitzers.[9] Although the resultant "torrent of metal" pounded the defenses of the Somme region "till it looked for all the world like nothing more than a ploughed field," the expected breakthrough never came.[10] Instead, the British Army suffered 60,000 casualties in one day, including almost 20,000 dead.

As Champagne, the Somme, and many other battles showed, mass alone could not win battles. In fact, mass often created as many problems as it solved. Larger armies armed with large numbers of sophisticated weapons forced nations into making some very difficult decisions. Every man held back for industry in order to manufacture weapons meant one less man in uniform. Similarly, every man put into industry or the army meant one less man growing food. Stopgap solutions such as hiring female workers, bringing in workers from overseas, and furloughing small numbers of men to help bring in the harvest eased, but did not solve, the essential problem, which only grew worse with each bloody battle.

Larger armies were also harder to feed, clothe, equip, and control. The British army had consumed 3.6 million pounds of meat and 4.5 million pounds of bread per month in 1914. By the end of the war, it was consuming 67.5 million pounds of meat and 90 million pounds of bread per month. The astonishing number of bullets, artillery shells, boots, horses, fodder, and uniforms that armies went through placed tremendous demands on economic structures. The failures of many of the lesser powers to meet these demands formed the root causes of their failures. Armies that did not receive enough food or appropriate clothing were often among the first to surrender or flee in battle.

The gigantic battlefields of the First World War, moreover, were extremely difficult to command. Officers at the front saw too little of the battlefield to make reliable judgments, and officers at higher headquarters were too far removed to see matters for themselves. There is no other way to explain comments such as Haig's "This was a fine day's work" and "wounded very cheery indeed" in his diary on the first day of the Third Battle of Ypres (Passchendaele) in 1917. The same diary entry claims that the British had taken 5,000 German prisoners. None of this optimism would have been justified had Haig been in possession of all the facts.[11] Moreover, moving masses of men and supplies across the limited number of usable roads and railways near the front lines proved a sometimes insurmountable challenge for staff officers.

Nevertheless, there were just enough examples of victory through mass to convince some generals to keep at it. Most notably, in Eastern Europe, the Germans concentrated an entire army, supported by more than 2 million artillery shells, against a weakened Russian corps between the towns of Gorlice and Tarnow and tore a huge hole in the Russian lines. By attacking the resulting exposed flanks, the Germans were able to force a retreat along the entire Russian line and capture all of Poland. In just two weeks of May 1915, the Germans moved the entire 700-mile-long line, from the Baltic Sea in the north to the Carpathian Mountains in the south, more than 95 miles to the east. They captured 153,000 Russian soldiers, and by the time the operation finally ended in September, the front line on the eastern front had moved 300 miles to the east. Still, the Russians were not beaten, proving (depending on one's point of view) either that mass could win big victories under the right circumstances or that even big victories did not necessarily win wars.

Fighting with machines instead of men became an alluring solution to the practitioners of what French historian Michel Goya calls "the scientific method of war." Under these new methods, "the goal to be achieved remained the same, namely breaking through the organized defenses of the enemy's line, but under the form of a long-term operation that comprised a series of methodical attacks on successive positions."[12] Versions of this system included the French *grignotage* and the British "bite and hold" tactics whereby a unit seized a key piece of high ground, then enticed its enemy to attack it on disadvantageous terms.

New technologies often featured prominently in such methods. Nevertheless, technology, then as now, offered no guarantee of victory. Technology, moreover, required an industrial system that could support it. Poison gas, tanks, airplanes, flamethrowers, and newer, larger artillery pieces all promised to provide important advantages. New technologies also came with important drawbacks. Gas had an unfortunate tendency to blow back on one's own position if the winds shifted, and it often proved ineffective against veteran troops well trained in how to deal with it. Tanks were slow, cumbersome, and prone to mechanical failure. In their early days they were as liable to make men scream with laughter as with fear, although they eventually developed into important weapons. Airplanes, too, frequently proved to be more dramatic than effective. Lacking reliable communication methods with ground forces and often unable to deliver munitions accurately, planes were still in their infancy; it is important to recall that a mere eleven years before the outbreak of the war, the Wright brothers had yet to make their first flight at Kitty Hawk, North Carolina. Aviators had come a long way in the war years, but they still had a long way to go.

Perhaps most importantly, with the exception of tanks, there was no technology one side could possess that the other side could not also either possess or counter. The technological edge in air warfare continually changed hands, as did the relative power of poison gas and the masks designed to neutralize it. The Germans lacked the capacity to manufacture tanks on the scale of the Allies, but once they learned to master their original fear of them, they learned ways to deal with them on an individual basis. The tank became a decisive weapon only when it could be massed in large numbers and placed within an effective combined-arms system of armor, artillery, aviation, and infantry.

The German economic system by 1918 was clearly inferior to that of the Allies, a circumstance that grew more serious after the United States' entry into the war. America's enormous financial and industrial systems gave the Allies an edge that the Germans could neither match nor neutralize. The Germans therefore sought to develop high-risk methods for doing much more with what they had. These methods, which involved devolution of command and required highly trained infantry, will be covered in greater depth in chapter 3. As we will see, these methods could provide only temporary and ephemeral success. They did not, in the end, compensate for Germany's inability to keep pace industrially and economically with the Allies.

The Germans were also instrumental in developing yet another method of war fighting, attrition. As a strategy, attrition was not new to the First World War. The North had used it in 1864 and 1865 to win the American Civil War. It had worked in that case because of the North's much larger population and industrial base. Such numerical discrepancies rarely existed on the western front. To take one snapshot, by the time of the Second Battle of the Marne in July 1918, the Germans had approximately 3,156,000 men on the western front, compared to the Allies' 2,972,000 men, even without the Americans, who contributed 618,000 more.[13] Such small numerical margins of difference argue strongly against a strategy of trying to kill your enemy at an acceptable ratio, safe in the knowledge that you can more easily replace your losses. As we have already seen, the British and French were in no position to do so given their manpower crises. The Germans, as the next chapter will show, were in just as dire a manpower dilemma by the time of the Second Battle of the Marne.

Attrition could therefore become a strategy of choice only under one of three conditions. First, it could work if the army doing the attriting was not your own. Thus both sides sought to find allies big and small such as Italy, Romania, Bulgaria, the Ottoman Empire, and, the biggest prize of all, the United States. Thus also the strenuous efforts of the British and French to keep the staggering Russian giant in the ring and punching. David French goes so far as to argue that Lord Kitchener's strategy for the New Armies was to hoard them and train them until at least 1917, by which time the French and Russians would have worn down the best units of the German Army. The fresh, well-trained British divisions could then enter the fray and win the war for Britain against a tired enemy at relatively low cost.[14]

Attrition might also work if one side could figure out a way to kill faster than it could itself suffer casualties. Such was the logic of German General Erich von Falkenhayn's supreme attrition plan at Verdun.[15] Falkenhayn had calculated that by enticing the French into futile and disjointed offensives against well-sited positions at Verdun he could kill the French at an acceptable ratio to his own losses. Once worn down by repeated attacks, the French would have little choice but to agree to peace terms the Germans would find not only acceptable, but favorable. Without the French to act as England's "best sword," the British would not be able to fight, and would also have to come to terms.[16] Germany would then be able to close off one front, and end the blockade, giving the Germans a chance to focus their resources exclusively against Russia.

The final way attrition might become a central strategy was if one could convince oneself that it was working. The British high command proved to be especially adept at such self-deception. At the end of 1914 Lord Kitchener ordered the director of military operations to "prove that the Germans will run out of men in the next few months." The DMO, Sir Charles Callwell, duly complied by using "statistical sleights of hand," knowing as he did that the purpose of the paper was political, not military. "I could just as easily have proved that they [the Germans] were good for another two years," he told Sir Henry Wilson. The British government bought the arguments in Callwell's "statistical conjuring trick" and "swallowed Callwell's (disingenuous) conclusions whole."[17]

While some skeptics, including Callwell's successor, General Sir George MacDonogh, rose to challenge these rosy proclamations, the notion that the Germans must be close to wearing out remained tantalizingly close to the surface of British strategic thinking throughout the war. Haig chose a bright, but too eager to please, young staff officer, John Charteris, to be his chief of intelligence. Charteris consistently presented evidence that his boss wanted to hear, and he "constantly bombarded Haig with over-optimistic reports of an impending collapse of German morale. Based often on thin rumors, the reports had the effect of building up Haig in times of difficulty, leading him to believe that the constant application of more pressure would cause decisive victory."[18] One such report from 22 August 1916 (that is, seven weeks into the bloody Somme fiasco), actually claimed that a British division wore out a German division in four and a half days as opposed to the three weeks required by a French division![19] Such reports convinced Haig that even if his plans for breakthrough had become manifest failures, he was nevertheless "wearing out" the German army faster than he was wearing out his own army, a dubious conclusion at best.

Under any circumstances, attrition was a long-term strategy. It could not produce a cheap or quick victory, nor could it reliably be used to

compel one's enemy to make peace. In short, attrition could not notice-
ably change the status quo and, as the Germans learned at Verdun and
the British learned at Passchendaele, the deadly strategy of attrition had
a logic all its own, and often defied the efforts of generals to control it.
In the end, attrition played an enormous role in deciding Allied victory,
largely because of the influx of hundreds of thousands of Americans, a
situation the British and French could not have confidently relied upon
until 1917. Even then, the Americans took their time shipping men to
Europe in numbers large enough to make a difference in the macabre
calculus of attrition.

Learning the Art of Defense in Modern Warfare

As the armies of the western front were learning to attack, they were also
learning to defend. The "learning curve" of defenders has not received
the same scholarly attention as that of attackers, but it should. Defending against enemy attacks became a specialized science of its own, with
its own methods, technologies, and command arrangements. Successful defenses also required units to dominate No Man's Land, conduct
successful trench raids, and have air forces capable of reporting on
enemy dispositions and movements. Defending could be quite stressful
and quite bloody. Defenders did not control the timing of combat, nor
is it true, as is often believed prima facie, that defending units always
suffered fewer casualties than attacking units.

The construction of defensive lines represented major investments
of time, energy, and resources. More importantly, such lines usually
were sited near places with strategic value. In many sectors, they protected lateral lines of communication, normally trunk rail lines and
canals that ran parallel to the front, without which nations could not
feed the ravenous needs of their large armies. Many Allied offensives
on the western front were designed to cut these lines of communication, thus forcing the Germans further east to their next set of lateral
communications. For this reason, critical rail junctures such as Arras,
St. Quentin, and Amiens became the scenes of major operations. The
Marne sector was virtually defined for military purposes by its two main
rail junctures, Soissons and Rheims.

In other cases, trench lines were established on high ground well
suited for defense. Behind these lines often sat flat, open country ideal

for conducting an effective pursuit. Thus defending territory, although it might seem easier than attacking in the environment of 1914–1918, presented real challenges of its own. A breakthrough on any part of the line could create exposed flanks that would threaten an entire army's position. As the case of Gorlice-Tarnow in 1915 showed, the collapse of one Russian corps forced Russia to abandon all of Poland. Thus it was not enough for an army to select high ground, dig in, and expect to hold on forever. Defense had to become a science all its own.

Because trench lines protected valuable ground, one means of defense involved placing as much firepower as far forward as possible. This method, if successful, also had the advantage of not ceding any territory to the enemy and thus allowed generals to make grand proclamations of "not one step backward." For Allied generals especially, the notion of holding every inch of unoccupied territory had important symbolic value. Thus when generals ordered their men to stand in place or die trying they were not necessarily being pigheaded or needlessly stubborn. The famous French rallying cry at Verdun, "They shall not pass," represented one example of inspiring men by ordering them to hold on to all territory at any cost.

This method had two important drawbacks. First, it made one's army immobile and thus a stationary target for enemy artillery. Armies that adopted it, as the Germans did on many parts of the Somme front, often took enormous casualties. Second, if, despite a concentration of power in the front lines, one's position yielded, there were few defenses left to guard rear areas. Armies that could rush reserves into threatened areas, as the Germans did successfully at Neuve Chapelle in 1915, could compensate for such weaknesses, but there were no guarantees that one's own reserves would appear on the battlefield before the enemy's.

A variant of this strategy involved absorbing the enemy's attack, then defending by counterattacks with forces held back specifically for the purpose. The theory assumed that an attacking army would tire itself out and in the end be in an exposed position with no trenches to protect them. They would therefore be in a dangerously exposed place if attacked in force. Armies thus concentrated reserves behind the lines and waited for the right opportunity to attack with fresh units against the weakened units of an enemy's attack. Such counterattacks also had the benefit of disrupting the enemy's timing and, where successful, regaining lost ground. The Germans developed two different types of such counterattacks, the *Gegenangriff*, a centrally planned counterof-fensive with larger operational goals, and the *Gegenstoss*, a hastily orga-nized local counterattack to disrupt enemy forces before they have an opportunity to consolidate their gains.[20]

Although it remained popular with generals, especially those in areas without much ground to cede, counterattacking did not always work. Foch and Haig had both used it with success at the First Battle of the Marne, but they had done so before the organization of the western front into two relatively solid lines. The Germans, by contrast, had suffered most of their casualties on the Somme after July 1 in local counterattacks, many of which were disjointed and unnecessary.

A final, and increasingly popular, method of defense involved the defense in depth. Under this scheme, defensive systems might include as many as five separate parallel trench lines, with the real strength be-ing in the middle or even the rear of the system. The first lines would slow down and tire out an enemy attack before it struck the main defen-sive positions, many of which were hidden on reverse slopes of hills out of the enemy's view, sometimes several miles behind the front lines. In areas such as Flanders, where digging in proved to be extremely difficult owing to the nature of the terrain, defense in depth provided the protec-tion that trenches could not. The best defense-in-depth systems took advantage of existing features, fortifying villages and turning stone farm-houses into miniature fortresses. Some regions featured 360° redoubts capable of all-around defense, so that even if they were surrounded and cut off they could still offer resistance and fire support.

Some defense-in-depth networks were formidable; others looked better on paper than they did in reality. One of the best, the Hinden-burg Line, called the *Siegfried Stellung* by the Germans, was a "deep defensive position characterized by thousands of concrete machine-gun positions, interlocking arcs of fire and dense belts of barbed wire that ran south from Arras to Laon," just in front of critical lateral railroad lines.[21] To increase the Hindenburg Line's power, the Germans destroyed all towns and villages within 10 miles. "Trees were felled, streets mined, and wells poisoned" in order to slow any Allied advance toward the line and to provide even greater strategic depth.[22] The line required the Ger-mans to give back 1,000 square miles of now ruined French territory, but by shortening the line and adding such power to it, the Germans were able to reassign an amazing ten to thirteen infantry divisions and fifty artillery batteries to other parts of the western front.

Although it became the preferred method of defense for many of the war's most insightful generals, not all armies could put defense in depth in place. As a method it had much to recommend it, but it also required a heavy commitment of manpower and resources. Trenches had to be dug, tons of concrete poured, telephone lines buried, and soldiers trained in the new methods. Not all armies had the time, the spare manpower, or the materiel to build effective defense-in-depth systems. In other cases, generals argued that they did not possess enough strategic space to do so, especially if they were defending a nearby town, rail juncture, or river crossing.

Moreover, placing scarce resources into defense networks was a tacit admission that defense had become the dominant mode of warfare. In other words, an army that settled in to defend was sending a message that it did not intend to attack in the near future. For the Allies, this message implied giving up on liberating lost territories (and, by extension, giving up the essential precondition for winning the war); for the Germans it demonstrated the basic failure of the grand strategy of the war. For men on both sides, it augured a long-term incarceration in the miserable world of the trenches.[23] Sitting underground in well-prepared defenses might have been better on an individual level than conducting more bloody and futile attacks, but it would not win the war, either.

In just over four years, the armies on the Marne had seen these and many other transformations. Some version of all of these strategies for offense and defense appeared at the Second Battle of the Marne. Like coaches with a playbook, the generals involved in the battle drew on them to find ways to create advantages and mismatches on the battlefield. Their success or failure indicated their level of mastery over the modern science of war in all of its many variations and permutations.

Saving the Allies from Defeat:
The Arrival of the Americans

The only army that had not been through this evolution, the American, had had the opportunity to learn at least some of the intricacies of modern war, but had failed to do so. Until its entry into the war in April 1917, the United States Army had made no sustained studies of the western front and had developed no methods to learn from European experiences. President Woodrow Wilson had gone so far to protect American neutrality in thought and deed that he exploded in anger when he discovered in 1916 that the army's general staff had been drafting contingency plans for a possible American entry into the war.

The Americans thus found themselves embarrassingly unprepared for modern war. Secretary of war Newton Baker, who, like President Wilson himself, had very little understanding of the technical workings of the military, noted that few of his critics had any "comprehension of how hard it is to expand industrially an unmilitary country into any sort of adequate response to such an emergency as we are now facing." Baker was right, but the government's own failure to take the necessary steps to prepare the nation was much to blame. The efforts of private citizens, most notably in forming and staffing the Plattsburg camps designed to train officers, often far exceeded those of the government.

The tasks the United States Army faced in April 1917 were truly "stupendous," as Baker realized.[24] The army had just 18,000 regular and National Guard officers when Congress issued its declaration of war. The total size of the regular American army, including more than 80,000 members of the National Guard called up to federal service, was just over 200,000 men at a time when the German army alone contained more than 3 million men. Over the next year and a half the United States had to train 182,000 officers to lead an army that grew to approximately 4 million men, half of whom eventually served overseas.[25] The speed with which the Americans raised, trained, and shipped their first army ever to fight in Europe was dizzying, but it was accompanied by a shamefully high occurrence of "delays, mistakes, and confusion," as well as a good deal of old-fashioned American political corruption.[26]

Nine American divisions fought at the Second Battle of the Marne as part of the larger American Expeditionary Forces (AEF). They included four prewar Regular Army divisions, the 1st, 2nd, 3rd, and 4th. The backbone of these divisions came from veteran professionals of the prewar army, but because of the twin needs to distribute their officers and NCOs to new units for training purposes and to rapidly augment existing divisions with draftees, their status as "veteran" units ought not to be exaggerated. More than 85 percent of the men in the Regular Army 2nd Division had less than one year of service.[27]

The other five divisions were formed out of National Guard regiments, augmented by volunteers and draftees. Coming out of the locally based American National Guard system, they were, like many British and French divisions, closely tied to a given locality. The 26th (Yankee) Division was raised among men from the New England states; the 28th (Keystone) Division from Pennsylvania; the 32nd (Wolverine) from Michigan and Wisconsin; and the 77th Division from New York City and its suburbs. The one exception was the 42nd Division, whose men came from twenty-six different states in virtually every part of the nation. As a symbol of its diverse origins, it adopted the rainbow (stretching from sea to shining sea) as its logo. Famous alumni, such as its chief of staff, Douglas MacArthur, and poet Joyce Kilmer, have since added to its distinctive nature.

The American high command made a series of controversial decisions at the outset of its belligerence. First, it decided that an American division would be twice the size of a European division. The Americans concluded that having to reinforce and resupply divisions over long distances and an unreliable communications network required that each division be given "greater driving power in the offensive."[28] Larger divisions, the Americans hoped, could stay in the field longer by rotating personnel in order to give them rest. This decision complicated command and control, but did allow the American divisions on the Marne to stay in the field for longer periods of time.

The second key decision came directly from the White House. In an effort to maintain a high degree of independence both on the battlefield and at the postwar peace conference, President Wilson insisted that American forces not be "amalgamated" into European units. In practice, amalgamation meant placing the newly formed American units into existing European command structures. Doing so would, its proponents argued, have simplified supply and command arrangements, while at the same time giving novice American soldiers the opportunity to learn modern warfare by serving side-by-side with veteran British and French soldiers. Only through amalgamation, some Europeans argued, could American manpower be integrated into the larger Allied system before it was too late.

Nevertheless, Wilson, Baker, and Pershing were surely right to conclude, as Pershing repeatedly told his European counterparts, that amalgamation would have been terribly unpopular with American soldiers and civilians alike. Most American soldiers had ambivalent feelings toward the aristocratic British, and few could speak French, although in the end the Americans developed strong ties with their allies, especially the French.[29] More than the young nation's pride was at stake. Few Americans wanted to see their sons and brothers fed into the murderous European war on European terms. With not a little naïveté, the Americans presumed that, their inexperience notwithstanding, they would be more than equal to the British, French, and Germans alike. As Major General Clarence Edwards told the men of his division, "I am an awful ingrained Yankee, and I know that one American could lick four or five of these Dutchmen (Germans)."[30] Wilson's diplomatic desire to stand apart from his European allies reinforced his opposition to amalgamation at almost any level, even to the extent of giving Pershing a written order to that effect.

Pershing needed little convincing. He had already settled upon a training program of "open warfare" that looked, certainly to the Europeans, more like that in use on the battlefields of 1914 than those of 1917 and 1918. The open-warfare doctrine disdained training in trench and position warfare in favor of offensive principles "so thoroughly taught at West Point for a century."[31] At least at first, Pershing's principles formed the basis of American training, in part because they so closely overlapped those of division and regimental commanders. The Yankee Division staff "insisted that the men be given thorough training on the range and with the bayonet," a policy that did not immediately change upon the American units arriving in France despite the French "continually dinning into the ears of the Yankees the dangers of overconfidence" and the inappropriateness of their methods.[32]

The Americans set off for France confident, eager, ill-equipped, poorly trained, and stubborn. Although the Europeans claimed, not without some reason, that the Americans were moving too slowly, the divisions that fought on the Marne were assembled and shipped out hastily. The 42nd had to absorb men from New York, Iowa, Georgia, Minnesota, and twenty-two other states, train them, and get them ready to go to France. The unit assembled at Camp Mills, New York, in August and September 1917, and was in France by the end of October.[33] The Yankee Division did not face the same geographic challenges, but it too had to assemble quickly. War Department authorization to create the unit came in mid-August 1917, the ranks were full within one week, and by mid-autumn it had become the first division to be fully organized in France.[34] The 3rd Division, one of the prewar Regular formations, did not even establish a headquarters until late March 1918 and had no horses until May.[35] The Yankee Division assembled in France with just thirty-six trucks for 25,000 men.[36]

Thus despite Pershing's insistence on marksmanship and rifle training, the haste with which the Americans dispatched their units often
meant that they had had no time to complete even rudimentary training. One survey of American units in France in June 1918 found that
40 percent of the men in the 4th Division and 45 percent of the men in
two surveyed regiments of the 77th Division had not even fired a rifle
in training. Although American frontier fascination with guns would
suggest that the Americans already knew how to shoot, not everyone
was impressed. Sergeant Alvin York, one of the army's best shots, was
astonished at the lack of familiarity with guns shown by urban recruits.
"They missed everything but the sky," York noted ruefully.[37]

Given the almost complete lack of preparation for modern war,
the American units had perforce to learn from their European allies.
Upon arrival in France, most American units went either to dedicated
training areas or to relatively calm sectors of the front, where they could
learn how to fight an industrial war. In March 1918, for example, the
Yankee Division was matched with a French brigade and sent to the
generally inactive Toul sector, where it fought two small engagements,
at Apremont and Seicheprey. The Rainbow Division went to Baccarat,
where it relieved the 128th French Division, which in turn went to a
more active sector.

Other units went directly into action. The 1st Division was, appropriately enough, the first American unit into action, the first to suffer
casualties, and, after the armistice, the first to enter Germany. The
American 2nd Division, which included a brigade of marines, fought
at Belleau Wood in June, suffering the most casualties in one day in the
history of the United States Marine Corps until the Battle of Tarawa
in 1942. American troops also fought at Le Hamel on July 4 alongside
Australians. The Americans fought hard and impressed friend and foe
alike, but their tactical and operational shortcomings were obvious.

Junior officers and enlisted men alike soon realized how poor their
training had been. Pershing's open warfare doctrine notwithstanding,
the Americans proved to be eager learners. French and British soldiers
helped the Americans to rid their heavy packs of unneeded gear, taught
them how to recognize signs of an impending German attack or raid,
and instructed them in modern forms of command and control. They
also taught the newcomers how to use weapons like hand grenades,
breaking the Americans of their habit of throwing grenades baseball-
style. The flat trajectory of such a throw made it likely that the grenade

would skip along the ground and miss its targets. Against their will and instincts, the Americans learned to lob the grenades on high trajectories to give them a better chance of landing inside a trench. In the case of the 4th Division, their stint of training with the French in June 1918 was the first time they had seen grenades and automatic rifles.[38]

Under such conditions even Pershing and Baker realized the futility of leaving the Americans entirely to themselves. Modern staff arrangements, moreover, were far too important to leave to chance. As such, the American high command agreed to place American divisions inside French corps and armies. In exchange, Foch promised Pershing that once the immediate crisis of the German offensive had passed, he would support the creation of a separate United States First Army with its own dedicated sector of the western front. Such a compromise arrangement kept American soldiers commanded by American officers up to the divisional level, while permitting the Americans to make use of the much more experienced French staff system.

Placing American units inside French corps, however, meant that the Americans would be physically separated on the battlefield. The American 1st and 2nd divisions went to the French Tenth Army sector under their most aggressive commander, Charles "The Butcher" Mangin. The 3rd and Keystone divisions were sent miles away to the east as part of the French Ninth Army, while the 4th and Yankee divisions went to the French Sixth Army. This arrangement was far from what Pershing envisioned, but he had little choice, and his decision to accept limited amalgamation undoubtedly saved American lives.

Pershing played a rather limited personal role in the battle to come. His units had been distributed among French corps and French armies, complicating his ability to control and monitor their actions. Partly due to his own insistence on open warfare, his men were also unprepared for the battle to come, although, to be fair, most of the Americans had not had much time to complete their apprenticeship. General Robert Bullard's comment on the arrival of the United States Marine Corps at the Battle of Belleau Wood in early June encapsulates the meaning of the AEF to the French and British before the Second Battle of the Marne. "The marines didn't 'win the war' here," he wrote, *"but they saved the Allies from defeat."*[39] At the Second Battle of the Marne one month later, the Americans would do that and much more, but as part of a large coalition effort, not as the independent force that Pershing and Wilson had envisioned.

Figure 1. American Expeditionary Forces Commander General John Pershing (*left*) meets French General Ferdinand Foch. Pershing agreed to follow Foch's strategic guidance, and Foch in turn agreed to Pershing's insistence on a separate American presence on the western front after the Second Battle of the Marne. Library of Congress.

Figure 2. General Ferdinand Foch was given authority to direct the strategic operations of the Allied armies in March, 1918. More than any other single person, he is responsible for the Allied victory on the Marne. Library of Congress.

Figure 3. General Henri Berthelot spent more than a year away from the western front. His performance as Fifth Army commander at the Second Battle of the Marne was mediocre at best. Soon after the battle he was dispatched to the Balkans. Library of Congress.

Figure 4. Charles Mangin, "the Butcher," had fallen into disgrace in 1917, but his career resurged at the Second Battle of the Marne, where his offensive tactics helped to win the campaign. Library of Congress.

Figure 5. Highly respected for his meticulous approach to war, General Marie Émile Fayolle had his doubts about Foch's aggressive plans for the battle, but Foch won him over. His army group alone was as large as the entire British army. Library of Congress.

Figure 6. The kaiser's son and an army group commander, Crown Prince Wilhelm had learned a great deal about modern war by 1918. After the battle he urged his father to accept any terms the Allies might offer because he knew that Germany could not win the war. Library of Congress.

Figure 7. A group of German prisoners in Soissons. Their gaunt appearance reveals the failure of the German supply system in 1918. Library of Congress.

Figure 8. The rail and road communications of Soissons made it a target for the artillery of both sides during the battle. Library of Congress.

Figure 9. French wounded leaving the Second Marne sector arrive at Châlons sur Marne. French medical services improved tremendously during the war, but still left a lot to be desired. Library of Congress.

Figure 10. These rudimentary trenches on the Aisne were a far cry from those the Germans had enjoyed in other phases of the war. They suggest the war of movement that had returned in 1918. Library of Congress.

Figure 11. France provided all of the armor used on the Second Marne front as well as the vast majority of the heavy and medium artillery pieces. U.S. Army Military History Institute, Carlisle, Pa., Clarence G. Anderson Collection.

Figure 12. Combat artist interpretation of fighting on the Second Marne front. The shelling came from German airplanes, which often targeted vulnerable supply lines. Library of Congress.

Figure 13. This destruction in the Aisne valley shows the power of modern artillery to reduce entire villages to rubble. Many *villages détruits* were never rebuilt. Library of Congress.

Figure 14. Henri-Philippe Pétain (*left*) and his good friend John Pershing. Pétain was among the most cautious French generals, but Foch overruled him and ordered the French army into battle on the Marne. Library of Congress.

Figure 15. 2nd Division commander Major General James G. Harbord in French helmet. He was shopping in Paris when informed of his promotion. He led aggressively, taking many objectives, but many casualties as well. Library of Congress.

Figure 16. Widely respected and one of the most senior officers in the war to be wounded in battle, General Henri Gouraud won the instant admiration of the Americans he served with, especially the men of the 42nd (Rainbow) Division. Library of Congress.

Figure 17. German prisoners of war provided critical information to Allied soldiers during the battle. U.S. Army Military History Institute, Carlisle, Pa., Roy Coles Collection.

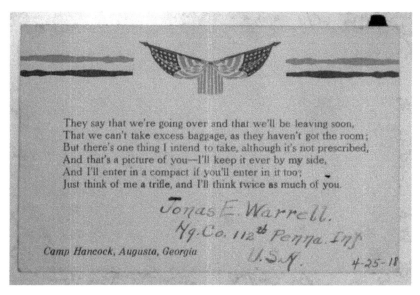

Figure 18. Less than three months after sending this postcard from a Georgia training camp, Jonas Warrell was fighting on the Marne with the 28th (Keystone) Division from Pennsylvania. U.S. Army Military History Institute, Carlisle, Pa., Jonas Warrell WWI 601.

Figure 19. The arrival of thousands of healthy American soldiers proved to be a needed tonic to the tired British and French. Here, members of Company G. U.S. Army Military History Institute, Carlisle, PA, Roy Coles Collection

Figure 20. Mutt, the YMCA dog, brings cigarettes to the men in the front lines. U.S. Army Military History Institute, Carlisle, Pa., Roy Coles Collection.

Figure 21. German anti-aircraft gunners helped to ensure that the Allies could not regularly identify the locations of German artillery batteries. Courtesy of Christian Pinnen and family.

Figure 22. German soldiers build a road on the western front. The need to improve logistical networks drove the Germans to attack in the Marne region. Courtesy of Christian Pinnen and family.

Figure 23. This humorous look at aviation notwithstanding, German airpower caused serious problems for the Allies on the Second Marne. Courtesy of Christian Pinnen and family.

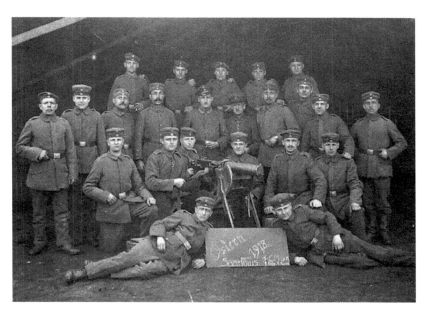

Figure 24. A German machine gun unit celebrates Easter on the western front. Courtesy of Christian Pinnen and family.

Figure 25. Extremely young prisoners of war captured on the Marne front revealed the desperation of the German war effort by summer 1918. U.S. Army Military History Institute, Carlisle, Pa., Roy Coles Collection.

Figure 26. Ruins of Fismes, one of the towns liberated by the 28th Division. U.S. Army Military History Institute, Carlisle, Pa., Allen J. Stevens Collection.

Figure 27. A German field funeral. After the war the Germans were allotted minimal space in France in which to bury their dead, usually in regions they themselves had devastated. Courtesy of Christian Pinnen and family.

Figure 28. The horrors of combat on the Marne front. U.S. Army Military History Institute, Carlisle, Pa., Clarence G. Anderson Collection.

THREE

GERMAN DESIGNS
ON THE MARNE

THE GERMAN ARMY that fought the Second Battle of the Marne had undergone a transformation no less dramatic than those of the British, French, and American armies. In 1914, the German army had taken on a combination of enemies that together had more people, more money, and a larger industrial base. The Germans had done so alongside one ally, Austria-Hungary, with whom they had not even coordinated war plans and another, Italy, that had dissociated itself from the alliance and instead decided upon a transparently self-serving neutrality. Few German generals lost much sleep over Italy's defection, although the decision did allow the French to move more than 80,000 men away from their Mediterranean front, and it forced the cancellation of plans to move Italian forces to the Rhine River in support of the German invasion of France.[1] In Italy's place came a new German ally, the Ottoman Empire, which had recently been humiliated in wars against second-level powers and would seemingly require a serious investment of German resources in order to be able to make any significant contributions to the combined war effort. Not for nothing was the Ottoman Empire known across the continent as the "sick man" of Europe.

These seemingly awesome constraints did not deter even the most pessimistic of German commanders from entering into a continental war. The prewar chief of the German general staff, General Helmuth von Moltke, normally considered to be among Germany's most dour and gloomy senior leaders, argued in 1912:

> If war occurs, there can be no doubt that the main weight of responsibility
> will be on Germany's shoulders which will be gripped on three sides by her
> opponents. Nonetheless we can *under the current conditions*, still face even the
> most difficult tasks with confidence, if we manage to formulate the *casus belli*
> in such a way that the nation will take up arms united and enthusiastically.[2]

Moltke had his own private doubts, but he rarely voiced them in forums
that mattered, for fear of being labeled a defeatist. Although others may
have had similar private doubts, German diplomats and generals expected
to win the war, notwithstanding the enormous tasks before them.

German confidence emerged from more than Teutonic arrogance.
The German general staff was certainly aware of its great triumph in
its last major war against France in 1870–1871, but the generals were
not simply resting on their laurels. Indeed, the Germans had a healthy
respect for the French army, nourished as it had recently been by the
extension of conscription from two years to three years and a revival
of nationalist spirit that brought about new military appropriations.
Moltke's oft-cited May 1914 comment to his Austrian counterpart,
Franz Conrad von Hötzendorf, reveals German concerns. When Conrad pressed Moltke to divulge his plans for a western campaign in the
event of war, Moltke flatly told him, "Well, I will do what I can. We are
not superior to the French."[3] The remark reveals not just Moltke's lack
of confidence, but a fatal inconsistency in his own thinking about the
relative strength of the German army.

German actions and planning further demonstrate the soldiers' ac-
knowledgment of their own weaknesses. Knowing that they had to find
ways to increase their chances of winning quickly, the Germans resorted
to extreme measures that could provide enormous payoffs if they succeeded. Placing German reserves into front-line offensive units represented one such gamble, providing extra offensive punch at the sharp
end of the sword, although it also put reserve troops into dangerously
exposed positions. The decision to invade neutral Luxembourg and Belgium (but not Holland) was another.[4] If it worked, allowing Germany to
outflank French defenses and surround the major French field armies,
then it would make a significant contribution to winning the war. If it
failed, it almost guaranteed the long war the Germans so dreaded.

German war planning thus involved an unusual degree of high-
stakes gambling. In 1914, however, the gamblers in this game believed
that they could even the odds by playing with marked cards. The

German general staff knew it could control the timing of the outbreak of war by acting quickly. Indeed, the Germans had long planned to get the jump on their enemies by a rapid mobilization and early movements. A lightning *coup de main* against the powerful Belgian fortresses at Liège was so important to German planners that movement against the town's defenses was to precede even a formal declaration of war. The Germans were unusually fortuitous in that the immediate causes of the war were in Eastern Europe; thus the British and the French, both only indirectly touched by the July crisis, were likely to think first and shoot later.[5]

Not so the Germans. Once they had decided on war, an intricate and delicately calibrated machine went into action. The German declaration of a "state of imminent war with Russia" allowed the Germans both to prepare for war before a declaration of mobilization and to send mixed signals to the French and British.[6] While the Germans prepared their *coup de main* against Liège, the British were still debating. On August 4, Britain finally decided for war. In Barbara Tuchman's memorable phrase, a still confused Britain "went to bed a belligerent, if something less than bellicose."[7] The Germans, by contrast, were already in place and ready to attack Liège by the time the British government awoke from its slumber the next morning.

Such rapid concentration was possible because German mobilization functioned as smoothly as it had done the last time Germany had gone to war, in 1870. The Germans needed less than two weeks to mobilize 3,822,450 enlisted men, 119,754 officers, and 600,000 horses, then move these forces to the front in 11,000 trains. More than 560 trains crossed the Rhine River every day from August 2 to August 18. Princess Evelyn Blücher, an Englishwoman who had moved to Berlin with her German husband just before the outbreak of the war, was surely not alone in witnessing the "overpowering" process of mobilization and concluding that the Germans "take to war as a duck takes to water."[8]

What she saw, however, was less a nation with a "genius for war" than a nation that knew it had to gamble and win quickly, or probably not win at all.[9] The Germans accordingly had marked more than one card in the deck. They played another by deploying for war an officer and NCO corps that had been rigorously trained to the same standards and in the same system. Consistent with a strategy of winning quickly, Germany had put unusual energy into its peacetime training programs. Only by being better at their jobs could German officers and NCOs expect to win a war against such a large combination of enemies.

But when the Germans could not win the hand even with their marked cards, their advantages began to fall away. As the war ground into stalemate, the Germans had to learn new methods of war just as their opponents did. In some ways, the rigorous planning and training of the prewar German army may have inhibited the search for new solutions by making it harder for new ideas to germinate in a relatively rigid intellectual environment. In this context, Falkenhayn's gory attrition plan for Verdun appears even more the result of a general staff that had run out of ideas yet could not even contemplate the notion of a compromise peace. The failure of the Germans to master industrial war in 1915, 1916, and 1917 led to an increased reliance on the navy to win the war with submarines. That decision, itself another long-odds gamble, blew up in their faces when the United States responded with a declaration of war.

The industrial war of 1916 and 1917 in particular bled the German army as badly as it bled the French and British. The Somme has for too long been associated with British loss, but for the Germans it was, as one of their officers famously dubbed it, "the muddy grave of the German field army."[10] The Somme caught the Germans at a critical juncture of their own learning curve.[11] Having learned from their 1915 experiences the danger of placing all of their forces in forward defenses (what was sometimes called a "shop window" defense), they had developed on the Somme an intricate defense-in-depth network. The German defenses on the Somme were ideal: deep both in their coverage of territory behind the front lines and in the distance underground they could be buried in the chalky soil of the Somme.

Nevertheless, the Germans suffered terribly at the Somme. The initial British bombardment may have been far too ineffective from the British perspective, but it was still deadly to the Germans who had to endure it. The German policy of defense by local counterattack, put in place after July 1, also inflicted high levels of casualty. There is no exact figure for German losses on the Somme, and no breakdown of when those losses may have occurred. The low figure appears to be around 400,000 total casualties, with some historians (including the official British historian, Sir James Edmonds) placing the figure closer to 680,000. Even if one accepts the low figure, it is obvious that the Germans suffered as badly on the Somme as did the British, who had taken 419,654 casualties there.[12] Thus one can understand the "muddy grave" comment as meaning that the Somme destroyed the finely tuned, well-oiled German war machine that fought Germany's 1914 and 1915 battles.

Nor was the Somme the only "muddy grave" for the Germans. Even if one accepts the lowest reputable figures for German losses at the Somme, it still becomes higher than comparable figures for the bloody battle of Verdun. At that battle, German casualty figures are normally estimated at between 337,000 and 373,000. Thus the Germans were undergoing two murderous battles at the same time; if one includes the operation to relieve the Austro-Hungarians in the wake of the Brusilov Offensive of June, then the Germans were in fact dealing with three large offensives simultaneously. Accepting both low-end estimates for the Somme still puts German losses in just two battles close to 750,000 men. Germany took 217,000 more casualties turning back the British army's inexcusably ruinous assaults on the Passchendaele Ridge in 1917.[13]

These losses were especially traumatic for an army that had prided itself on a uniformly high level of training and preparation. Replacing such losses essentially turned the German army from a finely tuned professional force into a large, conscript field force. Or, to return to the analogy of the gambler, the German army of 1917 was playing without the marked cards that had given it a relative advantage in 1914 and 1915. The Germans were still an innovative force, developing a 1,000-yard defense-in-deep system at Passchendaele, with reserves held even further back for local counterattacks. Still, it is noteworthy that at that battle the Germans had to rely heavily on yellow cross (mustard) gas and the torrential rains of the summer of 1917, which Crown Prince Rupprecht of Bavaria called "our most effective ally," to even the odds. German losses had been high enough to force a reduction in battalion strength from 750 men to 700 men.[14]

The need to find replacements placed Germany in an even more tenuous economic position than Britain or France. The British blockade increasingly cut into Germany's access to raw materials, at the same time that the length and cost of the war placed the German financial system under unprecedented stress. Unlike France or Britain, Germany could not use manpower from the colonies either to make good shortfalls of industrial workers or to fill non-combat positions. Because they controlled at least the surface of the oceans, the British and French could both import workers and soldiers from Asia and Africa and deny that ability to the Germans, whose own colonies were smaller and less developed in any case. Under China's "laborers as soldiers" plan, developed in 1915, France was also able to use tens of thousands of Chinese laborers.[15]

All of the armies tried as well to turn to a more industrial style of warfare, substituting firepower for the lack of manpower. The Germans, however, had difficulty matching the French and the British in the development of several key types of heavy weaponry. The discrepancy in tanks shows this problem most acutely. Whereas the British were able to concentrate six hundred tanks at one battle (Amiens, in August 1918) and the French were able to fill an order for one thousand Renault FT tanks, the Germans manufactured only about twenty tanks, and had to rely on a small number of captured British models to fill out their inventory. In part, the discrepancy in tanks was a function of the German desire to concentrate on the construction of expensive items such as submarines and super-heavy artillery pieces. The final result for the German army, though, was that it had to win the war with men, not machines, as neither submarines nor super-long-range artillery pieces provided the kind of power on the battlefield that tanks could provide by 1918.

The Germans tried to compensate for the shortages caused by the British blockade by squeezing the territories they occupied even more tightly. The harsher the occupation, however, the more troops the Germans needed to quell opposition to their increasingly draconian policies. This dilemma became most acute in Ukraine, but was a factor in the west as well. As a result, the Germans needed to divert troops from the western front for internal security.

Finally, the Germans faced the possibility of having to fight a new, fresh enemy in the United States. Senior German admirals made bombastic claims that the German submarine fleet could sink American transport ships en route and thereby prevent American soldiers from landing in Europe. The kaiser accepted the navy's conclusion, telling his advisers that America's entry into the war was "irrelevant." Few German field generals put much faith in these patently absurd claims. They knew that the Americans, who eventually landed in Europe an average of seven soldiers, with their equipment, *per minute*, would make the difference in sheer numbers, if not in quality.[16] The Germans increasingly understood that they were playing with a smaller and smaller deck. They therefore decided to mark some more cards.

The Great German Gamble of 1918

To solve their essential strategic dilemma, the Germans decided on another high-risk gamble. Unable to win the war by *Materialschlacht*, the Germans turned to a method of warfare that had been in development in several armies. The central idea was to create small groups of light infantry that could infiltrate enemy lines, move quickly, and exploit opportunities as they arose. The development of powerful portable weapons allowed such soldiers to bring increased levels of firepower with them. These elite infantry could target the enemy's lines of communications, company and platoon command posts, and supply dumps. After the elite soldiers had weakened the enemy's command and supply networks, regular infantry units could assault the enemy's now isolated front-line units with a much more reasonable chance of success.

All of the armies had experimented with some form of this new method of war, but it fit German needs and German understandings of war most closely. Indeed, infiltration tactics promised to return Germany to its traditional strengths. By focusing on quality over quantity, leadership at the small-unit level, and initiative, these infiltration tactics recalled German prewar doctrine and ideas about warfare. Hew Strachan's observations of the mid-nineteenth-century Prussian army's method of war still holds largely true for 1918: "The telegraph [and, by 1918, the radio] allowed at least some communication between units in the field. And technological development itself forced flank attacks, since the growth in firepower precluded frontal assaults. Envelopment caught the enemy in a crossfire. Thus the operational and tactical requirements fused."[17] Storm troops in 1918 aimed to force breaks in the enemy's front lines, which in turn might create flanks that less highly trained infantry could then exploit.

The development of small, elite units had been at the center of German tactical innovation for three years. As early as 1915, the Germans had organized the first *Sturmbatallione* (storm troop battalion). By the time of Verdun in 1916, each *Sturmbatallione* contained companies based around mobile weapons such as light machine guns, flamethrowers, and trench mortars (*Minenwerfer*). Elite units could be used both in the attack and as counterattack units that were part of larger defense-in-depth networks. The Germans quickly decided to focus the training and equipping of their storm troop units on attacking.

The Germans experienced tremendous early success with storm troops, most of whom were volunteers. Specialized artillery developed to support the storm troops, usually relying on gas instead of high explosives, because the former left the ground unbroken for the infantry assault. Consistent with Germany's need to husband resources carefully, most of these artillery bombardments were brief, but deadly. German shelling aimed less to destroy enemy positions than to neutralize them at least temporarily in order to give their elite infantry the chance to advance to unprotected targets.

The new method received a full test at Riga on the eastern front in September 1917. Both there and at Caporetto the following month in Italy, the new methods produced dramatic results at relatively low cost. Within two months of Riga, the Russian government had collapsed. The advance of German armies toward St. Petersburg after the fall of Riga had played no small role in the dénouement of the tsar's government. At Caporetto, an entire Italian army had been routed; only the limited German goals for the offensive slowed the advance.[18] Accordingly, the Germans assigned two men proficient in the new tactics, General Oskar von Hutier and Colonel Georg Bruchmüller, the mission of bringing the new methods to the western front. The Germans hoped that a mass application of these tactics might win the war on the western front before the Americans could finally tip the scale in the Allies' favor.[19]

The French and British were slower to infuse their armies with these new ideas, not because they were constitutionally slower to learn, but because they had no real reason to do so. They knew that as new tanks, planes, and other weapons became available in large numbers they would be well placed to win a war of large, set-piece battles. A war of machines placed their strengths against German weaknesses. The Allies therefore had far less incentive to experiment with storm troop tactics. After American entry in the war, the Allies also knew that time would eventually be on their side. If they could withstand the initial German assault in the spring, they could count on massive human and industrial help from the United States.

Still, the Allies were remarkably unprepared to meet the German assault. They had formed no unified chain of command, had established no functioning general reserve, and had failed to put defenses in depth in place uniformly across the western front. As late as 14 March 1918 (that is, just one week before the German spring offensives began) the British government and general headquarters were still unsure if the Germans would attack at all; less than a week before the German offensive began, Haig's headquarters had advised the Fifth Army not to expect any large attacks, and even authorized leave for almost 90,000 men.[20] Some British generals believed that the Germans would attack in the east, and possibly move on the Middle East, before beginning a massive assault in the west. Several British generals had even advocated going on the attack.

This confusion about German intentions helped to obfuscate a picture that should have been much clearer. The need for the Germans to play all their cards (both marked and unmarked) in the first half of 1918 should have been transparent. That the Allies were not fully prepared for the German onslaught that began on March 21 shows that their learning curve was not yet complete. The Germans used a combination of storm troop tactics and carefully directed artillery fire to tear open holes in the Allied lines. Some of the storm troops were veterans of the successes at Riga and Caporetto. One of Germany's junior officers, Ernst Jünger, recalled that day as the unleashing of a tempest:

> A flaming curtain went up, followed by unprecedentedly brutal roaring. A wild thunder, capable of submerging even the loudest detonations in its rolling, made the earth shake. The gigantic roaring of the innumerable guns behind us was so atrocious that even the greatest of the battles we had experienced seemed like a tea party by comparison. What we hadn't dared hope for happened: the enemy artillery was silenced; a prodigious blow had been laid out. We felt too reckless to stay in the dugout. Standing out on top, we gasped at the colossal wall of flame over the English lines, gradually obscuring itself behind crimson, surging clouds.[21]

A thick mist helped to blind British commanders to what was happening in front of them. By the time that they had divined the general picture, the initial German assaults had already done their job.

The Germans had decided to strike first at Britain, whom they saw as the smallest and in many ways the weakest member of the Allied coalition. Operation Michael, the first German attack, targeted the weakest part of the BEF, the British Fifth Army, under the command of General Sir Hubert Gough, a young protégé of Haig. Gough came from a distinguished military family, but had few ideas that would have seemed new to his distinguished ancestors. Supported by Haig, he had been promoted too quickly, becoming the youngest army commander on the western front. His inexperience showed when he did the Germans a great favor by placing most of his defenses far forward. This "shop window" system was too fragile and too thin to offer much resistance to the German storm troops. Having commanded at Passchendaele, Gough must have been well aware of the advantages of the defense-in-depth system, but he had neglected to put it in place in his sector. In his defense, Gough argued that he could not have put an elastic defense in place even if he had wanted to do so because his army had to cover 42 miles of front with just eleven under-strength divisions in line and one solitary infantry division (plus three cavalry divisions) in reserve.

Gough's pleading that his army had been stretched too thin in order to give aid to his French neighbors to the south had a ring of truth, but he was far too slow to respond to the German assault. The Fifth Army's lines broke, forcing it to retreat, although in most places it did so in good order, despite the morale-shattering fact of having to give back land so bitterly won on the Somme in 1916. In all, the Fifth Army retreated more than 40 miles, exposing the flanks of the British Third Army to its north and the French Sixth Army (a key player in the Second Battle of the Marne a few months later) to its south. By the end of the week Gough had been relieved of command. The Fifth Army received a new commander (Sir Henry Rawlinson) and even a new name (the Fourth Army) and began the process of reconstituting. Under its new commander and new organization it went on to play key roles in the final battles of the war.

The much stiffer resistance put up by the British Third Army to the north of the Fifth Army proved both the importance of competent senior leaders and the value of the defense-in-depth method, which the Third Army had put in place. Germany's second major offensive of the spring, in Flanders, gained far less ground, but threatened a serious German breakthrough of British positions, with a concomitant threat to vital British lines of communication along the English Channel. Although the Germans had failed to instill panic in the British and had also failed to achieve the operational goal of separating the British and French armies, they had still achieved dramatic results.

One of Germany's aims in this campaign was to force the British and French to sacrifice the juncture of their armies, which sat near the critical communications center of Amiens. More than 80 percent of British north-to-south rail traffic passed through Amiens, but David Zabecki's recent analysis of German action in March 1918 argues that the German army was slow to realize how important Amiens was to British logistics.[22] Instead, German planners saw Amiens as important because of its role as a presumably weak hinge between the British and French. The Germans hoped that, if pushed hard enough, the British would retreat north in order to protect their communications on the English Channel. Similarly, they hoped that the French would retreat south in order to protect Paris. Thus both the French and the British armies would have exposed flanks and would have their forces disadvantageously positioned to support one another.

Despite these expectations, the juncture between the French and British lines near Amiens held in large measure because of long-overdue decisions made by the senior Allied leaders at the civilian and military levels. Each of these decisions contributed to the eventual Allied triumph on the Marne months later. The most important of these decisions was the belated appointment of a single senior officer to oversee the various British, French, American, Italian, and Belgian war efforts. They man they chose, French General Ferdinand Foch, had a loose authority to supervise and coordinate Allied strategy, but no real ability to issue orders to national army commanders. He used his control over scarce reserves, his forceful personality, and his intuitive understanding of the German military's goals to direct the movements that helped to hold the Allied lines together. At the meeting where he was named to his new post on March 26, Foch told the gathered dignitaries, "I would fight in front of Amiens. I would fight in Amiens. I would fight behind Amiens." In other words, he would not permit the British and French armies to lose sustained contact.[23]

Foch met regularly with Haig, Pershing, and Pétain, establishing working relationships and building trust, despite tremendous personality differences between the men.[24] All of them recognized the need for high-level coordination and, disagreements notwithstanding, generally came to accept Foch's judgment. The trust that developed between the senior generals and their staffs became all the more important as subsequent German offensives pushed the Allies back further and further. That trust proved to be critical when Foch and Haig met for their lunch on July 15. Without it, the Second Battle of the Marne might never have been won.

On May 26, the Germans opened their fourth major offensive of 1918, attacking along the Aisne River, just to the west of the Marne sector. Operation Blücher aimed to force the French to move reserves to the south in order to make a renewed German attack on the British in Flanders more likely to succeed. Thus although the attack was aimed operationally at France, its strategic goal was still the defeat of the BEF.[25] The Germans had chosen well by targeting the French Sixth Army, commanded by General Denis Duchêne. Pétain had urged Duchêne to implement a defense-in-depth network in the Aisne sector, but Duchêne had stubbornly refused both Pétain and the urgings of British officers who had been part of the March retreat. Duchêne explained to the Army Group North commander, General Louis Franchet d'Esperey, that he preferred to place his main line of defense on the crests of the Chemin des Dames ridge, even if it meant placing his back dangerously on the Aisne River itself. Duchêne feared the negative effect on public opinion if he ceded the symbolic Chemin des Dames, and he also saw a value in issuing a order to his units that they would "remain in place until overrun."[26]

The entirely predictable result was a major setback like the one suffered by the British Fifth Army in March. With all its defenses placed as far forward as possible, the French Sixth Army was in poor position to react to a heavy and accurate German artillery fire. More than four thousand German guns fired shells to a depth of 12 kilometers for two hours and forty minutes, making it one of the heaviest artillery barrages of the war thus far. The Germans possessed a 3.7:1 advantage in artillery pieces, the largest they ever enjoyed on the western front.[27] Once the artillery had torn holes in the Allied lines, storm troops could probe their enemy's lines, looking for avenues to exploit and opening wider holes for the next wave. German regular infantry advanced easily into the holes the artillery and the storm troops tore open. Duchêne fatefully responded not by directing an orderly withdrawal (for which he had made no preparations in any case), but by ordering troops forward to fill in the holes. The Germans, moving much faster than the Allies, were able to thwart these efforts with ease and keep moving.

These German offensives had succeeded beyond even Ludendorff's greatest hopes. Instead of the 20 kilometers he had hoped to gain, the Germans advanced the line more than 55 kilometers, driving a deep wedge into the Marne sector. Duchêne's policy of defense by counterattack also led to needless French and British casualties, which played further into Ludendorff's hands. Duchêne, like Gough before him, was relieved of command and blamed for exposing the Marne, and thus the approaches to Paris, to a German advance.

On the strategic level, however, the success of the German offensive created as many problems as it solved. German advances in Operation Blücher had formed a dangerous and untenable salient. Rail communications into the sector were too weak to sustain the number of German soldiers inside. As in many of their other operations in 1918, the Germans tried to ease the pressure on rail lines by prioritizing ammunition over food and requiring the men to live off the countryside, but the rail network was still insufficient. The food problem, moreover, would grow worse after the German army had finished requisitioning what was available. As early as May 5 the Germans had begun to realize the dangerous logistical restrictions the salient imposed. Ludendorff and Crown Prince Wilhelm were disinclined to abandon the salient they had won despite the difficulties of moving supplies into it. By the end of May, they had begun to look at the rail center of Rheims as the answer to their logistical problems, even though the crown prince doubted that Germany had the strength to take it.[28]

The immediate decisions taken by the Allies to stop the Germans established most of the key players and places of the Second Battle of the Marne. Pétain replaced Duchêne with General Jean-Marie Degoutte, a relative unknown, but seemingly an improvement over the arrogant Duchêne. Foch agreed to release two armies, practically his entire general reserve, to the threatened sector as well. They were the Tenth Army under the hyper-aggressive General Charles "The Butcher" Mangin, whom Foch had recently brought back to senior command, and the Fifth Army under the inconsistent General Henri Berthelot.[29] These units, plus the French Ninth Army under General Henri de Mitry, formed the operational front for the Allies at the Second Battle of the Marne.

Although the four armies carried French names and had French commanders, they were all multi-national in character. Foch asked Haig to move three (later four) divisions south of the Somme River to be ready to move to the Marne sector if needed to replace tired French divisions. The Americans, with 650,000 men in France in early June, but few divisions in the front lines, agreed to send the 2nd and 3rd divisions to the Marne sector in late May to guard the crossings of the Marne River near Château-Thierry. The fresh, energetic men in their brand-new uniforms made one French officer note that "a magical transfusion of blood was taking place."[30] Pershing might not have appreciated the imagery, but he understood well enough how important the Americans would be to any defense of the Marne.

The exposed wedge that the German offensive had formed looked on a map like a flattened U. Inside the U on the western edge, the Germans had overrun Soissons and Buzancy, and had also crossed the Ourcq River. On the southern edge, the Germans had finally stopped at Château-Thierry on the Marne River itself. To the east the Germans had chosen to advance just west of the thick Forêt de Rheims, meaning that they did not move on the cities of Rheims and Epernay. The new Marne River salient was thus bordered on the west by the massive Forêt de Villers-Cotterêts, on the east by the Forêt de Rheims, and on the south by the Marne River.

From the Allied perspective, the situation in late May looked as bleak as it could have been. Officers in French headquarters spoke openly of the war ending in German victory in a matter of weeks if the Germans could pull off one more large offensive; General Degoutte could be seen weeping over tattered maps, and the normally confident General Edouard Noël de Castelnau warned Pétain and Foch that his Army Group East would most likely be forced into a massive retreat if attacked, because it had no reserves.[31] There had been a few positive signs, including a much better performance by French and British soldiers in repelling the fourth major German offensive near Noyon. Solid performances by the Americans in stopping local German offensives at Catigny, Belleau Wood, and Château-Thierry also provided glimmers of hope. Still, no one on the Allied side in mid-June knew where the Germans would strike next or how the Allies would respond.

The German Army Returns to the Marne

The German army that arrived on the Marne in June 1918 looked almost nothing like the one that had fought on the same ground four years earlier. Its losses had been astounding, and the bloody combats of 1918 only served to increase its casualty rosters. Although 21 March 1918 represented the return of mobility to the battlefield, it had also been Germany's bloodiest single day of the war to date. The Germans suffered 39,329 casualties on that day alone, as opposed to 38,512 British casualties. During the remainder of March the Germans suffered a further 192,678 casualties, bringing the total figure for the month to 232,007. Just how high these numbers are becomes clear when one considers that March 1918 was the bloodiest month of the war for the

Germans, even though major combat operations were limited to the month's final week and half.[32]

Lost in the maze of statistics and debates about the exact levels of German casualties is the critical fact that the German offensives may have returned mobility to the battlefield, but as long as German casualties remained roughly equivalent to Allied casualties, they only represented attrition on a larger and more mobile scale. Given that Germany could not replace its manpower losses as quickly as could the Allies, the German offensives were actually bringing Germany closer to defeat, not victory. The German storm troop units, in the first waves of most attacks, suffered the highest levels of casualties, meaning that over time the Germans lost both their quantitative and their qualitative advantages. Only if the Germans captured a truly vital objective such as Amiens could this method possibly result in victory.

April proved to be even costlier for the Germans than March, further underscoring the essential bankruptcy of German grand strategy. This realization struck many Germans hard, as it carried with it the implicit recognition of ultimate defeat. Senior officers tried to keep the poor state of the German army from becoming public knowledge in Germany itself, but the soldiers knew just how bad their condition truly was. If they needed any more evidence, they found it in the well-stocked British trenches and supply depots they overran. German troops saw eggs, "which we sucked on the spot," recalled Ernst Jünger, "as eggs were little more than a word to us at this stage." Jünger and his comrades also saw "stacks of canned meat, tins of delicious English jam, and bottles of Camp coffee," as well as tomatoes, onions, and "everything to delight an epicure's heart."

Some units had enough discipline to take what they could carry and then resume the attack. Others stopped to loot and fill their empty stomachs. Units that overran depots containing wine and whiskey often became ungovernable for days. Even for units, such as Jünger's, that kept attacking, the mere sight of "the enviable circumstances of our foes" was enough to lower morale considerably. Not only were the enemy's men better fed and cared for than they were, the ample stocks proved beyond a shadow of a doubt that the German policy of unrestricted submarine warfare was not working. Moreover, if British soldiers were so well supplied, then the home front must not be nearly as close to starvation as German propagandists claimed. If the morale of the British home front held, then a battlefield victory would be all that much harder for the Germans to win. Jünger noted that the sights of those British depots stayed with him and his comrades for the rest of the war, "when we lay for weeks in trenches, on meager bread rations, watery soup and thin nondescript jam."[33] The German decision to give ammunition priority over food on the already overtaxed German supply lines greatly exacerbated this problem.

Senior German leaders recognized how far the quality of the army had declined, although they seemed curiously unable to take the blame for it. Ludendorff later noted that "the German Army of 1918 was no longer the wonderful weapon of war we had put in the field four years before. It had not as keen an edge as in 1914, but it was by no means dull! If the war should continue much longer, however, the quality of the troops was liable rapidly to decline."[34] Allied intelligence reports suggested as well that the German capability to attack was declining, but that it would continue to be a formidable foe on the defensive. At best, then, the German army by mid-1918 was an instrument for defensive warfare. At worst, it had played its last cards.

Quantitatively, the decline of the German army was obvious for everyone on both sides to see. French intelligence estimated that the Germans had actually increased their total number of divisions on the western front, from 186 on March 21 to 207 by mid-July, by moving troops from the Russian front. Of the total German force, however, the number of German divisions considered "fresh" had declined in the same period from 78 to 43. Twenty-six German divisions were designated "reconstituted," meaning that they had accepted massive reinforcements from other, cannibalized units. The French further estimated that 35 German divisions had lost 1,000 to 2,000 prisoners of war each and a further 23 divisions had lost 2,000 to 3,000 prisoners each. As evidence of the crisis, Germany had reduced the number of men per company first from 150 to 120 and then to 70.[35] Other French intelligence reports noted that some German companies could not even maintain that number and were down to as few as 40 men.[36]

The four German armies in the Marne sector show this decline. Constituted together as Army Group Crown Prince Wilhelm, they were, from west to east, the Ninth under General Johaness von Eben, the Seventh under General Hans von Böhn, the First under General Fritz von Below, and the Third under General Karl von Einem. According to British estimates drawn up in early July, the Seventh Army, by far the largest, had just three fresh divisions and thirty-two tired divisions;

the First had three fresh and eleven tired divisions; and the Third had three fresh and six tired divisions. Army Group Crown Prince Rupprecht, to the north of the Marne sector, had just ten fit divisions and eighty-one tired divisions.[37]

Such reinforcements as were arriving from Germany did not generally impress veterans in either quality or quantity. The expected transfusion of forces from the eastern front provided less succor than it might have, because of both the number of German units needed to enforce harsh occupation policies in Ukraine and Russia and the thousands of German soldiers who simply got off their trains in Germany and went home. The German army thus had to depend upon very young men and men previously exempted from military service. These new draftees struck Crown Prince Wilhelm as "no longer of the best stamp."[38]

Standing starkly against this decline of German forces was the growth of the American Expeditionary Forces (AEF). Ludendorff knew that by July 1, the Americans would have one million men in France. He also knew that these Americans were being used to replace tired French units in need of rest and refitting. He had been impressed with what he had seen of the Americans, noting that "wherever the American soldier had made his appearance on the front, he had proved himself not very well trained, but extremely eager and even too rash, with apparently inexhaustible energy." Ludendorff concluded that the best chance for Germany lay in the inexperience of American officers; only their mismanagement of their own men could negate the sheer power of American numbers.[39] Foch, Haig, and Pétain shared his concern about the inexperience of American leaders from the other side of the hill, thus their desire to amalgamate American units with European corps and armies.

The state of German morale on the eve of the Second Marne offensive is harder to gauge than the sheer size of the army. As noted, Ludendorff knew how large the AEF had become by early July. Indeed, any senior German officer who could have found one of the many American newspapers that came to Germany through neutral nations could have seen the headlines. American, British, and French newspapers (many of them not more than a few days old) were common sights in Berlin cafés and among German intelligence officers. By late May, these newspapers were claiming that 650,000 Americans had landed in France, and on June 16, the New York *Times* announced the American government's plan to have one million men in France by the end of July. Ludendorff expressed surprise at the numbers, but evidently he accepted them; Hindenburg was "dismayed," knowing as he did that the arrival of the Americans meant that Germany's window of victory was closing fast.[40]

German senior leadership went to great lengths to hide this picture from German soldiers. One German deserter told an American in the 28th Division that he had been told that "there are scarcely a thousand Americans in France, [and] that the submarines are sinking them as fast as they come over. Can you imagine that!"[41] The realization that the Americans not only were in France in large numbers, but were taking an active role in combat must have been as demoralizing to German soldiers in June as the discovery of ample provisions in British depots had been in March.

Other German soldiers knew through instinct that their grand offensive had failed. Ernst Jünger, who had participated in the March offensive, knew that "in strategic terms it (the offensive) had failed."[42] The declining quality of German rations brought the strategic failure closer to home. German front-line soldiers in 1918 were supposed to receive a daily ration of 600 grams of bread, 200 grams of meat (served five days a week), 50 grams of fat, and 100 grams of honey or marmalade. This diet was supposed to provide a daily intake of 2,500 calories, below the 3,100 of the war's early months, but presumably still adequate.[43] But German forces, often 90 miles or more from their already insufficient railheads, rarely received even this relatively sparse ration, and the Germans had already stolen what little the locals still had.[44] By July, Ernst Jünger was eating "vegetarian sausages" (cucumbers) and little else. Every meal of cucumbers, sometimes supplemented by thin soup or coarse ersatz bread, demonstrated Germany's failure to the men better than any intelligence report could have done. Jünger was perceptive enough to conclude that with the declining quality of their diets, German soldiers would surely be more susceptible to the spreading influenza virus than the British, French, and Americans.

May and June had also been costly and bloody months to the German army. Overall losses were 138,574 men in May and 163,348 in June, for meager gains.[45] The fourth major German offensive, in the Noyon-Montdidier sector from June 8 to June 12, had failed to deliver results similar to the previous three. The Germans had to disband fourteen battalions of storm troops (with an on-paper strength of 18,000 men) after the battle, and German intelligence began to pick up on alarming signs of indiscipline and insubordination in the ranks.[46]

By the end of June, British intelligence reports had concluded that the German army was in its poorest condition of the war. German troops, exhausted from months of attacks and racked by influenza, were often too tired to dig into their newly won positions. Although Ludendorff claimed that influenza did not affect German troops, captured British reports showed that many German divisions had 2,000 men or more in hospitals owing to the disease. Many troops, the British noted, went days without eating anything at all. Thousands more had only recently been released from Russian prisoner-of-war camps and, consequently, had very low morale.[47]

Nevertheless, not all German soldiers greeted the idea of yet another offensive with trepidation. Some, like the deserter who believed the reports of submarines sinking American troop transports, may have concluded that German methods were in fact working. A German order captured along the Marne front before the offensive told German soldiers not to fear the coming offensive because the new German artillery and infantry methods had guaranteed that there would be no sustained opposition.[48] Others were told of intelligence reports suggesting that Allied morale was ready to crack.[49] Surely veteran soldiers greeted such comments with a healthy dose of skepticism, if not outright derision, but they may have helped to bolster the morale of new soldiers.

Even jaded and cynical soldiers might have their spirits lifted by the hope that with one more push, they might yet win the war. After all, the Germans had come within shelling distance of Paris and had forced the evacuation of much of the city. As it had been for the Germans on the Marne in 1914, the French capital seemed to be the ultimate prize, and it sat so tantalizingly close. Moreover, the "raw, but instinctively brave" demeanor of some of the best of the new German recruits heartened even a grizzled combat veteran like Jünger.[50] By the middle of July, news had spread that the kaiser himself had come to the Marne front to witness the final triumph of German arms. That battle, known to the Germans by the name "Peace Offensive" (*Friedensturm*), might just be the chance to end the war and go home as heroes.

FOUR

THE PEACE OFFENSIVE

IF THE SITUATION in June looked bleak from the German side of the lines, there seemed little immediate cause for optimism on the Allied side either. On June 3, French forces completed the withdrawal of their units to the south bank of the Marne River. Engineers then destroyed the final bridge over the river in the hopes of slowing down German pursuit. Thousands of refugees with their "goats, dogs, kittens, burros, pigs, milch cows, and crates of chickens" wandered "in ragged columns" toward Paris, only to find more than one-third of the city's residents gone and police urging the new arrivals not to stop in the capital because of major shortages of food.[1] On June 4, French Premier Georges Clemenceau tried to rally the people of France with a speech in which he declared, "I will fight in front of Paris. I will fight in Paris. I will fight behind Paris." It was a powerful speech from a charismatic and energetic man, but it was just words if the Allied armies could not stop the Germans.

A measure of relief came on June 6 when the American 2nd Division attacked German positions on the southwestern end of the Marne salient. Three weeks of fighting around a mile-long hunting preserve known as Belleau Wood stopped German momentum and proved that the Allies, especially the fresh Americans, were capable of doing more than organizing retreats. Losses had been heavy, especially among the Marine Corps brigade, but the clearing of Belleau Wood marked a significant setback for the Germans and provided some much-needed good news for the Allies. It also put the Allies in control of dominant high ground, positions critical for observation of German movements in the Marne valley.

Notwithstanding Allied ability in June to stop the fourth German drive, known as the Noyon-Montdidier Offensive, the great question among Allied commanders revolved around what the Germans might do next. Few of them expected the Germans to stop and regroup; the pressure to win quickly was too great to allow them to take much time to pause. The longer the Germans waited, the more Americans would arrive in line and the deeper the Allied blockade would cut into the ever-growing problem of feeding German civilians.[2] The imminent collapse of Germany's allies provided another motivation to act quickly. Italy had shown signs of definite recovery from the Caporetto disaster of the previous autumn, foreshadowing even greater external pressure on the faltering Austro-Hungarian Empire. In the Middle East, British forces, with significant help from Arab irregulars, continued to move almost at will against Ottoman forces. Only a German victory on the western front could redeem these losses. More immediately, if Germany's allies collapsed, then the Allies could redirect forces to the western front, or even create a new front on the undefended approaches from Austria. A resurgence by the Allies might even bring the Russians back into the war in an attempt to regain lost territory.

Thus the Allies knew that another German offensive could not be too far off. Both sides clearly recognized that the coming battles would be large, bloody, and protracted. The practical question for the Allied high command revolved around where to send precious reserves. The battles of March through June had left almost all units well under their authorized strength and in need of reinforcement. Forty days of active defense had cost the British 239,793 casualties.[3] Parts of the Allied line, especially on the British front, were only weakly held. Without reserves, true defense-in-depth networks could be neither built nor manned in sufficient strength. As the past few months had shown, the creation of such networks greatly increased the chances of stopping a German offensive; perhaps more starkly, the absence of such networks virtually guaranteed failure. With their backs on Paris and thus with less strategic space to yield, the Allies could not afford another massive retreat.

Not unreasonably, each commander feared that the next German attack would come in his sector. Haig and the British command feared for the six main English Channel ports that were the BEF's lifeline to its communications back to Britain. Rouen, the largest of the six ports, was out of Germany's immediate reach, but the loss of even Dunkirk (which carried 17.5 percent of British supplies) would be a major hindrance to British operations.[4] The British, moreover, knew from their intelligence reports that the Germans had a new offensive in the north at the top of their priority lists. Haig accordingly was reticent about moving British units too far south and even asked Foch to move "one or two good French units near Dunkirk . . . in case of necessity."[5]

The French were, naturally, more concerned about the safety of Paris, notwithstanding Foch's boasts that he had fought for the Channel ports in 1914 and 1915 and would do so in 1918 as well.[6] Foch told Haig in late June that the French government was "alarmed" about the city's situation and wanted extra measures taken to ensure its security. These measures included sending a French army detachment (the *Détachement de l'armée du nord*) from Flanders to the Paris region. Haig did not care for the idea, complaining that "this would mean extra risks" in the British sector. Still, he knew how important Paris was and understood that "the risk must be taken."[7] The insecurity of British dispositions in the Flanders sector, however, remained a source of considerable British anxiety throughout the summer.

By the end of June no large German offensive had yet occurred, as the Germans regrouped and reinforced. The pause gave the Allies some much-needed breathing room; Haig took personal leave to England on July 6, indicating perhaps that he did not expect a major German assault in the immediate future. The lack of German activity also allowed the Allies to conduct several small local counterattacks. These attacks had several important effects: they kept some pressure on the Germans by forcing them to expend energy and resources creating defensive networks; they helped the Allies straighten out their lines and seize critical local strong points; and they helped Allied morale by showing that they still maintained the capacity for attack.

The most significant of these local attacks occurred at Le Hamel on July 4. Using tanks instead of artillery, a combined Australian and American force, under the overall direction of the British Fourth Army, recaptured six square miles of territory, including a strategic ridge. Using armor in place of artillery kept the crucial element of surprise, left the terrain intact for the infantry, and provided fire support on the move.

The plan, meticulously designed by Australian General John Monash, captured all Allied objectives and took 1,500 German prisoners in just over an hour and a half. Armor and aviation worked well as part of a true combined-arms force. The success at Le Hamel led to immediate planning for a larger operation, based on the same principles, to take place around Amiens in early August.

The success at Le Hamel notwithstanding, the Allies were planning for defensive operations more than offensive ones. Most Allied officers were still thinking in terms of winning an attrition-based war in 1919 with what they expected would be overwhelming resources. The Americans hoped to have eighty fully trained and fully equipped divisions in France by April 1919. New fleets of tanks, trucks, and airplanes would provide mobility for this new force, while new machine guns and artillery would provide fire support. In late June, not even Foch was thinking in terms of winning the war in 1918.

He was, however, thinking in terms of resuming the offensive. He was waiting for the "culminating point," when the Germans would have so exhausted and outstretched themselves that they would be ripe for a powerful counterattack. Perpetual defensive operations were not in Foch's nature, nor were they consistent with the larger strategic goals of eliminating the threats to Paris and the Channel ports. Foch also hoped to gain some critical ground before the onset of bad weather halted operations for the year and gave the Germans a chance to regroup. Most Allied generals were afraid that the Germans might use the winter of 1918–1919 to construct a new line of powerful defenses like the Hindenburg Line. If the Allies could not prevent the line from being built at all, they at least wanted that line built as far east as possible. Only a successful offensive before fall could achieve that aim.

As early as June 10, Foch and Pétain had begun to think about the possibilities of a counterattack. General Marie Émile Fayolle, who had worked closely with both generals in the course of the war, was not surprised to find the two disagreeing. Foch, true to his nature, urged an offensive as soon as it could be arranged, while Pétain was more cautious. "Pétain arrives in his turn and says nothing [about attacking]. Obviously, one pushes for a counterattack and the other holds to his defensive spirit."[8] Fayolle had reason to watch this debate closely because he was then commanding the *Groupe d'armées de réserve* (GAR), which included the Tenth and Sixth armies on the western edge of the

Marne sector. The GAR, which, contrary to its name was a front-line formation, not a reserve formation, would likely play a major role in any offensive Foch ordered.

Debate continued, but at the end of the month, Foch directed Pétain to prepare for a major Allied offensive. Foch's grand vision called for twelve American, twelve French, and seven or eight British divisions to take the field sometime in August.[9] The two most obvious locations for a possible offensive were the bases of the large salients jutting toward Paris. The Château-Thierry salient in the Marne sector struck Pétain and Tenth Army commander General Charles Mangin as the more attractive option because Allied communications into the sector were much stronger than German communications. The Allies still held the large rail centers of Rheims, Châlons, and Epernay on the outside edges of the salient. They could also use the intricate rail network of the Paris region as a massive roundhouse to move men and supplies to the region from all over northern France.

The Germans, by contrast, could rely on only two local rail lines running from Soissons, one south to Château-Thierry and the other east in the general direction of Rheims. The latter line was of limited utility because the allies still held Rheims itself. Consequently, all twenty-two trains the Germans used daily to move supplies to men in the salient came through Soissons. If the Germans lost Soissons, they would lose all of their rail communications and the entire salient might quickly become untenable. Even if the Germans stopped the Allies short of Soissons, the Allies might still get close enough to shell the rail lines leading out of the city, thus rendering it much harder for the Germans to use. The only other usable rail line under German control ran southwest from Rheims to Ville-en-Tardenois and then to Dormans and Château-Thierry. As the Allies held both Rheims and Château-Thierry, these lines had limited utility as well.

As with the railroads, so too with the highways. Except for the roads in and out of Soissons, most of the major roads in the German part of the Marne sector ran west to east. The road system was therefore good for moving supplies from place to place within the pocket but ill-suited to moving supplies from major supply depots into the pocket itself. The Allies, on the other hand, could take advantage, as they had at Verdun, of major highways running to the pocket at Lucy le Bocage, Le Ferté Milon, Dormans, and elsewhere.

The Allies could also benefit from their enormous investment in motorized transportation, meaning that they could move supplies on the outside of the salient more quickly than the Germans could move supplies inside the salient. Thus, by mechanizing their movements, the Allies could negate the classic military advantage of operating along interior strategic lines. Because they were using so many trucks, and had access to a superior road and rail network, the exterior lines of the Allies proved to be no disadvantage. As we will soon see, the importance of effective lines of communication at the Second Battle of the Marne allowed the Allies to concentrate men and equipment much more rapidly than the Germans thought possible. Not for nothing did the Germans code-name their upcoming offensive *Strassenbau* (Road Building).

These constraints on German communications set the context for most of Germany's strategic thinking about resuming the offensive in the Marne sector. The German offensives in the Marne sector had created a difficult salient to supply and reinforce. With Soissons being the only reliable rail center in the salient, the Germans were faced with either attacking to obtain another rail center (with Rheims being the most likely target) or evacuating the salient altogether. As the latter was unthinkable, the former became the most attractive option to German planners.

Because it was Germany's only reliable center of communications, Soissons soon became the focus of Mangin and the staff of his Tenth Army. Foch saw the situation in the same terms, later writing, "It was clear, therefore, that if we made ourselves masters of Soissons, or if we were able to keep it constantly under fire, we would prevent the provisioning of troops in the 'pocket' and render the German positions on the Marne untenable."[10] As early as July 3, Mangin had concluded that an attack in the Soissons region "not only would present the best chance for success, but could also result in immediate exploitation." In other words, a breakthrough at Soissons could lead to an opportunity to pursue the Germans over open country. Mangin also noted that the Allies might be able to achieve surprise at the operational level near Soissons because of the chance to concentrate forces behind the Forêt de Villers-Cotterêts, and thus out of German view. German attention on their own operations in Flanders and around Rheims, Mangin believed, left them exposed to a major flank assault that, if as successful as he believed it could be, might liberate the entire Château-Thierry pocket. At a meeting on July 9, Foch revealed that he was thinking along the same lines, telling army commanders that an attack near Soissons "not only presents the best chance for success, but also is susceptible to creating a breakthrough." Foch directed Mangin to begin intensive planning for an attack should the opportunity arise.[11]

Mangin began making preparations both in theory and in practice. He ordered French forces to cross the Savières stream and take command of the heights on both banks. This four-day operation removed a barrier to future Allied movements and denied the Germans the ability to observe French movements in the valley below. Other operations captured the town of Vaux and part of the strategically critical Hill 204 west of Château-Thierry. The Savières crossing and almost forty other minor operations were, however, too small to distract much German attention from their own plans to attack, and thus did not give away growing French interest in the region.

Foch called the period from June 13 to July 15 "the period of waiting."[12] His choice of words is apt. The Allies were waiting for the Germans to show their hand and, hopefully, expose their weakness. They were also hoping for time to develop solid defensive networks in threatened areas while at the same time concentrating forces in the Tenth Army area for a massive counteroffensive. Both sides were waiting for supplies and reinforcements to fill in for the massive losses of the previous few months.

Several French commanders hoped that the Germans might not be planning to attack at all until August. If the Germans waited a bit longer, then the French might themselves be ready to attack first. If the Germans did attack out of the Marne sector, the Allies would be faced with a critical decision. They would need to determine if such an attack constituted a major assault of its own or if it was merely a diversion to draw resources and reserves away from other fronts, especially Flanders. If they guessed wrong, the Allied high command might denude a critical area of needed men and supplies. Haig in particular worried about the Germans using a move toward Rheims or Paris as a feint to draw attention away from the British sector in the north.

For his part, Foch believed that he had figured out the new German way of war, at least at the strategic level. For all of the German success in gaining territory, Foch believed that they had erred by reinforcing the wrong sectors.[13] Numerically, Flanders offered the Germans their best chance of success in late June. Yet Foch concluded that the Germans would resume their attack in the Marne sector in order to relieve the supply problems affecting the German soldiers there. While other generals worried about the Germans attacking Paris, Foch saw that they would in fact have to attack east, away from Paris, for the important but less dramatic reason of improving their logistics by capturing Rheims.

The British high command was just as divided as the French command about German intentions. Most British generals presumed (correctly, as it turned out) that an attack in the Marne sector would have the strategic purpose of moving Allied reserves away from Flanders, allowing the Germans to break British lines there and perhaps approach Paris from the north. Haig and several other senior British generals were so concerned about Flanders that they doubted the Germans would attack on the Marne at all. Thus, the Allied generals disagreed on what might happen next, even if almost all of them admitted at least the possibility of a renewed German offensive on the Marne.

Foch was almost alone in concluding that the main blow of the next German offensive was bound to come in the first half of July. He had also concluded that the offensive would be aimed at both sides of Rheims (and therefore away from Paris) because of the need for the Germans to control the Marne sector's railway network. He and Mangin had agreed that not only would the German offensive fail, but it would also expose the Germans to a vicious counterattack on their western flank. Thus the two men were thinking not just about defending, but about attacking. As Mangin and Foch both remembered, the Germans had exposed their western flank on the Marne in 1914 as well. The rapid Allied response in 1914 had saved Paris and changed the momentum of the war. Foch and Mangin now hoped that the Germans would expose a flank again and that the results would be just as dramatic.

German Planning

Georg von Hertling, the former Bavarian prime minister who succeeded Georg Michaelis as German chancellor in November 1917, held out great hopes for the fifth German offensive, which he had been told would begin in mid-July. After the war he wrote, "At the beginning of July, 1918, I was convinced, I confess it, that before the first of September our adversaries would send us peace proposals. . . . We expected grave events in Paris for the end of July."[14] Hertling obviously wanted to believe, evidence in front of him notwithstanding, that Germany was capable of winning the war with one more major offensive.

Had Hertling more closely studied the strategic situation at hand, he would have seen how slight the odds of a German victory truly were. With German forces so far ahead of their railheads, exploitation of any gaps created by storm troops would have been very difficult for regular infantry to sustain. This problem had confronted armies since the beginning of the war. Creating a gap in enemy lines, difficult in and of itself, was easier than supplying the soldiers who would have to move through that gap and attack the enemy's exposed flanks. As David Zabecki has pointed out, armies could create occasional break-ins, but they could not create break-throughs.[15] In the Marne sector, with the Allies so close to the major supply centers in and around Paris, exploiting a gap would be that much harder.

Moreover, the Allies had now seen most of the facets of the new German way of fighting. Most Allied commanders had by July become convinced of the value of defense-in-depth networks. The fates of Gough and Duchêne provided extra motivation for generals to reconsider any opposition they had to such systems. Several of the best defense-in-depth networks, including one on the Marne front, had become quite sophisticated. With the Allies on alert for another German offensive, moreover, surprise on the level of March 21 was out of the question. Lastly, the one million Americans in France gave Foch an astounding resource that he could use to fill in gaps, conduct local counterattacks, and provide operational flexibility.

Before the Germans could hope for a big victory, they had to improve their supply arrangements. Thus the Germans had first to look for an important local success. The biggest local prize, as Foch had divined, was the rail network of the Marne salient. To gain full control over the network required seizing three rail centers: Rheims, Epernay, and Châlons. The last sat east of Epernay and also commanded the eastern half of the Marne River. The three cities together formed a right triangle with the line connecting Rheims and Châlons (northwest to southeast) forming the hypotenuse. Inside the triangle sat the thick Forêt de la Montagne de Rheims, through which both highways and railroads ran. The Germans would therefore need to dominate the forest as well.

If the Germans could succeed in capturing these goals they could cut the Paris to Verdun trunk line. Doing so would in turn isolate Verdun and the French and American armies in the east, making them vulnerable to an attack. Control of the Marne rail network would, of course, be a critical step for any large operation toward Paris, although there is no evidence that Paris was an immediate, or even medium-range, goal of the Germans in July.[16] From a technical logistic stand-point, a successful attack in the Marne sector could produce some favor-able results, even if an advance on Paris might not follow immediately behind it.

On the strategic level, the Germans had to create a numerical mis-match to give them numerical superiority somewhere on the western front, preferably against the British. Pressure on the Marne front might, as Haig feared, induce Foch to move reserves away from the north to reinforce the Marne. French politicians might also insist on forces being shifted south in order to insure the safety of Paris. Finally, a threat to the symbolic city of Verdun might just cause the French to reinforce that sector as they had done in 1916. These troop movements might leave the British armies in Flanders open to an attack and isolated from rein-forcement. Given the presence of the Americans, the Germans' hope for the latter was probably no more than a pipe dream, but it continued to haunt British officers even after German intentions on the Marne became obvious.

A German order from mid-June indicates that at that time the Ger-man Supreme Headquarters saw a Flanders operation as the main attack and the Marne operation as merely preliminary. The order, dated June 14 and entitled "Disposition of German Armies for Marne Operations," notes that Operation Hagen, the codename of the Flanders offensive, would begin "about July 20." The Marne deployments in Crown Prince Wilhelm's sector were identified merely as "preparations" for Hagen. It also directed the German First and Seventh armies to develop plans not only to attack the Marne sector, but to defend it as well, a further indi-cation that the Germans were not thinking of an immediate move on Paris. It set the date for the Marne offensive at July 10, enough time to allow the Allies to reposition forces from Flanders to the Marne. Then Hagen could begin in Flanders with a greater probability of success.[17]

Although this order reinforces the conclusion that Paris was not a short-term goal of the Marne operation, German army planners recog-nized the need to take steps preliminary to a major offensive in the direc-tion of the French capital. The rail network of Rheims, which Crown Prince Wilhelm recognized was "essential some time or another" if the Germans were to move on the city, thus became one of the two foci of planning, along with Flanders.[18] Until the Germans could dominate the communications of the Marne, they knew, Paris could not seriously be threatened from the east.

Still, Paris was a long way off from German planning in July. Rheims had to be taken first. In late June the crown prince's staff envisioned a double envelopment to capture the city and its rail lines. The German Seventh Army would cross the Marne west of the city between Château-Thierry and Chambercy. Such a movement would cut the main roads leading into Epernay, thus isolating that city. The German First Army would attack to the east of Rheims and head toward Châlons. Rheims would thus be surrounded, Epernay cut off from three directions, and Châlons threatened.

Two elements of the plan would determine its success or failure. First, surprise had to be maintained because the Allies had to be kept guessing about whether the Marne operation was the main assault or a feint to distract attention from Flanders. If the Allies did not move reserves away from Flanders, then Hagen could not possibly succeed. Thus, in Crown Prince Wilhelm's words, "if the factor of surprise was lacking for any reason, the whole operation would fail with the opening move." Second, the crown prince's army group would have to succeed without large numbers of reserves or reinforcements. All reserves went north to Flanders to be ready to exploit the expected mismatch of numbers to be created when Foch moved Allied reserves to Paris and the Marne. The attack would be handicapped by less generous supplies of artillery and a reliance on generally second-rate units, but Ludendorff "had [nevertheless] convinced himself that another massive tactical victory in July in this otherwise non-decisive sector would collapse French moral and cause them to sue for peace."[19]

Unlike Ludendorff and Hertling, Crown Prince Wilhelm did not expect this offensive to result in a quick victory. Neither did his staff, whom he found "prey to a certain mental depression as we faced our new task." Wilhelm knew that the plan asked too much of tired German troops, and he also knew that however close it looked on a map, Rheims, to say nothing of Paris, was beyond Germany's reach: "Speaking generally, therefore, this new offensive also had no great strategic purpose in view of a kind to decide the campaign. Its purpose was rather a series of separate attacks at different times and in different places, with a view to improving the line which circumstances had imposed on us."[20] Even despite his occasional bouts of optimism, Ludendorff at times agreed, noting that a twin-axis attack on either side of Rheims "made great demands on our troops, but in our position there was no other course possible."[21]

If the two men most responsible for the attack did not expect big results from it, why did they order it to be conducted at all? The most logical answer is that they had concluded that the risks of waiting were greater than the risks of acting, even if they had to launch their offensive under unfavorable circumstances. The arrival of the Americans and the continuing pressure of the blockade forced the Germans to press their advantage even if the commanders themselves believed they might be pressing too far too fast. Even should the offensive succeed, the crown prince knew that "the contemplated Marne-Rheims blow . . . was probably the last great effort of which we (Army Group Crown Prince) were capable."[22]

Neither the crown prince nor Ludendorff seems to have known exactly what he wanted the Marne offensive to accomplish. There remained confusion at the highest levels about whether the offensive's main goal was to denude the Flanders front of Allied reserves in preparation for a major German offensive there or whether the operation was to be limited to improving logistical networks in the Marne salient. More fundamentally, supply and logistical arrangements could not be completed in time to meet the start date of July 10. Each day lost, the commanders knew, reduced the overall chances of success. Still, the increasingly unstable Ludendorff held out great hopes, noting later that a German victory in Champagne in July "would have changed the whole war situation in favor of the fatherland," although he is less than clear as to exactly how it would have done so.[23]

Speed became an essential factor in German planning, but the German army of July was no longer capable of the speed and suppleness of maneuver that had characterized it in March. Moreover, German intelligence concluded that the Allies could man the sector between Château-Thierry and Verdun only lightly, but that they were likely to reinforce the sector quickly if they suspected that the Germans intended to take the offensive in that area. Any offensive had to begin quickly. In the larger strategic sense, of course, Allied ability to move forces into the Marne sector did not concern German planners. Indeed, the Germans wanted the Allies to shift large numbers of men and supplies south in the hopes that such troops would come from the Flanders sector. They presumed, however, that large-scale troop transfers would not begin until the German offensive itself had begun.

The appearance of an intelligence report to the contrary on July 11 appears not to have caused undue alarm on the German side. The report noted that several captured Allied soldiers informed German officers of massive troop concentrations behind the cover of the Forêt de Villers-Cotterêts on the western edge of the Marne salient.[24] Ludendorff later noted in his memoirs that he was aware of the possibility of the Allies attacking Soissons on the western end of the salient in order to disrupt his efforts against Rheims on the eastern edge of the salient. But if he was aware of the danger, he did little to plan for it, dispatching just one division that had recently redeployed from the eastern front to guard Soissons. The rest of the units near Soissons were tired and in need of rest; thus they were designated to defend, not to take part in the offensive to come. They would have their work cut out for them because German prepared defenses in the area were, even by Ludendorff's own admission, "not far advanced."[25]

The crown prince wanted as much time as possible to prepare his armies for a new offensive. The poor state of rail and road communications in the salient made it difficult for the Germans to supply their men. The crown prince would have preferred to wait until August to attack again, but the speed with which the Americans were arriving in France made waiting that long impossible. In the end, the crown prince was able to buy only a few extra days. The start date for the offensive was set for July 15; the kaiser's staff began making the arrangements for Wilhelm II to be present to witness the expected triumph of German arms. Given that July 14 fell that year on a Sunday, the Bastille Day holiday weekend would be officially extended to Monday. Celebrations would, of course, be more muted than in years past, but the German attack, if it could maintain surprise, might catch the French and their new American allies at the end of three-day celebration.

The invitation to the kaiser, and all the staff work that would accompany it, provides yet another indication that at least a few senior German officials thought that the offensive would produce dramatic, momentum-changing results. Wilhelm's own understanding of the intricacies of modern war, as opposed to the staged war games he had witnessed before 1914, was notably lacking. In place of grand strategic debates, he had instead become prone to rambling tirades increasingly disconnected to reality. The kaiser, once so proud of his role as commander in chief of the German army, had become less and less relevant to German strategy and military operations. It is thus highly unlikely that the kaiser would have been invited to witness an operation designed solely to draw Allied reserves away from Flanders, because he was unlikely to understand it in all of its technicalities.[26] The capture of Rheims would be a much more dramatic accomplishment, and one worthy of the kaiser's presence.

After overseeing the invitation of his father to the Marne front, Crown Prince Wilhelm called the chiefs of staff of the First and Third armies "to make certain whether surprise was assured." They both assured him that the operation, scheduled to begin the next day, July 15, had an excellent chance of success because "the enemy had so far noticed nothing" out of the ordinary and had no idea that a German offensive was about to begin.[27] Ludendorff, too, had called the army headquarters, "anxious to know if, in their opinion, or in that of the troops, the enemy had any knowledge of our preparations."[28] The army headquarters informed Ludendorff, as they had the crown prince, that all was well and that surprise had been maintained. The Germans could not have been more wrong.

Allied Preparations

By the time the German attack began, the Allies had an almost complete picture of German intentions and capabilities. Despite the claims of the two German chiefs of staff, the Allies knew the key details of the German plan down to the minute. Their information had come from numerous sources. German staff work on this operation seems not to have been to the same high standard of previous operations. Ludendorff later noted that German confidence in the operation had led to a sloppiness about basic operational security and that "an attack on Rheims was discussed in the most irresponsible way throughout Germany."[29]

There is little evidence that loose lips in Germany were an important source of information for the Allies. Among the Allied generals, only American General Hunter Liggett even mentions the knowledge of the operation in Berlin, commenting laconically that the Marne offensive "had too many press agents."[30] Liggett and the other Allied commanders did not need spies inside Germany to tell them that something was afoot. They had plenty of other sources of information at hand.

As early as mid-June, deserters and aerial observations had revealed the telltale signs of a coming offensive. On June 28, air reconnaissance and prisoners of war taken in a recent raid provided important pieces to the puzzle. They informed the French Fourth Army intelligence bureau of a concentration of heavy equipment along a nine-mile corridor between Château-Thierry and Epernay. German prisoners confirmed the purpose of these concentrations to be a July offensive against Rheims as well as numerous local diversions. A later report confirmed the presence of large numbers of storm troops in the German plans for the first wave of the offensive. These reports appear to have provided Foch with the final pieces of information he needed to conclude that the Germans would strike the Marne before they struck in Flanders; by the end of the first week of July, Foch had overseen the movement of ten divisions from the general reserve to the Marne sector.[31]

On July 5, Pétain felt confident enough to issue an order to army commanders reading:

> The object of the anticipated German attack in the Champagne may be:
>
> To draw the mass of our reserves from the region of Paris and the zone of the Franco-British junction.
>
> To effect the fall of Reims and gain a foothold on the Montagne de Reims.
>
> To bring the Epernay—Châlons—Revigny Railroad within the range of its artillery.[32]

The order neatly summarized the main points of German intentions as the French understood them. Note also the use of the definite article when referring to "*the* anticipated German attack," indicating that the French commanders were already well acquainted with at least the prospect of a German attack.

Fayolle must have been privy to more information than just Pétain's order. On the same day, he noted in his diary the probability of a German attack. He also concluded that "if the Germans [le Boche] fail in this offensive, we will be three-quarters saved." Four days later he confided to his diary that the French army headquarters (meaning Pétain and his staff) "finally seems to have begun to prepare seriously this time for an attack south of Soissons. Will it be possible if the Germans attack first? I think so, because we will be able to do it (attack) with all resources."[33] His comments suggest both that the German attack was expected and that defeating it would represent a major turning point in Allied fortunes.

Knowledge of an impending German attack percolated down to the soldiers themselves. Rumors of upcoming offensives were, of course, commonplace, and units in the front lines had experienced numerous false alarms. One American field artillery unit from the 26th Division received orders to cancel their July 4th holiday plans and march 28 kilometers to Jouarre to help meet a German attack that was expected within forty-eight hours. The Germans were so close, the men were told, that they should not even smoke at railway stations for fear of being targeted by snipers spotting the glow of their cigarettes. The men believed the rumors, but clearly they had fallen prey to their own inexperience. When the attack failed to materialize, the men took advantage of the opportunity to swim in the Marne.[34]

Other American units put more faith in the alerts they received. Two American battalions returned to their units following July 4th celebrations in Paris to find the men in their part of the line convinced of an imminent German attack.[35] The men of the American Yankee Division who deployed that week west of Château-Thierry noted the rumors as well. Their commander, Major General Clarence Edwards, believed that his unit had moved to the Château-Thierry portion of the Marne sector for the express purpose of defeating an impending German attack.[36] His counterpart in the 2nd Division, Major General James Harbord, noted in his diary on July 9 that he had been aware of the imminence of a German attack for days.[37]

Information from demoralized deserters and prisoners taken in raids continued to come in to Foch's small and insular headquarters. Foch used these "reliable indications of the enemy's intentions" to guess that in the first two weeks of July, the Germans would attack along an approximately 75-mile front, with the main effort directed at Rheims and toward crossing the Marne River near Dormans. Foch directed that more raids and reconnaissance flights be conducted in order to gather even more information. He found that "the enemy was actively pushing his preparations" on the Marne, but that "in his haste he even neglected precautions which might have concealed them."[38] The picture was coming so clearly into focus that several Allied officers began to wonder if the whole Marne operation might not be a ruse. Divining German intentions had never been this easy. Perhaps it was too easy, and the Allies were walking into a trap.

For his part, GAR commander Fayolle grew increasingly confident. On July 12 he wrote in his diary, "The Germans are going to attack between Château Thierry and Reims. This is more and more certain. When they do, I can fall upon their back! For it to work, we must hold on the Marne without having to take away any reserves (from the armies designated for the attack)."[39] French Fourth Army commander General Henri Gouraud, who had lost an arm earlier in the war, was also confident. On July 7, his order of the day noted, "We may be attacked at any moment. You all know that a defensive battle was never engaged under more favorable conditions. We are awake and on our guard."[40]

The critical pieces of information came in just hours before the beginning of the battle. On July 13, a German officer had crossed the Marne River to scout French defenses on the other side. He found the defenders easily enough, but they found him as well, capturing him before he could make it back to the safety of the north bank of the river. He was unwisely carrying with him a complete copy of the attack orders, which he had not had time to destroy before his capture. In a separate incident, a July 14 raid by five soldiers of the French IV Corps was even more successful, yielding twenty-seven prisoners, one of whom gave his interrogators the exact minute that the German artillery and infantry phases were to begin. The French high command thus knew that the Germans would open preparatory artillery fire at ten minutes past midnight on the morning of July 15.[41]

Thus the key element of surprise, without which Crown Prince Wilhelm believed the offensive could not succeed, had been lost long before the offensive began. Even the letters of individual soldiers attest that the Allies were sitting and waiting for the Germans. A private in the American 42nd Division wrote home even while the battle was still raging that the "time and place (of the German attack) had been figured and worked out almost to the minute."[42]

Curiously, the private seemed to know more than two of the national commanders in chief. Pershing made no mention of the Marne offensive in his personal diary until July 17, despite Foch having told him a week before that he (Foch) expected the Marne salient to be reduced by September.[43] Haig's understanding of the situation is even more curious. On July 14 he wrote in his diary, "Apparently, without any definite facts to go on, Foch has made up his mind that the Enemy's main attack is about to fall on the French in the east [sic] of Rheims."[44] It is hard to reconcile the difference in knowledge about German intentions between a private from Pennsylvania and two national commanders, except to note that both generals had their attention fixed elsewhere. Fortunately, Foch's attention was not.

Allied preparations for meeting the German attack had been underway for months. The much maligned and largely anonymous staff
officers of the French high command had been working night and day
to concentrate forces around the Marne sector. Their job was intricate
and very difficult. They had to arrange for the movement of hundreds
of thousands of men and their equipment without giving away those
movements to the Germans or tipping their hands to any spies. Much of
this movement was conducted at night in order to hide from German air
reconnaissance. Staff officers faced a myriad of tasks including arranging for the appropriate rolling stock, buses, and trucks to be at entraining
and detraining stations; providing fuel for the vehicles, food for the men,
and fodder for the horses; and arranging for guides from units already
in the area to lead the new arrivals to their positions. The staffs also had
to deconflict rail schedules so that trains were not overloading the rail
networks. A traffic jam on any point of the network could slow down
the entire operation. The staffs also had to rework their arrangements
again and again as orders came from higher headquarters changing
destinations at the last minute. Their job was monumental, and although it received far less attention than the performance of men on the
battlefield, it was no less important to the battle's final outcome.

Given all of the constraints under which the staff officers were working, it is not surprising to find that some units were less than satisfied
with their transportation arrangements. One lieutenant colonel in the
British 51st Division complained that on arrival in the Marne sector
there were no guides to help his men find their front-line positions.
They had to complete a "night march in a strange country to destinations which local inhabitants had never even heard of!"[45] His commanding general, Sir W. P. Braithwaite, agreed, noting that "French staff work
was beneath contempt. Hardly a single thing came off as they said it
would. . . . How we ever managed to get ready for the initial advance
was not only a wonder to me, but to everyone else concerned."[46]

These complaints are comparatively rare, however, and came years
after the war from a 51st Division staff that had few positive words for
their French allies in general. The bulk of the evidence suggests that the
staffs had done incredible work, even if almost all of it was behind the
scenes. The British 62nd Division traveled from the general reserve in
forty trains (each made up of forty individual cars), the first one leaving
at 4:42 on the afternoon of July 14 and the last one leaving at 6:12 the

next morning. It took just thirty-two hours to move an entire division and all of its supplies to the battlefront, an impressive accomplishment in and of itself. The feat is all the more remarkable when one learns from the division's war diary that it was decided while the division was en route to move it from the Fourth Army area to the Fifth Army area.[47]

The staffs faced several unforeseen challenges. Some units even lacked commanders. Just hours before the battle Pershing decided to give Major General James Guthrie Harbord command of the 2nd Division. Although fifteen months earlier he had been a major and a student at the Army Staff College, the affable and efficient Harbord had impressed Pershing early on and had preformed well as commander of the Marine Brigade at Belleau Wood. Harbord, however, was in Paris shopping when the order came down from Pershing's staff naming him 2nd Division commander. He had to find his scattered division and prepare orders for his men, all during a driving rainstorm that turned roads to mud. Harbord also had very little solid information on the Marne sector itself. His sole intelligence report consisted of a "short memorandum" on the terrain written by a veteran of the First Battle of the Marne.[48]

Once on the Marne sector, men had to move quickly from train stations to the battlefront. Many had to do so at night, with guides who did not speak their language, and under tremendous pressure from higher headquarters to move quickly, as the battle was just hours away from commencing. A member of the Argyll and Seaforth Highlanders recalled arriving at the front in the early hours of July 15 to a scene of mass confusion. A last-minute change of destination rendered all of their preparations null and void. The maps they had originally been given were taken away and new ones issued. "*Frantic* preparations at night for a move to the south. Thousands of orders coming in, accompanied or followed by thousands of cancellations."[49]

The final movements to the battlefield had to be made on foot, and often at night. Many men of the British 62nd Division had to march as many as 30 miles to get to their start positions. Americans in the 26th Division completed a night march of 18 miles and entered a sector that the guides told them was a *pas bon* sector because of the routine German shelling and the expectation that it was in the direct path of any major German operation.[50] Hurried movements of men, horses, and machines continued even as the guns began to roar. Many men sprinted the last few miles in order to arrive at their designated places on time.

In the midst of this chaos, on the warm night of July 14, the communications officer of the American 42nd Division received a coded message from Fourth Army headquarters. The coded official part of the message read, "François cinq sept zero." The message confirmed that the long-anticipated German attack would begin at midnight. The official part of the message was soon followed by the words *bon chance*. The Second Battle of the Marne was about to begin.

FIVE

TURNING THE TIDE
OF THE WAR

AS THE PRECEDING chapters have shown, even before the Second
Battle of the Marne opened on 15 July 1918, the two sides had already
made many of the key decisions that would determine the battle's outcome. The Germans had already decided to fight a battle with unclear
strategic purposes and resources insufficient to achieve meaningful
operational success. Their sloppiness and haste had tipped their hand
and, unbeknownst to the German high command, had put their forces
at a tremendous disadvantage. For their part, the Allies had decided to
meet this offensive, the fifth major German offensive since March, not
just with a vigorous defense, but with an aggressive counteroffensive
designed not just to hold their line in place, but to change the tenor of
the war entirely.

Nevertheless, even the most optimistic Allied commanders knew
that none of their preparations guaranteed victory. The minor victory
at Le Hamel on July 4 notwithstanding, the Allies on July 15 were
still on the strategic defensive. Their gargantuan efforts to move men
and supplies into the Marne sector evened their numerical inferiority
somewhat, but the Germans still held important materiel advantages.
Moreover, many Allied units had arrived on the battlefield tired and
confused. Several regiments detrained and literally sprinted toward the
sound of guns to join the fight; many of them arrived in the wrong place.
The multi-lingual and multi-national command structure, moreover,

was still unproven in battle. The Allied high command was certainly optimistic, but generals had been optimistic before, only to have their high hopes dashed. Despite Allied possession of an accurate understanding of German intentions, the outcome of this battle was far from preordained. The battle might still devolve into another long, indecisive slogging match that did neither side any good while killing many thousands more men.

To guard against such an eventuality, the Allies endeavored to make the most of their intelligence. The Germans had planned to start their artillery barrage at ten minutes past midnight French time, ten minutes past one o'clock in the morning German time, on July 15.[1] The night before, German officer Kurt Hesse had overseen the final preparations of his unit, then drifted off to sleep before the next morning's offensive. He was awakened by the sound of heavy artillery fire: "I looked at my watch. It was 1:00 AM [German time]. Was our artillery mistaken? It was not to commence its fire until 1:10 AM. I jumped out of my shell hole to look around. Shells were falling in front and in rear of us. It was the enemy who had commenced."[2] Hesse soon found that the Allied shelling had cut his telephone lines and, by firing heavy barrages into the German first line, had mauled two of his battalion's companies. Allied shelling had also focused on German railroad junctures and road crossings where the Germans were most likely to concentrate their infantry, thus impeding the flow of reinforcements of men and supplies to the front.

Allied shelling had also instilled panic in the German lines because the men had been assured that the Allies did not know about the offensive. The result was confusion and demoralization. "The engineers had quit," Hesse recalled. "The boats [for ferrying German soldiers across the Marne] had been abandoned in place several hundred meters from the Marne." Worst of all, the ten minutes between the start of the Allied barrage and the planned start of the German barrage was too short a time difference to change intricate German planning. As a result, the German artillery plan went ahead exactly as scheduled, despite the obvious fact that surprise, considered so critical to success, was gone. Thus the German rolling barrage, intended to cover the advance of the German infantry (see below), went on as scheduled even though "nothing that had been foreseen could be carried out" under the new circumstances. German infantry officers hurriedly sought new objectives while Hesse sat listening to the sounds of Allied machine gun fire as he watched the German artillery barrage roll away from him to no effect. The Allied machine guns he heard could therefore fire with impunity into the ranks of advancing German soldiers. With no infantry available to follow the artillery forward, Hesse knew that the plan had failed even before it had had a chance to succeed.

On another part of the German front, German soldier Rudolph Binding had a similar experience. His unit had been less well prepared for its role in the attack. Binding noted that "the preparations for this hell consisted mostly of paper: the road to it was paved with paper. If we fire off as much ammunition at the enemy as we had paper fired at us he will have a bad time." Binding thought it "hardly credible" to think that the Allies did not suspect a German offensive, given how clumsy German preparations had been. He seems to have been one of the few Germans to have expected a difficult day on July 15. He was certainly right.[3]

The Allies had been able to blunt the German attack with a heavy counter–artillery barrage of their own, but the German attack still had powerful force behind it. The total battle frontage covered more than 65 miles, with the bulk of the German effort concentrated on either side of Rheims. The Germans had twenty-two divisions east of the city and twenty more divisions advancing on it from the west. The combination of the two artillery barrages was powerful enough to be both heard and seen in Paris. It even knocked pictures off the walls in some eastern Parisian districts.[4] One newspaper report of the battle noted that "when people [in Paris] rose from their beds they saw the northeastern horizon aglow with a pale, flame-colored light." Another report said that from the heights of Montmartre, Parisians could make out individual gun flashes.[5]

Although the Allies had managed to even the odds through their rapid redeployment of resources, the Germans still held a materiel advantage. On July 15, the Germans had a 1,047 to 360 edge in field artillery pieces and a 609 to 408 advantage in heavy and "super-heavy" pieces in the Rheims sector alone; they had over 2,000 artillery batteries to cover the entire Marne salient.[6] In phase one, the German artillery plan called for three hours of preparatory shelling with smoke, high explosive, and gas shells. The main targets of the barrage were the Allied front-line positions, but some targets were as far as seven miles behind the front line. The Germans had used this technique of a deadly, but relatively brief, artillery preparation phase to great effect earlier in the year. Ideally, it would pin down and disorient soldiers in the Allied front line and at the same time disrupt Allied communications in the rear. As we will see, however, Allied preparations had negated and diluted the impacts of this shelling by emptying the front line of men and equipment. The Allied shelling that began ten minutes before the German fire also caused major disruptions. Thus the first phase of the German attack was far weaker than the Germans had anticipated.

The first phase of the German artillery barrage was also designed to clear the way for the initial German crossing of the Marne and the seizure of key points on the south bank of the river. After one hour and forty-five minutes of the preparatory shelling had presumably removed all obstacles to a German crossing, the Germans would place scores of twenty-man boats in the Marne, the most formidable water obstacle the 1918 offensives had yet faced. Engineers would also build footbridges for the movement of the next wave of infantrymen and pontoon bridges for the movement of heavy equipment. German field artillery would then shoot at any targets of opportunity the gunners saw and fire dozens of smoke shells to make Allied observation of the crossing even more difficult in the predawn twilight.[7] The plan called for the German crossing of the river to take just fifteen minutes and for German pioneers to be in command of the railway embankments on the south side of the Marne by 2:30 AM. German soldiers would then reassemble under the cover provided by the predawn darkness, smoke, and tall wheat fields, reorganize their platoons and companies, and wait for the second phase of the artillery plan to unfold.[8]

The first phase of the German barrage had one other important goal. German super-heavy guns were to fire on Allied hangars in the hopes of destroying Allied aircraft on the ground. The Germans brought in an 11-inch gun dedicated to this purpose. The gun was so large that it could be moved only by rail. The Allies had anticipated this tactic and removed their airplanes from hangars that were within range of the German guns. The German guns thus obliterated the hangars, but the airplanes, having been flown safely away, were untouched.[9]

The second German artillery phase featured a rolling (or creeping) barrage, a standard part of any World War I offensive by 1918. Rolling barrages, as their name implies, preceded the infantry in a carefully choreographed tandem in order to provide fire support on the move. Each barrage was different, but all advanced by measured steps, focusing fire on one line or part of the line before moving forward to the next set of targets at a designated time in order to allow the infantry to advance into presumably clear areas. The exact speed and timing of rolling barrages varied according to the terrain and the strength of an individual enemy position, but a typical speed for advancing infantry by this stage of the war was approximately 250 meters in ten minutes.

The German rolling barrage on the morning of July 15 was intended to move five miles in all, far enough to cover German soldiers as they crossed the river and established solid defensive positions on the south bank of the Marne. A five-mile advance would also place the Germans beyond the suspected depth of serious Allied resistance and into open country. Because of the disruption caused by the Allied artillery barrage ten minutes before the start of the German barrage, however, the rolling barrage had no chance of succeeding. French counter–battery fire destroyed the careful German timing, causing the pontoon boats to go into the water as much as two hours behind the rigidly prepared schedule.[10] As a result, Hesse watched the barrage roll away on the south bank of the Marne far in advance of the infantry.

The Germans also expected to control the skies in the battle's early phases. German squadrons, including the famous "Flying Circus" squadron that had been commanded by Manfred von Richtofen until his death in April, had assembled in the region. A major German airbase near the town of Coincy, just north of Château-Thierry, was home to two elite squadrons, each consisting of twenty-eight planes. Its central location allowed it to roam the Marne sector almost at will, although the thick forests of the region limited pilots' ability to provide ground commanders with reliable and accurate intelligence about enemy numbers and preparations. German pilots therefore did not detect the massive concentration of men and machines from the French Tenth Army inside the Forêt de Villers-Cotterêts southwest of Soissons.

The air war over the Second Battle of the Marne also produced one of the most dramatic incidents of the war for the Americans. On 14 July 1918, Quentin Roosevelt, the youngest son of former president Theodore Roosevelt, was shot down over the Marne sector while strafing German lines near the town of Fère-en-Tardenois. He was twenty years old and had left Harvard during his sophomore year to volunteer for the army. His death hit Theodore Roosevelt hard, and made for banner headlines in the United States, France, and Great Britain. French President Raymond Poincaré sent a letter of condolence to the former president. Roosevelt responded in characteristic fashion by writing to Poincaré: "My only regret is that I am unable to fight beside my sons."[11]

For Allied soldiers facing the German advance, the presence of German aviation proved to be a major hindrance. One soldier noted in his diary for July 15 that "there are fully three hundred planes up close to here [Château-Thierry] and I'll warrant two-thirds of them are Boche."[12] Another veteran noted the "hordes" of planes the Germans used to support their advance. German aviation "swept here and there over the battlefield, machine gunning American defensive positions, bombing centers of resistance, [and] guiding the infantry. To the desperately fighting infantry there seemed [to be] no Allied planes in the world."[13]

In point of fact, the Allies did have large numbers of airplanes in the Marne theater. They were, however, dedicated to the mission of striking targets behind German lines instead of clearing the skies of German airplanes. French planes dropped more than fourteen tons of explosives on targets deep behind German lines on day one of the battle.[14] The inability of Allied aviators to clear the sky of German fighters and bombers, however, caused tremendous problems for Allied infantry. Numerous memoirs of the battle complain of the lack of Allied cover and the constant threat posed by German planes.

Despite Allied forewarning of the German advance, the power of the German attack took its toll on Allied units. Inexperienced units suffered the highest casualty levels, because many of their men did not know how to dig defensive positions strong enough to resist German artillery. The American 28th Division and the French 125th Division suffered heavily from the German barrage because, having arrived so soon before the battle, their trenches were "only partially dug" and they had "no deep bomb-proofs even for the points of command."[15] French soldiers called these positions *pas fini* (not finished) sections, and looked upon the prospect of serving in them with considerable dread. Compounding matters, some regiments and brigades had been told, in contravention of the prevailing wisdom at higher headquarters, to have their men defend the Marne with one foot in the river and to counterattack to recover any lost territory. Many of the casualties in the American 3rd and 28th divisions came as a result of these unnecessary tactics.

Unwise these tactics may have been, but the motives behind them were noble enough. Many French soldiers did not want to cede the strategic and symbolic Marne River without a fight, and many American

soldiers looked aghast at retreating under any circumstances, but especially in their first battle serving alongside their new allies. They much
preferred to display the "calm and perfect bearing under artillery fire,
endurance of fatigue and privations, tenacity in defense, eagerness in
counterattack, [and] willingness to engage in hand-to-hand fighting"
reported by a French liaison officer.[16] Where solid defense-in-depth
systems were created, they performed extremely well. Not all units,
however, had the time or the resources to build such networks.

Even among veterans, the uncertainty and chaos of this battlefield
was a far cry from the training they had received. The deadly accuracy
of German snipers concealed among tall wheat fields, combined with
reports that German storm troops were wearing American and French
uniforms, added to the confusion and sense of desperation.[17] One soldier in the American 2nd Division described the fighting as "hectic and
hard" and concluded that "the great Champagne-Marne *Defensive* is
on. There is something tremendous in the air. It brings ample supplies
of ammunition and prompt replacement of disabled howitzers. There
is desperate action and there are no excuses."[18]

The German infantry attack east of Rheims looked impressive on
paper. It involved twenty-two divisions under the overall command
of the German First and Third armies. Of those twenty-two divisions,
however, only five were classified by British intelligence as "fresh." The
remainder were still being reconstructed following the heavy losses they
had suffered during the spring offensives.[19] Eleven of these divisions had
to be held in reserve because they were deemed unfit for major offensive
operations. Moreover, the Germans had almost no armor support.

The early failures of the Germans had dire consequences for the rest
of the battle, and indeed, for the rest of the war as well. The Germans
succeeded in crossing the Marne in one sector only. They had created
a bridgehead on the south bank of the river that was seven to nine miles
wide, with the town of Dormans roughly in the center and the town of
Mezy marking its westernmost extreme. The bridgehead was no deeper
than five miles in any place, about two miles short of the first set of German objectives. The tenuous bridgehead was thus exposed on its west
by the powerful Allied forces around Château-Thierry and to the east
by forces concentrated around Epernay. For reasons we will explore
below, the Germans had made no progress at all against Rheims or the
heights surrounding it.

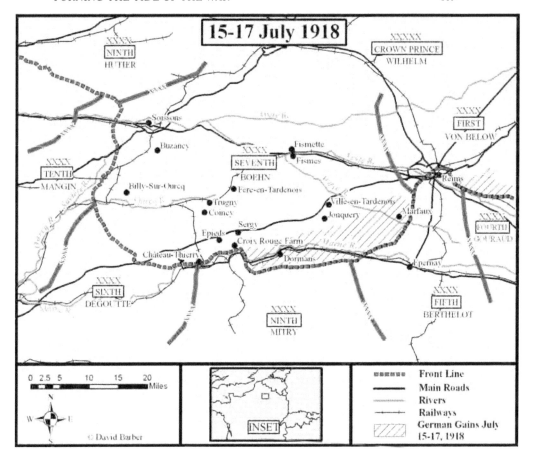

German progress had been too weak to allow for the exploitation of the Allies in open country that German senior leaders had expected. Instead, each successive wave of German attacks grew less and less powerful. With each failure, the morale of German soldiers who had been told that this "peace offensive" would end the war declined. Binding noted that "one could feel the panic of troops . . . gradually growing" as it became more and more obvious that the offensive was failing.[20]

Defending the Marne

The German offensive had made some important gains, but it had failed to achieve even its minimal first-day objectives. Much of the German failure can be attributed to Allied knowledge of the German plan ahead of time and the less than careful plans developed by the Germans themselves. But to stop an analysis of the battle's first stage there would be a disservice to the careful defensive arrangements put in place by the French in their sector east of Rheims. It would also underplay the key role played by units engaging in local counterattacks. The stubborn Allied defense on the Marne on July 15 not only ruined German objectives for the battle, but set the stage for the major Allied counterattack to follow.

East of Rheims, the Allies had put in place one of the strongest, deepest, and most innovative defense-in-depth networks of the war. The sector east of Rheims belonged to the French Fourth Army and held the key to the approaches to Châlons. Foch had therefore guessed that it sat at the heart of German planning. Intelligence reports and aerial observation confirmed German interest in the sector. Accordingly, Foch had dedicated precious reserves to the Fourth Army sector, and Pétain had ordered this sector to prepare an especially strong defensive network.

The French Fourth Army commander, General Henri Gouraud, seemed on the surface to be an unlikely man to execute an order to implement a defense in depth with vigor. A graduate of the French military academy at St. Cyr in 1890, Gouraud had grown up intellectually in the years of the *offensive à outrance* mentality, and, his maturation during the war notwithstanding, he still tended to look upon the voluntary ceding of French territory as a stain upon his, and his army's, honor. It is also worth noting that Gouraud had spent relatively little time on the western front after being wounded in the Argonne Forest in January 1915. A division commander at Gallipoli, he had been badly wounded by a shell burst that tore off one arm and broke both of his legs. After a period of convalescence, he served briefly in Champagne before spending the first half of 1917 in Morocco as governor general. He therefore had had little occasion to observe the learning curve of the Allied armies from 1914 to 1918.

Nevertheless, he proved to be an excellent choice. In April 1917, Pétain selected Gouraud to command the Fourth Army in part because of the innovative ideas he had seen during Gouraud's brief 1916 tour of duty in Champagne. During that period, argues French historian Michel Goya, the Fourth Army "was a model for pioneering studies, experimentation, and the distribution of recommended and prescribed proceedings from higher headquarters." Goya notes that the Fourth Army had maintained an offensive attitude, but it was an attitude "quite different from that of winter, 1914."[21] It had adapted to the new realities of trench warfare and understood the role of the defense in an overall doctrine for winning the war.

Gouraud impressed the French and the Americans alike. He had been on the short list of less than a dozen candidates to replace Robert Nivelle as French army chief of staff in 1917. American Colonel Douglas MacArthur, who served under Gouraud at the Second Battle of the Marne, and was no glad sufferer of fools, left a vivid description of Gouraud:

> With one arm gone, and half a leg missing, with his red beard glittering in the sunlight, the jaunty rake of his cocked hat and the oratorical brilliance of his resonant voice, his impact was overwhelming. He seemed almost to be the reincarnation of that legendary figure of battle and romance, Henry of Navarre. And he was just as good as he looked. I have known all of the modern French commanders, and many were great measured by any standards, but he was the greatest of them all.

Gouraud, wrote MacArthur, "was without a weakness."[22]

Although Gouraud, in the words of another American officer, "more nearly satisfied my conception of the greatest soldiers of the First Empire than any other commander I had met in France,"[23] he had developed the ability to change to meet the needs of modern war. Gouraud's willingness to adapt his method of warfare to the directives emanating from Pétain's headquarters made him an ideal choice for the Fourth Army command. Gouraud had been particularly effective in applying Pétain's Directive Number Four of 24 January 1918, whose salient points included these:

1. The placement of divisions should occur in two echelons, with the first line consisting of just two regiments, and very few heavy weapons. The first echelon should make use of local strong points like fortified villages to compensate for its inferior numbers;
2. The role of the first echelon should be to slow the enemy's infantry enough to disrupt his rolling artillery barrage and buy

time for reinforcements to come forward from division and corps
headquarters to threatened parts of the line;

3. The main "combat zone" of the division should be placed several
   kilometers behind the front line, and therefore out of the range
   of all but the largest German artillery pieces. The combat zone
   should consist of several fresh regiments and the overwhelming
   majority of the division's heavy weapons, especially its machine
   guns. This zone should provide the main resistance to an enemy
   that had become dissociated from its artillery support;

4. Smaller (37mm) field artillery guns, antitank guns, and mortars,
   placed just behind the combat zone should provide additional
   heavy support and a squadron of cavalry should stand ready to
   counterattack isolated enemy units.

5. Heavier artillery should be placed even further back and should
   be placed under regimental control in order to provide for
   immediate fire support where needed.[24]

Directive Number Four was a perfect encapsulation of the theory
of the defense in depth. Time and experience would prove its wisdom, but not all army and army group commanders heeded its warn-
ings. Gouraud, however, had taken the importance of the defense in
depth seriously, and, consequently, his Fourth Army had ceded the
least ground of any French army engaged in battle since the start of
the German offensive in March. By the time of the Second Battle of
the Marne, his Fourth Army had been extended to control 50 miles of
the front, and Gouraud had overseen the construction of a complex
defensive arrangement throughout.

Gouraud's staff took Allied intelligence reports concerning the imminence of the German attack seriously and planned accordingly. They
arranged for a massive artillery barrage to hit the German first lines at
ten minutes before the anticipated start of the German offensive. This
barrage would therefore strike the German first wave just as it was
organizing for the attack. The artillery did its job well, laying down "a
very destructive fire on the north bank [of the Marne], on the principal
avenues of approach, and on suspected places of assembly of troops."[25]

More importantly, the French Fourth Army had put in place a
defense in depth perfectly adapted to the terrain and in complete ac-
cord with the principles laid out in Pétain's Directive Number Four.
The first line was held only lightly, although it was held by specialized
troops with a specialized mission. The second line was held by large

numbers of infantrymen, including the newly arrived double-strength American 42nd Division, which was placed in the French XXI Corps sector alongside the veteran 13th, 43rd, and 170th French divisions. The bulk of the Fourth Army's defensive weaponry, including almost all of its artillery, sat in the third and fourth defensive lines.

The real key to the Fourth Army's defense in depth lay in the first line. Although it would be the first to feel the weight of the German assault, it was only lightly held, with most of the infantrymen in the first line withdrawn at the last hour to protect them from the power of the German artillery bombardment. The first line was, in fact, so weak that the men came to call it the "sacrificial trench." Nonetheless, when French Premier Georges Clemenceau visited the Fourth Army sector just days before the battle he came away overwhelmed with the dedication and courage of the men who had volunteered to serve in such positions. Their eyes, he wrote, "burned with an invincible resolution" as they prepared for the battle. "He who has not lived through such moments," Clemenceau noted, "does not know what life can give."[26]

The soldiers who stayed in these trenches met the German attack by throwing hand grenades and firing machine guns. When the avenues of German approach became evident, they fired rockets to help Allied units in rear areas place their reinforcements and direct field artillery. They were not to fight hand to hand to the death, but were instead to try to slow the German attack as much as possible in order to allow those in the second and third lines to be in the best position to fight. Slowing down the enemy attack would also have the virtue of destroying the precise timing required of the rolling barrage. Once it became obvious that they could no longer hold on to their sacrificial trenches, they destroyed their heavy weapons to prevent them falling into the hands of the enemy, then withdrew to fight alongside their comrades in carefully prepared positions in the second line.

All of the men who remained in the sacrificial trenches were volunteers, providing further evidence of the willingness of French soldiers to fight and sacrifice themselves to defend France. Lacking first-person testimonials, we can only speculate as to their motivations in volunteering for such a manifestly dangerous duty. Some of them undoubtedly volunteered out of the same spirit of self-sacrifice that impels a man to fall on a live grenade in order to save the lives of his comrades. They willingly fought against the German first wave in order to give their comrades in the second line the best possible chance of succeeding.

Others might have wanted to play a role in meeting the attack rather than wait in the rear areas in order to get the initial anxiety of battle over quickly. It is also possible that, as with many combat veterans, they had concluded rather fatalistically that they would not survive the war; fighting in the front line would at least give them a chance to sell their lives dearly and for a noble purpose.

Whatever their reasons for volunteering, the men in the sacrificial trenches performed their job with precision and succeeded beyond anyone's expectations. By the time the German attackers had suffered through the French counter–artillery barrage and fought through the first lines, they were already, in the words of the 42nd Division's chief of staff, Colonel Douglas MacArthur, "exhausted, uncoordinated, and scattered, incapable of going farther without being reorganized and re-inforced."[27] Once these men had made their way through the first line, they discovered that their horror had only just begun; they still had to face the full strength of the Allied defenses in the second and third lines. The Germans sent seven waves of attacks at the Allied second line, but none broke through.

Some Allied units were even in a position to counterattack by mid-day and recover the ground they had lost. By 3:00 PM elements of at least two American and three French divisions had taken the offensive, although they took heavy losses from German machine guns hidden in the wheat fields of the north bank of the Marne, a deadly harbinger of the offensive phase of the war to come. The American 42nd Division even retook its sacrificial trenches by nightfall.

The defense in depth ordered by Pétain and put in place by Gouraud had worked to perfection. Gouraud could rightly boast that his Fourth Army had not had a single man taken prisoner nor had it lost a single artillery piece on the entire first day of the battle, a remarkable achieve-ment in and of itself.[28] On the strategic level, the Fourth Army's stout defense made it possible for the Allied high command to think about starting the offensive phase of the battle.

Gouraud's order of the day on July 15 summed up the day's great achievements:

> Soldiers of the Fourth Army!
>   On July 15, you broke the effort of 15 German divisions, supported by ten others;
>   Their orders were to cross the Marne, but you stopped them. . . . ;

> You have the right to be proud, you heroic soldiers and machine gunners of the forward posts who signaled the attack and broke it up, aviators who flew overhead, battalions and batteries who destroyed it, staff officers who so minutely prepared the battlefield;
>
> This was a hard blow to the enemy!
>
> This was a great day for France!
>
> I count on you to act in the same way every time the enemy dares to attack and from my soldier's heart, I thank you.[29]

The Fourth Army's great stand boosted Allied morale. As the news spread of the heroic performance of the Fourth Army near Rheims, the men of the French 70th Regiment, stationed in the Tenth Army sector near Soissons, knew that the tide was at long last turning. "A great air of an offensive reigns everywhere. The German check in Champagne is affirmed . . . we have all given up the thought of being relieved and going into a rest area. Everyone's spirits await the next attack."[30] The French 74th Regiment had only recently left the Fourth Army sector. Its *journal de marche* for July 15 noted that the men had "learned of a new German push in Champagne. . . . We have learned that the Boche did not pass. . . . The hour of revenge will soon be here."[31]

Farther to the west, the French Fifth Army had not put as strong a defense-in-depth network in place as had the Fourth. The third and fourth defensive lines, where the Fourth Army had placed its strongest artillery, existed only on paper in the Fifth Army's sector. Because virtually all of its combat power was in just two lines instead of four, almost all French assets were within range of German artillery; forty-three of the Fifth Army's battalions were in the first two lines, with just eighteen held back in reserve. The Fifth Army, moreover, included two unreliable Italian divisions that the British were seeking to relieve as quickly as possible.[32]

The Fifth Army's defense, therefore, would have to rely on local counterattacks to keep the German invaders off balance. These attacks were designed to disrupt German timing, expose gaps in the German lines, and create a general sense of panic. As a method of defense, defending by attacking looked less sophisticated than the establishment of the kinds of defense-in-depth networks created by Gouraud, but counterattacks could be an effective method for slowing an enemy offensive if carried out carefully.

In some cases, the method worked as designed. One German regiment, the Sixth Grenadiers, crossed the Marne at 3:40 AM with only "slight losses" and reached a railway embankment shortly thereafter. Believing that they faced only light opposition, they regrouped and advanced, only to discover that the enemy was waiting for them. At 5:15 AM, "an enemy counter attack with greatly superior forces begins and rolls up the regiment from the left, which suffers heavy losses through the enemy machine gun and artillery fire. . . . As our own artillery is completely silenced by the enemy artillery, the remnants of the regiment are thrown back over the Marne at 6:00 AM."[33] By noon on day one, the regiment was down to just five officers and 107 enlisted men.

This German regiment had unwittingly played a role in what AEF commander General John Pershing later called "one of the most brilliant pages in our [American] military annals."[34] The Sixth Grenadier regiment was part of a larger attack by General von Böhn's Seventh Army against Allied positions east of Château-Thierry. As with most Allied positions west of Rheims, the positions near Château-Thierry had no defense-in-depth system worthy of the name. Instead, defenses consisted largely of isolated rifle pits and shell holes.

The line was held by the American 3rd Division, with the French 125th Division to their right and the French 39th Division to their left. The Americans had deployed by regiment, with each regiment placing one battalion in rifle pits along the river bank and behind a gentle embankment. Two other battalions from each regiment deployed into the hills and woods just to the south of the main line of resistance. The French units on either side, by contrast, had deployed all of their men forward, thus exposing them to the full fury of the German artillery barrage. The barrage also hit the Americans very hard. Relying heavily on poison gas, the German shelling caused some panic in the lines of the inexperienced Americans. One regimental commander even had to be taken from the field because of his panic and fear.

Two American regiments, the 30th and the 38th, felt the full fury of the German offensive. The 30th Infantry Regiment had been badly mauled by German artillery and had lost all contact with adjacent units. Upon receiving a report that his forward companies on the river had been destroyed, Colonel Edmund Butts ordered the men in his advance line to withdraw and then asked for Allied artillery to fire on the positions they had just yielded. The plan made good tactical sense and it kept the Germans from breaking the 30th Regiment's second line, but it dangerously exposed the flank of the neighboring 38th Regiment.[35]

The 38th Regiment's commander, Colonel Ulysses Grant McAlexander, was a hard-driving West Pointer who had once been relieved of his command on suspicion of sleeping in his command post, but was later reinstated by Pershing personally.[36] He had foreseen the exposed position of the French regiment to his right and knew that, French promises to him that they would hold notwithstanding, he and his men were in a dangerous position. By early morning, the French had withdrawn under heavy German artillery fire without informing McAlexander of their departure. The withdrawal of the 30th meant that both of McAlexander's flanks were now exposed. Despite the fact that his regiment would have to try to stop an entire German division, McAlexander not only ordered his men to stay, he ordered them to counterattack in order to improve his position.

McAlexander ordered one company to seize the heights of Moulins left empty by the French withdrawal on his right. He ordered another company to seize a key point of the rail line, then had his remaining men dig rifle pits to protect their flanks. It was a daring move that likely prevented a German drive through part of the Allied line in the Château-Thierry sector. One of McAlexander's fellow officers praised the decision: "Had the 38th throughout its distended lines, all of which were subjected at once to frontal, flank, and rear fire, merely clung to a stubborn defense, it in all probability would have been overwhelmed in that day of constant fighting."[37]

Instead of retreating and leaving a gap in the lines, the 38th fought for fourteen hours against repeated German attacks, stopping the German offensive in its tracks. The regiment took prisoners of war from six different German regiments and bought time for the Americans to regroup. By the afternoon, the 30th and the 7th American regiments had reformed and counterattacked, saving the line. The 38th's sector was the only one west of Gouraud's defense-in-depth network that held its place. The 38th has been known ever since as the "Rock of the Marne."

By the end of the day, the Sixth Grenadiers had seen their attack completely fall apart. The official regimental report read, "Regiment thrown back over the Marne, being outflanked on the left. Very heavy losses, some taken prisoner, some crossed back over the Marne. As scarcely any officers are left, units must be reorganized." The report also noted that as German soldiers swam back across the Marne they became slow-moving targets, easy for American riflemen to find and kill. Kurt

Hesse recorded that "the cry of fear" among German soldiers on July 15 was "The Americans kill everyone" and that "for a long time it [fear of the Americans] caused our men to tremble.[38] The 3rd Division's official report on their defense of the Marne gave cold testimony both to the ultimate failure of the Germans and to the ferocity of the division's experiences: "On the front of the Third Division there are no Germans south of the Marne, except the dead."[39]

The great offensive had thus left the Germans with little more than a small and untenable bridgehead around Dormans. The Allied hinge points of Château-Thierry and Rheims had held solidly. Although the Allies lacked the strength to conduct an immediate pursuit north of the Marne River on the 15th, they were in an excellent position to begin regular and accurate artillery harassments of German positions. Isolated pockets of German soldiers south of the Marne posed no serious threat to Allied positions. General Fayolle recorded in his diary that the position of his army group on the 15th "had not become alarming," an understated way of noting that the Allies had the offensive quite well in hand.[40]

Such was the situation when Foch met Haig for lunch at 1:00 PM on July 15. By that point, Foch knew that he had divined his enemy's intentions perfectly. The main weight of the German attack had indeed been aimed at Rheims, where Foch had moved adequate reinforcements to not just meet it, but stop it dead in its tracks. Foch also knew that the Germans were now badly exposed to the massive offensive Mangin had ready to go on the western edge of the salient near Soissons against second-rate German units. Foch was "in the best of spirits" because his plan had come together almost perfectly. He had defeated the main German strike, and he could now unleash his own strike. Even Haig had become more optimistic, reporting on the results of July 15 favorably to Jan Smuts and stating that while he was still worried that the Germans would strike in Flanders near Kemmel, he considered the general situation satisfactory.[41] Foch was much more than merely satisfied. He was beginning to see the war in a whole new light. All he needed now was a couple of days for Mangin to complete his concentrations.

The Meaning of July 15

The Germans understood as well as Foch how important the day had been. As early as 4:40 AM reports began coming in to Crown Prince Wilhelm's headquarters indicating "that apparently the enemy had evacuated his front line according to plan, and that we were not getting forward." At a morning meeting, the crown prince's chief of staff "confirmed on the map what I already knew, that the French plan had been to evade our blow, so that our artillery preparation had destroyed a trench system which had been almost entirely evacuated." Reports also indicated that Allied shelling had been especially accurate and had destroyed a number of German ammunition dumps. "I saw," the crown prince noted, "my first doubts in the way of being confirmed."[42]

From the front lines, Rudolf Binding came to much the same conclusion. He wrote that "I have lived through the most disheartening day of the war." Criticizing German preparations, he concluded that "the French deliberately lured us. They put up no resistance in front. . . . Our guns bombarded empty trenches; our gas shells gassed empty artillery positions." The German advance thus moved over empty ground, revealing to all just how deftly the French and Americans had avoided the heavy German punch. "We did not see a single dead Frenchman, let alone a captured [artillery] gun or machine gun, and we had suffered heavy losses. . . . Everything seemed to go wrong."[43] Kurt Hesse agreed, calling July 15 "the most severe defeat of the war" for Germany.[44]

By the end of the day, Crown Prince Wilhelm had to face two difficult moments. He had to approve the order to withdraw most German forces back across the Marne, an order Hesse received as "a message of deliverance." As Hesse oversaw his unit's crossing to the north bank of the Marne, he noted, "I have never seen so many dead; never have I seen such a frightful war sight." Once north of the river, he received new orders to prepare to attack again. Consequently, he was prevented from ordering his men to dig in.[45] The German high command seems to have appreciated the strength of the Allies in defense, but seems also not to have expected the Allies to have the strength to launch an attack of their own.

The crown prince's next difficult moment came when he had to inform his father, who had come to the front to witness the capture of Rheims, that the offensive had failed. "It is a terrible moment," he wrote, "when the commander can no longer hide from himself that an operation of such importance has not succeeded." It must have been just as terrible to break the news to the kaiser, but the crown prince could no longer hide the "bitter truth that the offensive had failed."[46] As more discouraging reports came in during the course of the day, the crown prince took the dramatic step of ordering all attacks by the German First and Third armies to stop. Local German attacks continued during the time it took for the orders to work their way down the chain of command. One Allied officer noted that each successive offensive had less and less power behind it. "There was a hopelessness in the last few efforts, then it stopped."[47]

The next day, July 16, the crown prince ordered the Seventh Army to stop its offensives as well. Local counterattacks by German forces had failed everywhere that day. Ludendorff supported the decision, noting that "a continuation of the offensive would have cost us too much."[48] By July 17, the crown prince's headquarters became focused not on attacking, but on evacuating the remaining German units south of the Marne to the presumed safety of the north bank within the next four days. Ludendorff himself left the Marne sector on the 17th, still hoping that the crown prince might be able to resume the attack once the German armies had regrouped. Presumably, German desires to resume the offensive explain why German forces did not dig in once they had reached the north bank of the Marne. Ludendorff then headed to Flanders in order to supervise the final preparations for his offensive there. He seems not to have realized that the failures of July 15 made his cherished Flanders offensive an impossibility. Nor did he realize just how badly exposed the crown prince's army group was to an Allied counteroffensive.

While German senior leaders were deciding what to do next and their subordinates began to take stock of the full magnitude of their defeat, Foch set to work. Like a chess player he began moving his pieces around the board, thinking one step ahead and concealing his intentions from his opponent. The Fourth Army had held its ground well enough that Foch knew the Germans would not try again, and even if they did, the result would likely be the same. He therefore redirected the British 62nd Division, then en route to the Fourth Army sector, to the Fifth Army sector, where it could play a key role in the counterattack to come. The fast change meant "a heavy burden on the administrative staff" and a forced march of 30 miles on July 17, but it put the 62nd in a key position on the Ardre River in time for the attack.[49]

Most importantly, the shift of the 62nd Division placed powerful forces on the German front for which they had not accounted. The 62nd was soon joined by the British 51st, which arrived on the 19th. Its artillery had to be moved through a rain storm 80 miles in three days, but the division had all of its brigade headquarters functioning by the time the final pieces arrived.[50] The two divisions together formed the British XXI Corps under the command of General Sir Alexander Godley; his uneven record at Gallipoli had made him unpopular, but by 1918 the British command was ready to give him another chance. The experience at Gallipoli had also given him the chance to develop a close friendship with fellow Gallipoli veteran Henri Gouraud.[51]

The Americans were also on the move. The 42nd Division, after having performed so well as part of Gouraud's defense in depth near Rheims, went to the Château-Thierry sector to regroup and prepare for its role in the offensive to come. The 28th Division moved forward from the general reserve into the sector as well, with the mission of preparing to clear the south bank of the Marne of German forces.[52] The American 4th Division, then headed toward the relatively quiet Vosges sector, was rerouted in transit to the Marne and placed into the line southeast of Villers-Cotterêts. From there it would be in perfect position to strike into the exposed western flank of the German salient.

These moves were almost for naught. Despite the success of the very Allied defense in depth that he had ordered to be created, Pétain remained concerned about the presence of the German bridgehead near Dormans. He sent orders to the French armies canceling preparations for the offensive and ordering defense preparations made instead. These orders reached Marie Émile Fayolle's *Groupe d'armées de reserve* (GAR) headquarters at 10:00 AM on July 15.[53] By coincidence, Foch arrived at GAR headquarters to meet with Fayolle shortly after the orders had arrived. Foch immediately countermanded them, or, in Foch's words, "I at once sent a message to [Pétain's] General Headquarters which ensured the necessary corrections, and the preparations for the counter attack were pursued without any delay being occasioned."[54] The offensive would go on as scheduled as soon as all of the pieces on the board were in place. Foch may not have been able to hope for a checkmate just yet, but he was clearly ready to change the nature of the game.

SIX

THE ALLIES STRIKE, JULY 18–21

MEN ON BOTH sides knew how badly the German offensive of July 15 had failed. Only the Allied high command, however, knew the full details of the next step that was to come. In order for the Allies to take maximum advantage of their success on the battle's first day they would need to move quickly. They could not afford to give the Germans time that they might use to resume the offensive either in Champagne or in Flanders, nor could they expect to maintain the secrecy of their preparations for much longer. In order to be successful, they would need to get their final pieces in place in a matter of hours.

The resulting constant shuffling of Allied units back and forth across the Marne salient, while unavoidable, caused a great deal of confusion in Allied ranks. Orders had been given and countermanded so often that troops might have been forgiven for wondering if the staffs had any idea at all what they were doing. The men of the American 2nd Division, for example, had marched for 50 hours in a 72-hour period in order to arrive at their designated place in the line west of Buzancy. Even after just the first day of this exhausting march one soldier had written, "Hiked all day . . . the boys sure are tired." Still he and "the boys" had two more hard days of marching ahead just to get in position to fight.[1] The American 26th Division did not even receive orders to move until 10:15 PM on the rainy night of July 17, leading to a frantic scramble to get in line through the mud and darkness.[2] Owing to the need for secrecy and the driving rain, the men of the American 1st Division had to complete a forced march to the front with no hot food, leaving them "in a state of mind to fight anybody."[3] The rain at least had the welcome advantage of reducing the number of German planes overhead.

The confusion and chaos of the front line existed in the rear as well. Railway stations were a mass of frenetic activity as men detrained, looked for the buses that would take them forward, and searched for their ration carts. When the roads ended or became too crowded, soldiers began marching through wheat and corn fields, often at night to avoid the peering eyes of German pilots. Civilians were moving, too, in the opposite direction, "clearing out as fast as possible with . . . crazy carts they were able to find for the transportation of their worldly possessions." Cities such as Epernay and Châlons quickly became ghost towns. "Not a soul was to be seen," noted a British soldier who passed through Epernay, which had theretofore avoided the worst the war had to offer.[4]

The confusion created by the refugee exodus and the advance of armies caused terrible traffic jams and considerable disorder, especially among men who had never even seen the terrain over which they were moving. Moving to the front with no maps was "trying beyond description" for the men of the American 4th Division, especially given the windy, rainy weather and roads "cluttered with transport—wagons, trucks, automobiles, mounted men, [and] front [line] troops" moving in all directions.[5] Because of the confusion, some regiments arrived at the front without the weapons they needed. Only four of the American 1st Division's twenty-four howitzers were in place to fire when the division attacked; many regiments were also without their light 37mm field guns, which were stuck somewhere in the massive traffic jams in the rear areas.[6]

Nevertheless, in retrospect, it is remarkable both that sufficient resources got to the Allied front lines as needed and that the Germans did not suspect the size and scope of the coming Allied attack. Many German soldiers, grown confident from four months of attacking almost at will, blithely dismissed the threat to their flanks. One German war diary dismissed the possibility of an Allied attack because "there was so much to argue against it," presumably the expected difficulty of concentrating sufficient firepower.[7] If the Germans could have seen the massive Allied effort opposite them, they might well have opened their eyes a bit wider.

On the Allied side, the sights and sounds of all this movement before the battle's second phase even began were unlike anything most men had ever seen. Much of the movement took place during the night and through heavy summer rains, adding a misty, eerie feel to an already surreal scene. Men of the American 1st and 2nd divisions entered into the line as part of the French XX Corps, considered by many to be among the most distinguished formations in the French army. The 1st Division had the leftmost position in the corps, with the highly respected Moroccan Division to their right. To the right of the Moroccans sat the American 2nd Division. Due to the need to find replacements, many of the reinforcements in Moroccan units were in fact Senegalese. Their transportation came from trucks and buses driven by Vietnamese laborers.[8] Thus the men of four continents (Europe, North America, Africa, and Asia) had come together to this small corner of France to fight a desperate battle to decide Europe's fate.

As a result of the confusion and rush to get units in line, the resulting order of battle for the Allies by July 18 was a mixed bag of units, commands, supply arrangements, and languages. The situation struck many men as a Tower of Babel come to life, with so many languages being shouted at once. Allied officers were giving orders in at least four languages (French, English, Italian, and Arabic for some of the French colonial and Moroccan units), and the general staffs of four armies were coordinating movements. The four field armies dedicated to the offensive were all French and commanded by French generals, but they were all multi-national in character.

The largest and most important of these four armies was the French Tenth, commanded by General Charles Mangin. A native of the "lost province" of Lorraine, Mangin had been one of the firmest advocates of the offensive. He had long argued for the French army to "shake off the mud of the trenches" and resume the attack.[9] But as antediluvian as some of Mangin's aggressiveness seemed, he was not stuck in the mindset of 1914. Rather, he had been at the forefront of tactical innovation in the French army, learning how to conduct rolling barrages and carefully preparing every foreseeable detail before attacking. Many soldiers saw serving under "the Butcher" as akin to a death sentence, but he was well-suited to command the powerful left hook that Foch envisioned for this offensive. He knew how hard he was pushing his men, but he remained confident that tired troops fighting with the element of surprise stood a greater chance of success than fresh troops spotted and detected by the Germans.

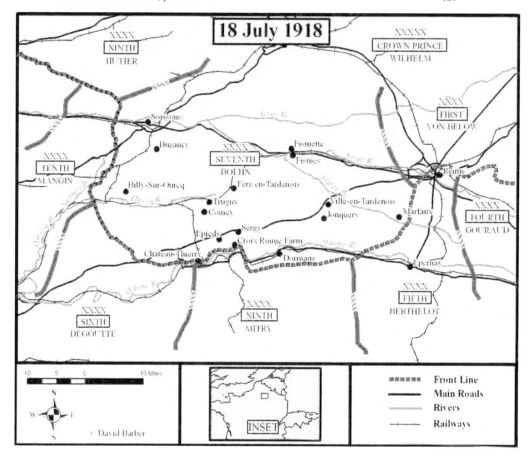

Mangin's Tenth Army was indeed a potent formation. It contained five corps, including France's elite XX and XXX Corps. Together those five corps contained twenty-two infantry and three cavalry divisions. The divisions included the 58th Division from Morocco, the 1st and 2nd American divisions, and the British 34th and 15th divisions. Unfortunately, the haste with which the units were assembled prevented the two British units from being placed together in the same corps. Instead the 15th went to the XX Corps, while the Americans and the 34th went to the XXX Corps alongside four French divisions. Sixteen of the twenty-two divisions would be involved in the attack's first wave, with the rest in reserve waiting to reinforce areas experiencing the greatest levels of success. The cavalry (acting as mounted infantry) could not do much to help create a breakthrough, but, if effectively used, mobile units such as cavalry could help turn a breakthrough into a rout by cutting off German lines of retreat and targeting vulnerable positions behind enemy lines.

Mangin's area of responsibility covered the western edge of the Marne salient, bordered to the north by the Aisne River, just west of Soissons, and to the south by the Ourcq River. Approximately 10 kilometers inside the salient sat the main highway and railroad that connected Soissons to Château-Thierry. The Tenth Army's main operational goal was to move generally southeast, cutting the German lines of communication as it went. If successful, the operation would leave German forces in the salient without reliable means of resupply.

Mangin and Foch were hoping for much more expansive results. They had already anticipated that a strong punch by the Tenth Army might cave in the entire German position and create panic and disorganization in German lines. Such a situation might make possible a full exploitation of German units in open country. Mangin's smaller operations in July had laid the groundwork for the larger offensive to come, but the aggressive general was already dreaming of the chance to pursue and destroy German units located in the Tardenois plain in the center of the salient.

As Mangin's Tenth Army moved southeast, the neighboring French Sixth Army of General Jean-Marie Degoutte would advance northeast toward the same Soissons to Château-Thierry railroad and highway. Its offensive would begin just south of the Ourcq River, with its lines extending toward Belleau Wood. The Sixth Army had eight divisions divided into three corps. They included the American 4th and 26th divisions, although the 4th was divided, with most of the division placed in the VII Corps, but the 7th Brigade placed at the opposite end of the Sixth Army front as part the French 33rd Division. Degoutte had commanded Americans at Belleau Wood in June and had already overcome his initial skepticism of their capabilities. His army on July 18 had 588 artillery pieces and 147 tanks.[10]

The French Ninth Army, under General Henri de Mitry, would hold the nose of the salient. Its primary mission involved not permitting the Germans to retreat from the bottom of the salient across the Marne River without taking a severe beating. The Ninth Army held the sector from Château-Thierry to Dormans. Its eastern part included much of the bridgehead across the Marne that the Germans had managed to create on July 15. To accomplish the mission of wiping that bridgehead out completely, Mitry had six French and two American divisions (the 3rd and 28th), plus 644 artillery pieces and 90 tanks.

The remainder of the German bridgehead sat in the sector of the French Fifth Army, which had taken the heaviest casualties from the

German offensive of July 15. Its mission was to attack northwest both to prevent German units opposite it from redeploying to the west and to seal off potential avenues of retreat for the units opposite the Ninth Army. The Fifth Army was also a powerful force, containing eight French infantry divisions, four French cavalry divisions, two Italian divisions, two colonial (Moroccan and Senegalese) divisions, and two British divisions, the 51st and the 62nd. Unlike their fellow Britons in the Tenth Army area, the British divisions in this sector were placed next to one another inside a new formation, the British XXII Corps, commanded by a British general, Sir Alexander Godley. The 902 artillery pieces and 45 tanks (all light tanks) added to the Ninth Army's combat power. French armor concentration was the greatest of the war so far, and impressive enough to lead one American to comment that the French had managed to assemble "more tanks than we knew were in the world."[11]

To give the offensive every chance of success, the Allies also moved powerful air assets into the theater. German ability to control the skies had been crucial to what limited successes they had enjoyed in the battle's first phase. Now that the general strategic and operational picture had come into sharper focus, the Allies could even the score by moving air squadrons to the Marne sector. By flying far to the west and south of the salient, Allied pilots could also safely avoid German observation aircraft. Thus they arrived at the front lines largely unaccounted for by German intelligence. The French 2nd Air Brigade, with 216 fighters and 78 bombers, was assigned to the Tenth Army, giving it a total of 581 planes of all types; the 9th Royal Air Force Brigade was assigned to the Sixth Army, boosting its air strength to 562 planes; two combat groups totaling 80 planes were assigned to the Ninth Army, giving it 182 planes; and one combat group of 39 planes was assigned to the Fourth Army.[12] American air assets also moved to the front from bases near the relatively quiet Toul sector. Allied soldiers continued to complain about German dominance in the air, but the Allies had clearly made a serious commitment to even the odds as much as possible.

One can understand the operational plan by envisioning the sector as an open paper bag. The Ninth Army would prevent the bag from collapsing from the bottom while the Tenth, Sixth, and Fifth Armies closed the bag by squeezing it at the sides near the opening. If done quickly and deftly, the bag might just close with large numbers of German units trapped inside with no possibility of help. In a perfect world, the advance guards of the Tenth Army, approaching from the west, would meet the advance guards of the Fifth Army, advancing from the east, somewhere north of the German supply center at Fère-en-Tardenois, roughly in the center of the Marne salient, thus closing the bag.

The key to this massive operation lay in operational and tactical surprise. To achieve the former, the Allies needed to assemble their key components without tipping their hand to the Germans. Here the Allies made excellent use of the thick forests of the Marne sector. Into those forests, Mangin had concentrated 16 infantry divisions, 1,545 artillery pieces, and 346 tanks. The Tenth Army could also count on the support of 581 airplanes.[13] Although isolated and rather vague reports of Allied armor concentration in the Forêt de Villers-Cotterêts reached higher headquarters, they remained unconfirmed and therefore were not taken too seriously at the crown prince's staff. Mangin also ordered the field artillery pieces needed for an effective rolling barrage brought forward into the woods at the last minute.

Achieving tactical surprise meant hitting the Germans with the full weight of the attack before they could take effective measures for their own defense. Accordingly, Mangin planned to eschew any preparatory artillery fire at all. Instead, the offensive would begin suddenly with a rolling barrage and a rapid infantry assault. Mangin knew from experience that the timing of rolling barrages could be calculated, but rarely relied upon, because the fog and friction of war too often disrupted careful timetables. Mangin had, however, used the minor attacks on the Savières stream to familiarize the men he planned to place in the first wave with his new methods. These operations also allowed gunners to preregister some of their artillery pieces well in advance. The men of the French 48th Division (part of the XXX Corps) recorded that, despite having lost 60 men killed and 1,132 wounded in the Savières operations, they had learned "the idea of attacking with only a very brief artillery preparation, or even no preparation at all."[14] They were also convinced that the German 40th and 115th divisions opposite them were unaware that the Savières operations were preliminary to something much bigger.

Mangin also planned to rely heavily on tanks, whose presence he had previously taken great pains to conceal from the Germans. The tanks would play several important roles: they could crush any barbed wire the Germans had put in place, serve as mobile machine gun platforms, and even fire light artillery rounds into farmhouses and other buildings that the Germans used in defense. The tanks would also serve a psychological role, instilling fear into German soldiers who had not yet faced them.

Allied preparations were so thorough that individual units were able to take advantage of the luck that comes from hard work. On the night of July 17, a lost German carrier pigeon arrived in Allied lines. It carried a message from a German regiment warning that it would have to retreat if not reinforced quickly. Within thirty minutes of the message having been decoded and translated, American and French gunners had worked together to pinpoint the location of the unit and prepare a massive barrage to hit the regiment as soon as the offensive opened.[15]

While the Allies put the finishing touches on the battle to this level of detail, the Germans showed by their actions that they had no idea what was about to hit them. German officers even ordered a series of local counterattacks, including a rather sizable one in the general direction of Epernay.[16] These attacks, conducted on July 16 and 17, seem to have had two goals. First, they were to probe for weaknesses in the Allied line that might later be exploited by a renewed German offensive. Second, they were to cover the withdrawal of the weakest German units to the north bank of the Marne. All of these attacks failed, with the one near Epernay stopped by a French counteroffensive and that on the Ardre River stopped at Nanteuil after minimal gains. That they were conducted at all indicates how little the Germans suspected of Allied intentions. Had they known of Allied plans, they would undoubtedly have pulled back, reorganized, and dug new defensive positions.

The failure of the Germans to dig in and prepare to defend is, however, entirely consistent with German military attitudes, even by this late stage of the war. Isabel Hull has persuasively argued that by 1918 the German high command had long lost touch with any realistic war aims other than complete victory. Because they rejected the possibility of ending the war by compromise or agreeing to seek partial victory (for example evacuating Belgium and returning Alsace and Lorraine to France in exchange for holding their gains in the east), preparing for another offensive came to seem the only possible alternative. Thus the Germans held "an ingrained bias against the defense," an ironic position for them to take given their "enormous success in defense in the first three years of the war."[17] Germany's continued quest for total victory blinded its military leaders to the possibility that the Allies might soon resume the offensive themselves.

Consequently, German forces opposite the Tenth Army were entirely inadequate to meet the force Mangin was set to unleash. The Germans had just eight divisions of uneven quality in the first line, with six more tired divisions in reserve.[18] These divisions had only the most rudimentary of field defenses, no armor, and very few anti-tank guns. Most importantly, they had no idea that they were about to be targeted, and, accordingly, they had taken no substantive measures to protect the Soissons to Château-Thierry lines of communications, which fed and supplied parts or all of forty German divisions. Most German reserves had instead been concentrated too far to the east, in the area near Fère-en-Tardenois. The French Fifth Army, if successful, could pin them there and prevent them from moving west to help defend Soissons.

An important indication of German ignorance about the coming Allied offensive rests in the disposition of German units. The Germans had twenty-two divisions in the Seventh Army area in the center of the Marne salient, and only five in the Ninth Army area, the one closest to the French Tenth Army.[19] Most of the German divisions, moreover, faced southeast, that is, toward either Château-Thierry or Epernay.[20] These dispositions show Germany's intention to resume the offensive in the near future; they are illogical for a solid all-around defense of Marne salient. Such dispositions also negated the interior lines of communications the Germans might have enjoyed inside the salient if their forces had been more properly arranged. Clearly, they expected nothing.

Late in the afternoon of July 18, noted British journalist Philip Gibbs sat down to write his dispatch for the day. He had heard of a massive Allied attack on the Marne (indeed, given Gibbs's ability to glean information from British officers, he probably knew about the offensive long before it began) and understood immediately how important it would be to Allied fate in the war. Writing from Flanders from the perspective of the British armies there, he observed: "Our own future depends intimately on the progress of that French counter-stroke. . . . So in the north of this western front the British and German armies are both hungering for news of what is happening in Champagne, knowing that upon events there depend their own action in the immediate future."[21] Evidently, Gibbs either did not know or was not allowed to put in print the fact that British and American divisions were also involved in the "French" counterstroke. He had, however, correctly divined that the course of the war was about to change.

"Glorious Day! The Dawn of the Final Victory."

Even the weather had switched sides.[22] In March the Germans had benefited from thick mists and cloudy weather. On July 18, heat and several preceding days of rain gave the Allies the advantage of a similarly strong morning mist. The mist added to the confusion in German lines when Mangin's Tenth Army began the second phase of the battle at 4:35 AM on July 18. More than 2,100 artillery pieces opened fire simultaneously on German positions. At 5:00 AM French artillery opened fire around Rheims as well to keep the Germans guessing about where the main attack might fall. The French First Cavalry Corps also conducted raids all during the day around the Montagne de Rheims to keep German attention focused on both sides of the salient.[23]

Unlike the German barrage just three days earlier, the Allied cannonade of July 18 caught their enemies completely by surprise. The Allied guns targeted fortified villages, German lines of communication, and likely troop concentration points, then began a rolling barrage to cover the advance of the initial wave of nine divisions. One Allied field artillery battery fired an impressive 1,400 rounds of ammunition in less than eight hours, covering the battlefield in "great clouds of smoke and flame."[24] Men of the French 74th Regiment watched as "in an instant the entire forest seemed embraced by the fire of the thousands of cannons it had concealed." Even veterans stopped what they were doing to watch the astonishing spectacle of so many guns firing such a dense barrage.[25] The American writer Edith Wharton, who lived in Paris during the war as a Red Cross volunteer, heard the barrage from her apartment near Les Invalides. She described it as "the level throb of distant artillery," a sound she had often heard on trips near the front, but never as far from the fighting as her neighborhood. A guest staying in her apartment turned to her and said, "It's the opening of Foch's big offensive."[26]

The smoke and mist of this powerful barrage helped to cover the next phase of the plan, that of the infantry and armor. As the infantry advanced, 321 tanks left the security of the Forêt de Villers-Cotterêts and moved east, headed for the bridges over the Savières and other streams in the region. The newly arrived air armada flew overhead, clearing the sky of German planes (many of which had been grounded due to the mist, as there was no suspicion of an enemy offensive) and locating target sets for the artillery. On July 19, when the weather cleared, Allied aircraft began strafing German troop concentrations as well.

Even had the Germans known what was coming, they still would have been faced with a massive Allied assault. The nine Allied divisions of the first wave attacked over a total frontage of more than 28 miles. Approximately 70 percent of the men in this first wave were French; the remaining 30 percent were American.[27] The tanks that accompanied the first wave appeared "like prehistoric monsters grown too heavy to progress easily on land," but they did their jobs. They panic they instilled was evidenced by the hundreds of signal flares that frightened German units sent up, lighting up the dawn sky.[28] The tanks soon proved to have an unforeseen capability that helped Allied soldiers advance over the terrain. With their machine guns placed high up in turrets or on the sides, they could shoot above or through the tall wheat and corn fields much more easily than infantrymen could.

Whether they were fully ready for this war or not, the Americans held central roles in this battle. Only the 26th American Division was classified as fresh, but General Pershing insisted that the American 1st, 2nd, and 4th divisions be involved on the offensive's first day. The latter three divisions were placed on the western edge of the salient, roughly parallel to the Soissons to Château-Thierry road. The American divisions were not placed together; in every case there were French units on either side of an American division. Most likely this arrangement was more a function of the hasty movements of the previous days than any lack of confidence among French commanders of the Americans' abilities.

The Americans had tremendous élan, but they also showed their inexperience. Too often they took unnecessary casualties by charging directly at German machine gun positions. They soon learned from the French to pause and call for field artillery support against the suspected machine gun position, then attack the position's flanks.[29] Despite high casualties, however, the American spirit remained undaunted. Near the end of the first day, one AEF staff officer asked 1st Division commander Major General Charles Summerall if his men could still attack or if they needed rest. He replied "Sir, when the 1st Division has only two men left they will be echeloned in depth and attacking toward Berlin."[30] Such bombast both pleased and bewildered the French.

It soon became apparent that the Allied offensive had caught the Germans completely flat footed. One Allied commander noted as his unit advanced that German trenches were "conspicuous by their absence," leaving the German defenders in the area particularly susceptible to the shrapnel shelling of the rolling barrage.[31] One French unit attacked the 115th German Division just as it was in the process of being relieved by the German 3rd Reserve Division. The French attack therefore caught the Germans at the most awkward moment possible. Nor were German reinforcements much material help to the men inside the salient. Attacking French units soon found that companies in the 3rd Reserve Division were down to as few as sixty infantrymen per unit.[32]

Allied soldiers were shocked at the poor condition of the German soldiers they captured. They were tired, demoralized, and hungry. One German field artillerist exchanged information on the location of German batteries and units for food, water, and a promise of several hours of sleep before being moved to a prisoner of war camp.[33] Many prisoners of war were suffering from the obvious effects of malnourishment and the influenza epidemic. They surrendered in such high numbers that one French Territorial unit assigned the task of moving them to prisoner of war camps found it could just barely handle a movement of prisoners and equipment that "never stopped flowing."[34]

Signs of a monumental Allied triumph were everywhere. That night Generals Pétain, Fayolle, and Mangin met to discuss the first day's events. Even Pétain, normally among the most pessimistic of men, found "that the results obtained exceeded all expectations." Nevertheless, Mangin came away with the impression that Pétain felt that "an exploitation is limited by the means available to him and the general situation (of the armies)." He therefore declined to send reinforcements forward. Foch once again disagreed, and sent the Tenth Army four divisions from the general reserve in order that the battle could be continued with the utmost vigor.[35] The next day he made clear to Pétain that he had big goals for the offensive, writing that "the battle now in progress should aim at the destruction of the enemy's forces south of the Aisne and the Vesle. It must be pursued with the utmost energy and without any loss of time, so as to exploit the surprise we have effected."[36] Now that he had the Germans back on their heels, Foch planned to give them no respite from the Allies and their offensive power.

For his part, Mangin was overjoyed with the Tenth Army's performance. He told his men in an order of the day that they had removed the "stain" of "the new barbarian occupation" from the "cradle of France" and had assured the safety of not just Paris, but the entire Île de France region.[37] Across the salient near Epernay, British General Sir Alexander Godley wrote to his wife from the luxury of the Château of the Comte de Chandon (of Moët and Chandon champagne fame) that "the French are, of course, very pleased with themselves, as they have every reason to be."[38] It was evident to all Allied commanders that the momentum of the war had just shifted in a dramatic and favorable way.

The first day of the Allied counteroffensive had been a massive success. In total, the Allies had captured 20,000 prisoners of war, 518 enemy artillery pieces, 300 *Minenwerfer* (trench mortars), and 3,000 machine guns. The Tenth Army alone had taken 12,000 prisoners and 250 artillery pieces.[39] One American regiment captured 3,000 prisoners from five different German divisions, an indication of the confusion in German lines.[40] The high number of prisoners indicated both the astonishing achievement of surprise and the low state of morale in many German units. The number of German prisoners on this first day exceeds the number of Germans taken prisoner at the Battle of Amiens, which began on 8 August 1918. That battle, which saw 17,000 Germans surrender on the first day, has justifiably gone down in history as, in Ludendorff's words, the "black day" of the German army. A black day it surely was, but in terms of both raw numbers of Germans who had surrendered and the tremendous shift in momentum, July 18 was significantly more important.

The events of July 18, moreover, badly unhinged an already unsteady Ludendorff. That night, Field Marshal Paul von Hindenburg, Ludendorff's superior, urged Ludendorff to attack the left flank of the new Allied line. Ludendorff called his commander's ideas "utterly unfeasible" and, later that night, dared to dismiss Hindenburg's strategic judgment as "nonsense." Ludendorff's insolence led to a frank one-on-one encounter between the two men in which Hindenburg "reminded his second to remember his place" in the chain of command. Two recent biographers of Hindenburg note that the incident was "an astonishing breakdown in discipline" on the part of Ludendorff, who had "dared to ridicule" the ideas of a German icon eighteen years his senior. The incident created an abiding tension between the two men that Hindenburg neither forgot nor forgave.[41]

The stress in the German high command was easy to understand. The line moved eight kilometers in the Allies' favor in some places, with the greatest gains made by the American 1st and 2nd divisions and the French Colonial Division that sat between them. The 2nd had in fact advanced so far that it had outrun its supply lines, a rare problem indeed on the western front. In moving the line so far, the Allies had liberated twenty French villages, although many of them were just piles of rubble by the time French and American units entered them. French artillery units had advanced far enough to begin shelling the Soissons to Château-Thierry highway, thus fulfilling a major goal of the operation. Without free use of that road, the Germans could not hope to supply the men stuck in the bottom of the "bag."

Ludendorff had not been in a position to see the results of the day firsthand. He had moved north to Mons in order to put the finishing touches on his next offensive, code-named Hagen, that he hoped to unleash against British forces in Flanders. He therefore had only conflicting and chaotic reports from which to judge the situation on the Marne. These reports told him of the effectiveness of Allied tanks, both in attacking and in quickly bringing supplies to men engaged in battle. He also learned of the Allied ability to threaten the security of German communications near Soissons, which he wrote was "most inconvenient." German troops thus had to detrain in the Ailette valley further north and march into the Marne sector, impeding the Germans' ability to reinforce.[42] Ludendorff, however, gave no indication that he saw the situation on July 18 as serious enough to lead him to cancel Hagen.

German soldiers who actually faced the Allied attack knew differently. Allied armor was faster, more nimble, and more effective than it had ever been. The German Seventh Army's war diary noted that the Germans "had underestimated the offensive value of tanks" and also "did not appreciate fully the number of his [the enemy's] troops." The "carefully planned and prepared" offensive thus possessed "enormous fighting means" and had achieved complete surprise. Even before July 18 was over, the staff officers of the Seventh Army had developed a full appreciation (certainly a much fuller appreciation than Ludendorff's) of what their defeat had meant:

> The effort to recover ourselves and support the front between the Aisne and Marne cost us so heavily that the Army Group German Crown Prince [Wilhelm] was forced to give up all intentions of continuing our offensive for some time to come. And here, we at once see an undoubtedly great strategic success for Marshal Foch and, based on this viewpoint, July 18, 1918 marks a turning point in the history of the World War.[43]

German soldier Rudolf Binding saw the situation in similar terms, writing in his diary on July 19 that "since our experiences of July 16th I know that we are finished. My thoughts oppress me. How are we to recover ourselves? *Kultur,* as it will be known after the war will be of no use; mankind itself will probably be of still less use."[44] Binding understood as well as anyone how important the events of July 18 had been.

Some senior German officials also understood the meaning of the Allied offensive. Hindenburg later wrote of the events of July 18, "How many hopes, cherished during the last few months, had probably collapsed at one blow!"[45] Imperial chancellor Georg von Hertling was even more melodramatic: "At the beginning of July, 1918 I was convinced, I confess it, that before the first of September our adversaries would send us peace proposals. . . . We expected grave events in Paris for the end of July. That was on the 15th. On the 18th even the most optimistic among us knew that all was lost. The history of the world was played out in three days."[46]

Officers at Army Group Crown Prince's headquarters saw the danger, but they reacted with measured, professional steps. They quickly realized that the Allies were in an excellent position to exploit the German mistake of leaving Soissons so dangerously undefended. Crown Prince Wilhelm also knew that his command "had not at its disposal sufficient reserves to strengthen the menaced front," nor were German communications in the salient sufficient to allow for the rapid movement of reinforcements even if they had been available. Accordingly, he saw July 18 as representing "certainly the most critical situation in which I had found myself during the whole war." He responded by ordering all remaining German artillery pieces south of the Marne pulled north of the river lest they be captured by advancing Allied troops. He also ordered all German soldiers south of the Marne evacuated to the north bank in order that they might be "saved from a Sedan."[47] What had begun as the offensive to win the war for Germany now risked becoming a tragedy of epic proportions.

German Forces on the Defensive

The crown prince was willing to sacrifice the bridgehead south of the Marne, but he was not willing to surrender the battle just yet. Nevertheless, he had far fewer resources with which to fight. The first two days of the Allied offensive had hit the Germans very hard. Deploying reserves the German high command considered unfit wore units out much faster than anticipated. By July 20, the Germans estimated that they had no fully fit divisions in the Ninth Army area. Instead they had three divisions in need of at least three weeks' rest; three divisions in need of four weeks' rest; two divisions in need of five weeks' rest; and two divisions in need of "indefinite" rest. All ten divisions needed immediate, if mostly unavailable, replacements.[48]

The crown prince could count on precious few advantages in this phase of the battle. To be sure, surprise was no longer an important factor as German units all over the western front went on alert. German pilots, furthermore, continued to challenge the Allies for control of the air. Finally, many Allied units were just as tired and in need of refitting as many of the German units. The two Italian divisions were in "an exhausted and shaken condition," and many French divisions were in little better shape.[49] Even the relatively fresh American 42nd Division needed time away from the line to refit and reorganize.

Germany's best ally in the defense of the Marne sector was undoubtedly the terrain. Germany's only significant defensive successes on July 18 occurred on high ground such as Hill 193, northwest of Château-Thierry. German soldiers had been able to use other high points to establish a defensive line and count on the numerous ravines in the region to slow down attacking Allied units. The high corn and wheat also provided places for snipers to hide, and, ironically, the devastation of villages and farmhouses caused by the Allied rolling barrage created excellent locations in which to conceal machine gun nests. Finally, the crown prince had ordered two divisions to move to Soissons in an attempt to bolster faltering German lines in front of that critical railroad junction.

By July 19 the crown prince and his staff seem to have realized that abandoning the bridgehead south of the Marne had become inevitable. They undoubtedly also saw the threat to the entire Marne pocket, but at this time did not envision having to evacuate the salient. In larger strategic terms, the crown prince's army group could still help the overall cause by slowing the Allied advance and drawing Allied attention to a slugfest in the Marne ravines while Ludendorff unleashed Hagen in Flanders. If Hagen succeeded, the momentum might change once again, perhaps with positive consequences for the situation in the Marne salient. Thus, if the situation looked grave, it did not yet look entirely hopeless.

On July 19, chaos still ruled the day in German lines. The Germans were still defending on a local level as well as tired regiments and battalions could. Typically, they relied on the rapid firepower of carefully concealed machine guns hidden among wheat and corn fields. Thus the British 51st Division fought for an entire day only to find that they "had done no more than drive in the enemy's outposts and reach the main line of resistance." Still, they had advanced one mile up the Ardre River Valley. Aerial reconnaissance reported columns of German troops moving north that were so large that they were creating traffic tie-ups, but the British could not pursue owing to the power of the machine gun nests.[50]

The Allied attacks of July 19 did not experience the success of the previous day. The experiences of the American 1st Division on July 19 illuminate the problems Allied units faced in continuing their pursuit. On July 18, the division had performed marvelously, advancing as many as six kilometers in places, capturing as many as 2,000 Germans along with thirty artillery pieces, and seizing the critical Missy Ravine. The division received profuse praise from French and American commanders alike. The offensive had been an astounding success by any definition.

Nevertheless, the offensive soon ran into problems common to many successful World War I offensives. The carefully designed battle plan for July 18 had now been overcome by events, and there had been no time to prepare another one of equal care and detail. Units would thus have to advance with no overall plan and with the risk of losing contact with neighboring units. Few units had new maps that accurately indicated friendly or enemy positions because no one knew where they were. Accordingly, artillery support could not be arranged, nor could units identify their final objectives.

Thus even the hard-charging commander of the American 1st Division, Major General Charles Summerall, issued conservative orders for July 19. He ordered steps taken to consolidate the gains of July 18 and warned his regiments to be ready for a German counterattack; notably, he ordered that the freshest battalion from each regiment be placed behind the front lines in order to stiffen defenses. The success of July 18 notwithstanding, Summerall remained cautious. Mark Grotelueschen, who has recently studied the division's performance in 1918, concludes that Summerall's actions are "consistent with his appreciation of defensive firepower and an awareness of the tired and ill-equipped condition of his division when the battle began."[51] Summerall was also aware that some units had lost 60 percent of their officers and that in many cases neighboring French units had not advanced as far as the 1st had, thus leaving flanks exposed to German counterattacks.

The Allies could thus force the Germans out of their positions, but with their combat strength "horribly depleted," they lacked the strength to turn the victory into a rout.[52] The Germans still held the Soissons to Château-Thierry roads, although Allied gunners could now regularly shell the roads. Ludendorff thought that July 19 had "passed quite satisfactorily" and hoped that the Germans had managed to stop the Allied offensive short of Soissons. He expected that once the initial panic had passed, German soldiers would fight better and offer a more organized and more stubborn resistance.[53] German pilots seem also have made a recovery, with one historian claiming that on July 19 German pilots were able to bomb and strafe Allied positions "completely unopposed."[54]

By July 20, the steam had largely gone out of Mangin's initial push. The men of one French unit noted that they had hardly advanced at all on July 19, but the news was still good because enemy artillery fire remained weak, and Allied shelling had made German use of the roads in and out of Soissons more difficult.[55] Still, the offensive had clearly slowed. Thus, despite Mangin's order of July 20 stating, "Tomorrow continue the attack. Same objective," the main axis of advance had to be switched. That afternoon, Pétain issued new orders, making Degoutte's Sixth Army the main offensive unit, because it contained the relatively fresh American 3rd, 26th, and 28th divisions.[56] The Tenth Army would continue to press east toward Soissons; the Ninth Army would attempt to cut the Germans off from their avenue of retreat across the Marne, even if its soldiers "had to swim" across the Marne to do so;[57] and the Fifth Army would move northwest along the Ardre valley to keep up pressure on the eastern edge of the salient. "Everyone must understand," the order read, "that no rest can be left to our enemy until we have obtained all of our objectives."[58] Those final objectives still included closing the bag around German forces inside the salient near the town of Fère-en-Tardenois.

The plan of attack for July 20 came together more hastily than that for July 18 or July 19. The haste undoubtedly contributed to the day's limited success. With the element of surprise no longer a possibility, Allied planners added a heavy preparatory barrage designed to clear

German first-line opposition. With gunners firing one thousand shells per day or more, and with supply lines badly congested, shell supply was extremely limited. The preparation barrage was therefore limited to just two and half hours. It focused mostly on suspected German machine gun nests, many of which were virtually impossible to pinpoint.[59]

Finding fresh troops to follow the barrage proved a tremendous challenge. The British XXII Corps was initially only supposed to relieve the tired Italians, but it received a new mission en route. As its commander, General Sir Alexander Godley, told King George V's military secretary, Clive Wigram, "Foch's counterattack had developed [while the XXII Corps was moving], and it was decided to attack all around the salient, so I was hustled in in a great hurry to go through the Italians, and two French divisions who were mixed up with them, and attack." The haste meant that his two divisions, the 51st and the 62nd, would have to advance with no reconnaissance and no chance to preregister any artillery. It was a daunting task, but, Godley judged, "under the circumstances, it was I am sure the right thing to do."[60]

With so little time to plan the artillery support, it inevitably failed to match the needs of the infantry, leaving many soldiers with too little protection. The barrage that was supposed to protect them had to be designed by British soldiers in the 62nd Division along with Italian and French gunners who used different languages and different systems. Consequently, the barrage fell too far forward, leaving untouched "the countless machine gun posts in the intervening space" between the barrage and the fortified village of Marfeux. The men of the 62nd therefore had to crawl through "impenetrable woods, in which the enemy still lurked." Although some senior officers had told the 62nd to prepare for open warfare, the conditions in front of Marfeux hardly resembled open warfare. "Guerrilla warfare was a more appropriate term," wrote one veteran.[61]

The men of the 62nd understood how important their attack was to the overall operational plan in the Marne sector. "Most of the officers," noted one veteran of the division, "realised the desperate position, and everyone realised we were in for a sticky show."[62] Although the attack had slowed and then stopped by 6:00 PM, the officers of the 62nd Division staff considered it a success. The division had advanced and had tied down large numbers of German soldiers, thus preventing them from moving west toward Soissons.

The 62nd Division's neighbor, the British 51st Division, had an equally difficult time getting ready for the attack. Their orders to attack did not arrive until 9:00 PM on July 19. They had to move through the thick Bois de Rheims with just one French guide, not arriving at their posts until 4:00 AM on July 20. Then they had to arrange a rolling barrage aimed at advancing 100 meters every six minutes, ambitious under any circumstances, but exceedingly so in light of their difficulties getting into position.[63] Still, the men of the 51st expected to make a good show of the attack, scheduled to being at 6:00 AM. The orders for the Black Watch regiment specified that "the attack will be made before the eyes of the French Army, and it is expected that [all ranks] will maintain the prestige of the British Army." As expected, the barrage was too fast for men who had had too little training appropriate to the mission, far too little sleep, inadequate rations, and no chance even to see the ground over which they had to advance. The 51st advanced about 600 yards before running into a line of German machine guns hidden in the woods. The attack stalled there, and for the rest of the day the men of the 51st faced German machine guns and strafing from German pilots.[64]

Given the limitations imposed on XXII Corps, its achievement is remarkable. The British advanced approximately 2,500 yards at their furthest point. They captured 1,084 German prisoners of war and 125 German machine guns. They also had the honor of being able to return to the French 32 artillery pieces previously captured by the Germans.[65]

The two British divisions had therefore put pressure on the eastern edge of the salient; the main attack of the day, however, was to be made in the center by the American 26th Division. The Yankee Division served as the "pivot" division of the July 20 attacks, holding the place in the line near Château-Thierry where the line turned east. The men of the 26th were to advance slowly and methodically behind a rolling barrage, keeping contact with the French 167th Division on their left. The French had the mission of seizing the critical high ground of Hill 193. The French division had a difficult assignment, as attacking up so steep a ridge left them open to the full fury of German fire. When the French advance bogged down, the Americans attacked to help clear the French flanks of German machine gunners. As they moved forward they saw terrible evidence of the previous two days of battle. There were "thousands of bodies" and "enormous quantities of ammunition brought in by the Germans for their offensive toward Paris. There were piles as big as houses, some of which the enemy had tried to blow up in his retreat, but without success."[66] Hill 193 remained a sticking point in the German lines. Although the French and Americans had greatly weakened German defenses on the high ground, the hill remained in enemy hands.

The Americans had had their baptism of fire, and for many it was a sobering experience. One soldier in the 2nd Division had written in his diary on July 20 that the men of his unit had advanced six miles and were "tired but happy." Two days later he was no longer so happy. "Impossible for me to describe the doings of these terrible days. Dead, dead, and more dead. [I] will probably be the next. . . . [Horse limber] teams were killed, guys blown up and tanks destroyed. The Allies are going on but paying a price."[67]

Despite local setbacks, there were positive signs. German soldiers continued to surrender in large numbers, leading one soldier to write, "everyone thinks the war will soon end now because the Huns are quitting cold."[68] The American 3rd Division commander, Major General Joseph Dickman, noted the air "of complete confidence in ultimate victory" pervading Allied lines.[69] Fayolle, characteristically, was more reflective, writing in his diary, "This is the start of a great victory. Merci, Mon Dieu."[70]

By the end of the day on July 21, the Allies could congratulate themselves on a marvelous success. They had indeed changed the tenor and tempo of the war. Allied units had advanced as far as 15 kilometers in places. They had taken thousands of prisoners and scores of irreplaceable German artillery pieces and machine guns. Advance parties from the American 26th and French 167th Division were close enough to the Soissons to Château-Thierry highway to see German forces moving along it and to help correct artillery fire aimed at the road and the nearby railroad.[71]

The victory on the Marne was even beginning to have effects on other fronts. On July 20, Foch had written to Haig telling him that the Germans would now have no choice but to cancel any offensive they had planned for Flanders. Haig, in a letter to his wife on July 19, showed that he was still worried about German intentions. He made no mention of the Allied successes of July 18, but wrote, "I still expect to be attacked on the Hazebroucke–Ypres front."[72] Foch's thinking was quite different. In his July 20 letter, he suggested that instead of worrying about meeting a German offensive, Haig should think about conducting two offensives of his own at Kemmel and Amiens.

Foch was starting to see the war in an entirely new light. His grand multi-national coalition had held. He now knew that if he handled both events and personalities with enough dexterity he could use the strength of five nations against a Germany that was increasingly alone and isolated. Nevertheless, he would need to be careful to take into account American and British interests. As the diaries of Haig and Pershing confirm, neither the United States nor Great Britain saw the Second Marne as its only (or even its most important) strategic problem. Foch sent two British divisions back to Haig on July 23 to calm the latter's fears about an attack in Flanders, and still had to deal with persistent American demands to create a separate American First Army with a dedicated part of the front. Foch would need to keep everyone focused on the task at hand, but he had proven that the coalition could work.

As badly as the Germans had been bruised, however, they were far from defeated. By July 21 they had successfully withdrawn the last of their troops in the Marne bridgehead north of the river and had begun preparations to make a stand on the Ourcq River. They had also established a new line of resistance along the line Epieds–Trugny–Bois de Trugny. The line was extremely well sited, lying just behind a half-mile-wide depression in the earth. From their positions on the high ground and inside numerous fortified villages, the Germans could see every movement Allied soldiers made; as one American soldier wryly noted, "not a rat could get cover from machine guns" in that depression.[73]

In some areas, German resistance had stiffened considerably. In many sectors, badly coordinated Allied rolling barrages and tank malfunctions had evened the odds for the defenders. Some German field artillerists had learned to improvise ways to use their guns against Allied tanks, neutralizing the important advantages that accrued to the Allies through their use of armor. The Germans had taken casualties, but they had inflicted them as well. They had thus been badly bruised by the end of the battle's second phase on July 21, but they retained significant combat power and planned to resist any and all Allied attempts to close the Marne salient.

SEVEN

THE BATTLE OF TARDENOIS, JULY 22–26

THE GERMAN HIGH command understood how fundamentally the events of July 18–21 had changed the German army's strategic situation, but senior leadership did not respond with panic or desperation. Realizing that the Allied attack was losing momentum, the Germans developed a new line of defense intended to slow, or even stop, the Allied advance. The most important part of this defense was a line running north to south from just west of Soissons to the town of Epieds, near Château-Thierry. These German defenses were of a different sort from those previously used on the western front, focusing on machine gun nests carefully concealed in tall grain fields and inside deep ravines. The Germans also hid machine guns inside the remains of buildings destroyed by artillery fire and even in broken-down trucks in order to create rates of fire so high that one British veteran described facing them as like being stuck "in an April shower" of lead.[1] Relying on these new defensive arrangements, the Germans did not dig in and they did not create standard World War I field defenses utilizing barbed wire. Instead, the Germans used these positions to create ambushes, trapping Allied units in ravines and woods as they advanced, then tearing into them with concealed machine guns.

In the southern part of the salient, the Germans planned to defend the bottom of the "bag" by holding onto the line of the Ourcq River instead of the Marne. Withdrawing to the Ourcq gave the Germans the advantage of the natural barrier the river provided, as well as the ability to use the high ground on the river's north bank for observation. German defenses in the Ourcq region also relied upon fortified villages such as Fère-en-Tardenois and Sergy; the latter town traded hands a dozen times before the conclusion of the Second Battle of the Marne. Rearguard units centered on machine gun nests concealed in farmhouses and woods were to slow the approaching Allied advance to the Ourcq as long as possible. Thus this phase of the battle involved the Allies making slow progress against German defenses that were themselves designed to buy time for the ultimate establishment of a new defensive line on the Ourcq. The desperate fighting in the Tardenois plain during this phase has given the battle its name: the Battle of Tardenois.

In the east, the Germans planned to defend by conducting a tough, slow, fighting retreat up the difficult terrain of the Ardre River valley. The Ardre, unlike the Ourcq, which runs east to west, instead runs southeast to northwest. Thus the river itself could not provide a barrier to Allied advance. Both banks of the river, however, feature sharp ravines, thick woods, and swampy ground. The marshy ground provided the Germans with a key advantage by negating much of the power of Allied armor. The Germans planned to fight on both banks of the Ardre, using ambushes to disrupt the advance of British units, thereby preventing them from advancing in tandem.

In addition to machine gun teams, the Germans planned to rely heavily on poison gas to defend their new positions. Being heavier than air, poison gas could seep down into the ravines of the salient, the very places where Allied soldiers were most likely to seek cover from German machine guns. Poison gas might also have its most important effects on the relatively inexperienced Americans. At the very least, poison gas could force Allied soldiers to don unwieldy gas masks, thus complicating an already difficult offensive. The strategy appears to have worked. The American 26th Division reported that by July 25 it had suffered 169 cases of men "seriously" gassed and another 699 "lightly" gassed. Virtually all of these cases had to be evacuated from the battlefield for treatment and rest.[2]

This defensive scheme necessitated abandoning the small German bridgehead south of the Marne, and with it any significant strategic or operational pressure on Epernay or Rheims, but it allowed the Germans to concentrate their defense on a new natural line of defense. The Soissons to Château-Thierry highway sat inside German lines, but it was within easy range of Allied artillery and, in some places, Allied snipers as well. The Germans could therefore still use the road, but they came under fire for almost its entire length. At some places, notably near the towns of Buzancy and Breny, the Allies occasionally placed forces over the road. The Germans therefore used the road mostly at night and when German air cover could provide protection to German supply columns.

Withdrawing from the Marne to the Ourcq also forced the Germans to abandon their most important air base in the region. All German airplanes at the Coincy base were moved further northeast near the town of Fismes, on the Vesle River, giving German aviators less time over the combat zone. American aviators, who in the words of Eddie Rickenbacker, were "overwhelmingly outnumbered, poorly supplied, and lamentably equipped," now had a slightly better chance against much more experienced German pilots flying more advanced aircraft.[3] Rickenbacker was among the Allied pilots moved into the Château-Thierry sector to support American infantry units as they advanced into the teeth of the new German defenses. Allied infantry continued to complain of the omnipresence of German aircraft, indicating that even with more distant air bases the Germans still controlled the skies.

The Allied advance across the Marne River also forced the Germans to move their largest "Paris gun" out of the sector, and out of range of Paris. This enormous gun, with its 75-mile range, had been part of a series of three guns across the western front that had fired 303 rounds at the capital, killing 256 people and injuring 620 more. The most important of the Paris guns was located near Laon, but one of the guns had been located on a railway siding in the Marne salient. The Germans moved this massive 200-ton gun out of the salient in order to prevent its capture (or destruction by artillery fire) by advancing Allied units.

The new German situation worried many senior leaders. It gave the kaiser nightmares that included "visions of all the English and Russian relatives and the ministers and generals of his own reign marching past and mocking him."[4] Crown Prince Wilhelm remained concerned, but he was not nearly as despondent about the new German position as was his father. Despite realizing that "in a few days a revolutionary change had come over the situation of the Army Group" and that the Allies had powerful forces on three sides of the Marne salient, he felt on July 22 that the immediate crisis had passed. He remained cautiously confident, although he was concerned about the loss of unfettered movement along the Soissons to Château-Thierry highway.

About this same time, the crown prince received more bad news in the form of a new intelligence report estimating that twenty-seven American divisions were then in France. He also understood that "the great losses incurred in the uninterrupted fighting since March could not be made good even approximately," given the precarious state of German manpower. Still, he continued to hold out hope, somehow believing that the change of momentum on the Marne "did not *per se* preclude the possibility of our resuming the offensive."[5] He must, however, have known that his army group would need a great deal of help from Ludendorff's planned Operation Hagen in Flanders.

Senior officers in the German Seventh Army agreed with the crown prince's optimism. They believed that the danger of being encircled by Allied armies had passed. They also knew that their lateral communications (that is, east to west) remained secure, even if the Soissons to Château-Thierry highway remained under Allied fire. The minimal Allied gains of July 19–21, moreover, gave them some confidence that the Allies were running out of steam.[6] Reports of high Allied casualties and increasingly effective German resistance to Allied tanks also bolstered spirits.[7] Throughout the war the Germans (and for that matter the Allies as well) had seen offensives slow down before, when supplies failed to come forward and attackers tired as quickly as the defenders. Thus, unlike the kaiser, few experienced German officers panicked.

Nevertheless, holding off the Allies with hastily constructed defenses would be challenging. This third phase of the Second Battle of the Marne bore few similarities to the trench warfare that had dominated the western front since 1914. Instead of static warfare based around sieges of well-defended enemy positions, combat in this phase, ironically, resembled the type of open warfare for which armies had trained before 1914. Small units (platoon- and company-sized) would need to make advances against individual enemy strong points. The nature of the terrain complicated communications and also made it difficult for adjacent units to keep contact with one another. The woods grew even thicker near the Ourcq, making rolling barrages harder to time and execute. Men were understandably reluctant to follow rolling barrages into woods, with the danger of splintering trees and the eerie echoes that shelling created inside forests.[8]

Despite their having much more secure lines of communication than the Germans, supply presented another monumental problem for the Allies. Most Allied units were low on everything from food to clean drinking water to heavy ammunition. The men of one American unit were temporarily reduced to stealing carrots from the garden of a château to supplement their demoralizing diet of hardtack (that tasted like it was left over from the Civil War, complained some soldiers) and tinned beef.[9] Despite efforts to neutralize German air power, German pilots could still bombard Allied supply columns with regularity "at all hours of the day, and at night they bombed the roads."[10] Many Allied units could thus be supplied only at night. Allied artillery put German supply lines under similar (but far less consistent) pressure. German laborers had to be dispatched every night to fill in the craters on roads caused by Allied shelling in order to make the roads usable for the next day's operations.

The reports German commanders had received about high levels of Allied casualties had been accurate. Even the aggressive and hard-charging Mangin grudgingly recognized that his Tenth Army could not advance again until it had reorganized and replaced its human and materiel losses. By July 22 it had just one fresh division left at its disposal. Some Allied units had lost half of their officers, and some regiments, normally commanded by colonels, were temporarily being commanded by captains. One French regiment reported that this period of fighting had been its most severe of the war because "it had been kept in the field to the maximum of its endurance." Still, it also noted that morale remained high because every soldier knew that "the war must end despite the sacrifices" and because for the first time in a very long time the Germans were on the defensive and showing signs of defeat. The French did not want to give the Germans any relief.[11]

Foch was of exactly the same mind, telling Pétain on July 23 that the battle could not be allowed to slow down no matter how much fatigue was affecting Allied units. Foch did not want to allow the Germans time to create more durable lines of defense, nor did he want to give the Germans enough confidence to launch an attack in Flanders. He also knew that the Germans were as tired as the Allies were. He judged that the Germans would use any time the Allies allowed them to bolster their flanks; thus he ordered all available reserves given to Mangin's Tenth Army for a renewed push on the western flank of the salient, with the immediate goal still being the capture of Soissons. He also continued to envision having the two wings of the Allied advance close the salient and trap German forces near Fère-en-Tardenois. Pétain seems not to have shared Foch's view. Fayolle noted in his diary on July

22 that Pétain seemed "disenchanted" with the idea of resuming the offensive.[12] Despite its gains, the Allied offensive had slowed down, and no rout of German positions seemed imminent.

Because of the fatigue of many French units and the small number of British divisions in the Marne sector, the success or failure of this phase of the battle would depend heavily on the Americans. The dough-boys were learning quickly how to fight a modern war. They were also coming to hate their enemy. The lethality of German snipers especially roused the anger of the Americans. So, too, did the German habit of de-stroying and looting as they retreated. One Pennsylvanian wrote home to his father to tell him, "You may talk about barbarism, but of all the men you could imagine there is no one like the Boche. They smashed works of art, beautiful furniture and everything they thought was useful and they ransacked and plundered everywhere. . . . I will not mention other outrages excepting to say that they are everything you have ever heard they were and nothing is exaggerated."[13] One officer in the 28th Division noted that the farther the men "penetrated in the wake of the Boche the more deep-seated and lasting became this feeling of utter detestation. . . . Had word come that peace was declared it is doubtful if the officers could have held them back. The iron had entered their souls."[14]

The biggest tactical problem for the Allies involved locating and eliminating the deadly German machine gun nests. The Germans made excellent use of the rugged terrain to conceal their guns. They then waited until the Allies, often unaware of their presence, came into point-blank range. One British company lost all of its officers in less than thirty minutes when it walked into such an ambush.[15] By the time small units recovered, found leadership from their NCOs, and called for support, the German gunners had often moved to another location in preparation for repeating the ambush somewhere else along the line.

The Germans also used concealed machine guns in ways designed to exploit American inexperience. In their rush to move forward, the Americans often failed to "mop up" all positions before going on to the next line of enemy defenses. The Germans learned to hide ma-chine guns in woods, in champagne cellars, and even in hastily dug underground bunkers, then wait for the American line to advance past their positions. The Germans could then open fire into the backs of the advancing Americans. The Germans had used this tactic at Le Hamel earlier in the month, although it is unlikely that any warning about it would have reached American units on the Marne. This tactic struck the Americans as being particularly cruel and cowardly, and they soon came to show little sympathy for the men who used it. The Yanks learned to advance more carefully and deliberately, clearing out areas where the Germans might have concealed machine guns before moving forward to the next assault.

In many places along the line, the Germans also used high ground to observe Allied movements and direct fire upon them. Following the experience of the 1/8 Battalion of the Argyll and Seaforth Highlanders on July 23 gives an appreciation of how difficult the situation was for Allied units. Part of the British 15th Division, they were located near the Soissons to Château-Thierry road opposite the town of Buzancy; they were ordered to advance against German high ground positions at 3:15 AM. They had had no time to send scouts or patrols forward to reconnoiter German positions, nor did they have adequate maps of the region; one British soldier had been issued a map that was dated 1884 and had "only hatching to indicate hills and valleys."[16] Worst of all, German positions in the Château de Buzancy on top of the region's most dominating hill (147 meters high) afforded excellent observation of Allied movements.

The unit's war diary traces out the disaster that soon befell the battalion. The Highlanders had unknowingly walked into one of the ambushes that characterized German defenses in this phase of the battle. No sooner had they left the safety of the woods than German artillery and machine gun fire (no doubt directed from the château) opened on them. The day's first entry in the battalion's war diary reads, "Right front coy [company] heavily shelled and disorganized. Patrol platoon moved out but was unable to proceed on account of shelling." Within a few short minutes, both company commanders had been wounded and taken from the battlefield. Because there had not been time to prepare written orders, all directions had been given orally to the two officers; thus, when they left the battlefield they took with them any notions of the battle plan or overall operational goals.

The division tried to overcome this problem by sending orders forward to the battalions by runner. German observation of the British positions, however, was so good that by 5:30 AM no runner had yet been able to get to the battalion to give it orders. At 6:10 AM the war diary records: "Continued very heavy artillery fire on whole Battalion area forward of ridge. Slightest movement observed and countered with heavy artillery and machine gun fire. All efforts of front coys [companies] to get forward frustrated. . . . The caliber [of the German artillery fire] was heavy and appeared to be at short range. The observation must have been exceptional." Even pairs of men who moved forward were "immediately harassed by the most accurate fire. Machine gun fire was heavy on all movement and on roads."

The battalion, without leaders and believing itself to be a sitting duck, needed help. Two runners left their positions to tell division headquarters of their plight, but both were killed within five yards of entering open terrain. Consequently, no more runners left the battalion's position until midday, when one managed to get through. By 12:30 PM German resistance seemed to have grown weaker, so one company tried to move out of its dangerous position, but the Germans had simply set another trap. No sooner had the company moved out than "artillery immediately opened," sending men scurrying for cover. For the first time that day, the shelling included gas, a tactic designed to kill those soldiers who took refuge in shell holes and ravines. Thus pinned down, the battalion could make no more advances. Eventually, a runner got through to the battalion from division headquarters with orders to stay where they were until dark. At 1:30 AM on the morning of July 24, the 13th Royal Scots Battalion came forward to help the Highlanders get safely out of the line.

The battalion's after action report blamed several factors for the disaster. The loss so early in the day of the two company commanders responsible for leading the attack left the unit without leadership and without detailed orders. The unit also suffered from "entire ignorance of the ground" and inaccurate maps of the area and German defenses opposite them. The French battalion to the left of the Highlanders had not even been informed of the British attack and thus had not been prepared to support it. When the afternoon British advance ground to a halt, however, the French rendered what assistance they could, firing heavy artillery and gas shells into caves and ravines where the Germans might have located machine guns. The French also sent their medical teams to render help that was "gallant in the extreme." One French doctor treated seventy wounded British soldiers in a single afternoon.[17]

The bloody setback suffered by the Highlanders underscores the difficulties faced by Allied units in this phase of the battle. French gunners praised the "remarkable tenacity" of the Scots, and lamented their own inability to support the attack as well as they might have because

German airplanes had prevented them from being resupplied with ar-tillery ammunition.[18] Lacking accurate intelligence and working with hastily cobbled plans presented tremendous challenges to tired units. So did the switch to open warfare. Men so long accustomed to trenches and static warfare had to make adjustments to the new more fluid and mobile offensive warfare that the situation demanded. The commander of the British 51st Division noted that his unit's advance up the Ardre Valley was "practically our first experience of open fighting."[19]

Many lessons therefore had to be relearned. Changing the settings on artillery fuses, for example, could cause the shells to explode on their first contact with tree trunks, thus sending down a lethal shower not just of metal, but of wood as well. Four years of fighting in treeless conditions on the western front had caused that lesson to be forgotten. One British commander noted, "When an enemy is found in woods hastily occupied artillery bombardment with H. E. [high explosive shells] is likely to produce important results (an old lesson rather lost sight of as the result of attacks [made] on woods under trench warfare conditions)."[20] French fuses, being more sensitive, exploded almost on first contact with trees and were thus significantly more effective in this regard than were British shells. Thus British units came to place even greater emphasis on coordinating their artillery with neighboring French field artillery units.[21] One British officer noted that his men "were loud in their praise of the accuracy, intensity, and effectiveness" of a French barrage called in to support one of their offensives.[22] British commander Sir Alexander Godley also heard his men praise French (and even Italian) shells, writing to King George V's private secretary that "our men like it (French shelling) much better. They say that it is the best barrage that they have ever seen or ever had."[23]

Even this excellent artillery fire did not always remove the most obstinate obstacles to Allied advances. Fighting the hidden German machine gun nests proved to be the most daunting task the Allies faced as they advanced toward the Ourcq. A single machine gun left unac-counted for could hold up several platoons. The ravines and woods also created odd echoes and sounds that further complicated efforts to pin-point enemy positions. Allied soldiers came to fear, and in some cases even grudgingly respect, enemy machine gunners. One British soldier from the Black Watch regiment noted that German infantrymen "sur-rendered very simply," but the machine gunners did not, and instead "fought with great gallantry and stubbornness."[24]

Other Allied soldiers saw little gallantry in the stout defense of the German gunners. They believed instead that German infantry were ordered to abandon the machine gunners in place, in an effort to force the gunners to fight furiously for their lives. There is little hard evidence to prove this assertion; the stout defense of machine gun units likely comes from the fact that machine guns are crew-served weapons. Men thus had learned to fight together in small groups. Consequently, they faced less of the loneliness on the battlefield that new infantrymen experienced. They also understood the importance of staying and fighting to protect the lives of their fellow crew members. Finally, in a small-group setting, the wavering of one member of the crew could become obvious to his crewmates, who could then step in to bolster his courage.

Heavy artillery often proved too inaccurate to hit small and determined machine gun positions, and tanks could not reach into the tough terrain in which many gunners concealed themselves and their weapons. French units thus resorted to smaller weapons, relying heavily on grenades against German machine gun nests. The French had used grenadiers to great effect at Verdun, and they had become critical to most French offensive plans since. A lone French officer in the 23rd Colonial Regiment took out three machine guns with grenades, opening a path for his comrades to take Méry farm, along with the sixty Germans and four artillery pieces defending it.[25] The 74th Regiment also used grenades when its artillery preparation failed to quiet German machine guns near Hill 184.[26]

Allied advances were therefore slow, but in places they did exist. Most attacks occurred on narrow fronts because of the difficulty of arranging rolling barrages and the shortages of men in many units. The barrages themselves were slower and much more deliberate, holding fire on areas where the Germans were most likely to have hidden machine guns. Miscommunications, however, often put barrages hundreds of yards away from their intended targets.

One of the largest operations of this phase of the battle shows both the successes and the failures of Allied operations. The British XXII Corps planned a joint advance on both banks of the Ardre River, moving northwest toward the heavily defended town of Marfeux. Steep ravines cut into both banks of the Ardre, and north of the river sat the Bois du Petit Champ, an extension of the massive Forêt de la Montagne de Rheims. The British 62nd Division would have to advance into the imposing Bois du Petit Champ in order to clear out German positions that could fire into the flank of the attack. The Germans could also benefit from the château at Marfeux for observation and direction of fire.

The "thick, almost impenetrable woods" of the bois limited the effectiveness of the artillery preparation that began at 10:30 AM on July 21. The rolling barrage thus moved slowly and deliberately, at the relatively slow rate of 100 meters per ten minutes. Miscommunication put much of the barrage in the wrong place, thus leaving most of the German defenses in the area untouched. The failure to destroy German defenses meant that men of the 9th/Durham Light Infantry and the 5th/King's Own Yorkshire Light Infantry stepped into "a perfect inferno of machine gun fire."[27] One battalion reported losing forty men to enemy fire before it even saw a German soldier.[28] Some British platoons made minimal gains, "cut[ting] their way through like jungle," while others failed to advance at all, leaving an uneven line.[29] Aware that "no troops could withstand that murderous machine gun fire," British officers ordered the line consolidated, which in practice meant giving up even the small gains made that day.[30]

The next day (July 22) the British attacked again, using a rolling barrage that advanced at the same slow rate as the day before, 100 meters per ten minutes. The advance also received the support of five French tanks and numerous gas shells. The British planned to strike Marfeux simultaneously from the north and the south. They timed their attack for 11:30 AM, hoping to surprise the Germans by not attacking at dawn. The initial advance by the British provided some cause for optimism, but the British soon learned that they had been lured into a trap. Approximately 200 yards inside the Bois du Petit Champ, the British hit a line of German machine gun nests, intentionally kept off the front line in order to protect them from the rolling barrage. They discovered two more German machine gun lines within the next 100 yards.

Through bloody lessons acquired in places like the Bois du Petit Champ, the British developed methods for advancing through such positions. The British learned to attack machine gun nests by encircling them, using the woods to conceal their own movements. This kind of fighting was "quite unlike anything the Division had hitherto experienced in France," but they learned to make it work. In this case, they also benefited from a bit of calculated luck, as their late attack had in fact caught the Germans in the midst of a relief. On July 23, the 62nd Division, supported to their left by the 51st Division, cleared the Bois du Petit Champ and entered Marfeux, although the Germans were able to keep up a steady artillery fire on the town.[31] One shell (probably dropped from a German plane) struck an Allied ammunition dump, which continued to explode for twenty-four hours and provided light powerful enough to read by 15 miles away.[32]

The capture of the Bois du Petit Champ and Marfeux showed that carefully prepared and executed attacks could succeed. The staff of the 62nd Division had made a virtue of a necessity, selecting a small objective, knowing full well that its men lacked the strength to do much more. As a result, the attack compares favorably with that of the Argyll and Seaforth Highlanders on the opposite end of the salient, examined earlier. Still, to advance no more than a few hundred meters, the British 62nd Division had taken casualties amounting to 91 officers and 2,722 enlisted men. The seizure of the Bois du Petit Champ thus also shows the strength of German positions and the costs involved in attacking.[33]

The problems involved in advancing were thus easy to identify and common to many units. On the western side of the salient, the problems were the same as those encountered in the attack on the Bois du Petit Champ on the eastern side. Few units had reliable maps, and almost no one knew anything about the terrain, leaving advancing infantry danger-ously exposed to machine gun fire from the woods and the ravines. The British 15th Division arrived at front line positions at 3:00 AM on July 23, just three hours before their artillery was supposed to begin. The men arrived to find that "the front line as taken over from the French and the American troops by no means coincided with that shown on the map, and even its approximate position was extremely difficult to find in the dark."[34]

The speed of the battle also contributed to mistakes. Attacks had to be arranged on increasingly short notice in order to take advantage of newly arrived units and the availability of artillery support. Often, the pace of the battle outstripped commanders' ability to make timely decisions. Marc Bloch, who fought at the Second Battle of the Marne, recalled an incident from this phase of the battle that highlighted the problems of command and control:

> On 22 July 1918 I was serving with Mangin's [Tenth] Army—in which meth-ods of intercommunication were particularly unsatisfactory. On one occasion I was appalled to receive for re-transmission an order to attack at such short notice that it was impossible to get it to the troops concerned in time. They were actually already on the move. When it did arrive, it was so late that

the battalion detailed to carry it out had no opportunity to reconnoiter the ground before daylight, advanced to the assault on a wrong bearing, and was slaughtered almost to a man, quite uselessly.[35]

Nor was communication between staff and line the only such problem. The crucial task of coordinating infantry with artillery also proved extremely difficult, especially when French field artillerists had to work with English-speaking American or British units. In the case of the 15th Division's attack, French, British, and American artillerists had to work together to lay down a rolling barrage. It marked the first time that the three nations had ever jointly prepared an artillery barrage. The weight of the barrage was impressive, but it struck the wrong target, as the German front line was 600 yards further back than the line indicated on the maps available to the gunners. As a result, when the British 15th Division's men left their positions after a twenty-minute artillery barrage, they attacked into the full fury of undamaged German artillery and machine gun positions.[36] The mistakes and difficulties of the Allied offensives were thus the same on both sides of the salient.

The Role of the Americans

In the center of the salient, the main weight of attack fell to the Americans. The 26th and 3rd divisions shouldered the load until July 26, when the 26th went to the St. Mihiel salient and the 28th and 42nd entered the line. The Americans found themselves short of most important heavy weapons, especially tanks, 155mm artillery pieces, and gas. They also had too few of the excellent Browning .30-caliber machine guns. Instead, they received mass quantities of the very unpopular French Chauchat light machine gun. The Chauchat had a much heavier than usual recoil and thus required a great deal of training, but few Americans had had that training. The Americans had purchased 34,000 Chauchats from the French while awaiting deliveries of the Brownings; to ease the transition, the French rebored the barrels of the Chauchats in order to take the Browning's 8mm ammunition, but the process produced poor results, resulting in inaccurate weapons universally detested by the Americans who had to use them.

The New England men in the American 26th Division had the most important mission. Their job was to break the bottom of the

German north-south defensive line at the village of Epieds. The mission was so important that Pershing himself made two visits to the division to impress upon them the gravity of the situation. Pershing might have been able to rally the men, but he could not do much to help their lack of air cover. The Allies could not prevent near-total German control of the sky, with the Germans able to concentrate as many as eighty planes at a time over the division's line. Most of those planes were the Fokker DR. I, whose rate of climb, maneuverability, and durability were superior to the Nieuport 27 biplane then in use by most Allied pilots. The newer Spad XIII was beginning to appear in small number to even the odds, but they were too few to make any serious contribution. Eddie Rickenbacker's famous "Hat in the Ring" squadron did not get their Spads until 8 August 1918, too late to help the men of the 26th.

Units of the 26th nevertheless forced their way into Epieds on July 23, but soon faced a strong counterattack. In order to give the men in the village some much-needed protection from a German counterattack, Allied artillery units had to organize and fire a hasty defensive barrage, but Allied soldiers still found the fighting rough going.[37] One inexperienced regiment had unwisely advanced too far into the woods near the village of Trugny, leaving its flanks exposed. The Germans saw the opportunity and attacked. Cut off, the regiment managed to send a runner back to division headquarters with a desperate message: "For Christ's sake, knock out the machine guns on our right. Heavy casualties. What troops should be on my right and left and where are they?" Division headquarters officers were understandably reluctant to fire artillery into the position because American and German units were too close to one another. By the end of the day, the brigade to which this regiment was attached had been able to provide some help, but it had suffered 1,226 casualties serious enough to require hospitalization, as well as an unknown number of dead.[38]

After experiences such as these, the Americans found themselves in less of a mood to be generous to their surrendering enemies. Advancing units also found the damage the Germans had intentionally created in order to cover their retreat. Mined roads, poisoned wells, felled trees, and burned fields all attested to the wanton German destruction. More importantly, Americans had quickly grown tired of the German habit of emptying their weapons at point-blank range against the Americans, then throwing up their arms and shouting "Americans! Kamerads!"[39] One veteran of the 26th reported that his unit treated German prisoners "roughly," with the exception of one sent back from the front who bore a note from the American who had taken him that read, "This man when captured was giving water to a wounded American soldier."[40] That the exception had to be pointed out to Americans further behind the line speaks volumes about the unwritten rules that must have been in place.

Later that day, the Allies realized that the Germans were preparing a final withdrawal to the Ourcq River, to be covered by a thick belt of German machine guns placed as close as seven yards apart from one another in places. Rather than attack the position, the 26th turned east and cut an important lateral road, then awaited relief from the men of the 42nd Division. They had taken their immediate objective, although the Germans had managed to escape north of the Ourcq, with rear-guards established behind a powerful defensive line. In one week, the 26th Division had advanced 10 miles at the cost of 4,108 casualties.[41]

Other American units advanced as well. One regiment of the 3rd Division, operating to the right of the 26th, improvised a pontoon bridge over the Marne using empty gas cans, thus securing the eastern approaches to Château-Thierry.[42] Speed served the men of the regiment well; their rapid crossing prevented the Germans opposite them from establishing defensive positions among the particularly steep ravines of the area. They thus were able to establish excellent positions on both sides of a 220-meter-high ridge west of Jaulgonne.

With each major action, the Americans improved their tactics. They still had to "learn to play the game," but they made fewer mistakes as they matured. Their dash and their aggressiveness led one French commander to comment that the American way of fighting was "glorious, it was heroic, but it was not war." It certainly was not the methodical, carefully prepared war of set-piece engagements that the French had learned to fight. But it did allow the Allies to become more aggressive, and it "infused new hope, new vigor, [and] new courage" in Allied operations. The costs continued to be high, but American recklessness slowly began to give way to a more careful method of war.[43]

The sights, sounds, and smells of the battlefield also forced the Americans to mature quickly. Young, inexperienced Americans advanced through woods "simply full of German and American dead and the stench is very, very bad." Bodies turned blue from exposure to poison gas, and the sheer number of unburied bodies and body parts were novel and terrifying sights. The damage that modern tools of war can cause to nature, a facet that Europeans on the western front had seen for years, also struck Americans. "Great woods that had once been green and beautiful were leveled to the ground and the dead leaves were black from the effects of the gas."[44] Towns and villages "that before had probably been some of the most picturesque in France were now in complete ruins," symbolic of the destruction of the war the Americans had entered. To many Americans, the sight of buried bodies uncovered by shelling proved to the most traumatic. It was all part and parcel of learning how to fight a modern war.

Foch's Memorandum

As the fighting in this third major phase of the battle was wearing down, the high commands of both armies took new stock of their situations. Although Allied territorial gains had been important, they had not caused the hoped-for rupture of German lines, and they had not closed the bag. Nevertheless, most signs were favorable for the Allies. A July 24 French intelligence report concluded that combat on the Marne since July 14 had completely exhausted twenty German divisions, and also reported that German battalions had been reduced in strength from 980 men each to 880 men each. The report also saw signs that suggested that the Germans might delay or even cancel their planned offensive in Flanders. Meanwhile, the continued arrival of fresh, double-strength American divisions meant an increasing numerical advantage for the Allies.[45]

These reports encouraged Foch, but he was taking no chances. He had met with French premier Georges Clemenceau on July 18, 19, and 22 to update him on the new strategic and operational situation. At these meetings he had urged the French government to call up the conscript Class of 1920 (mostly composed of men born in 1902) in October, that is, after most of the fall harvest had been collected. Foch argued that the battle had produced tremendous advantages to the Allies and dealt a crushing blow to the Germans. He wanted the Class of 1920 trained over the course of the winter in order to be ready to fight in the spring, 1919, even though some of these men would be as young as seventeen years old.

Foch took the occasion of a July 24 meeting of senior officers to announce a major shift in his strategy. He presented a memorandum to Pétain, Pershing, and Haig outlining his new thinking; the memorandum was so important to Foch that he devoted an entire chapter of his memoirs to it. He began by noting that the fifth German offensive of 1918 "had been halted at its very start" and could now conclusively be labeled "a failure." The counterattacks of the French Tenth and Sixth armies had converted this failure into a shattering battlefield defeat for Germany, and in so doing had created the "basis on which should rest the general attitude to be adopted by the Allied armies." The numerical situation in both men and weapons had begun to tilt in favor of the Allies, and alongside it the Allies were also developing a "moral ascendancy" which was every bit as important as the sheer numbers.

Accordingly, Foch argued, the time had come to change both Allied grand strategy and the general Allied attitude toward the war. The critical component of Foch's memorandum, which he highlighted in his memoirs, reads, "The moment has come to abandon the general defensive attitude forced upon us until now by numerical inferiority and to pass to the offensive."[46] Foch's memorandum then laid out a grand strategic plan based on offensive operations against rail centers and economic targets such as coal and iron ore mines. The first goal of Foch's plan was the Paris to Nancy railroad, which ran through the Marne sector. Thus in the short term the Allies would need to maintain pressure in the Marne sector in order to secure this critical rail line. The memorandum concluded by asking the generals assembled to envision what "retrograde movements" the Germans might make in the near future and what steps the Allied armies might take to frustrate those movements.

Foch later wrote that he thought the generals at the meeting had viewed his memorandum with "considerable surprise" owing to its ambitious nature and the number of offensives Foch envisioned before the onset of winter. Nevertheless, none of the generals objected to any of Foch's main points. At this stage, Foch was still envisioning 1919 as "the decisive year of the conflict," a conclusion consistent with his request to Clemenceau for the calling of the Class of 1920 a year earlier than planned. Years after the war, Foch told an interviewer that at the same time that he was preparing the memorandum he had already begun to think that the Allies could win the war in 1918, although there is nothing in the memorandum to suggest that conclusion.

Foch may have been alone in his ambitions for 1918, but he was obviously not the only optimistic Allied commander. At a meeting on

July 25, even the extremely cautious Pétain expressed optimism despite the limited ground the Allies had actually gained. He told British XXII Corps commander Sir Alexander Godley that he expected German foreign minister Richard von Kühlmann to offer new peace terms in the near future that would be much more attractive to the Allied governments. Pétain added that the Germans must understand how much the strategic situation had changed: "Until the present we have been fighting from a position of disadvantage, but now we fight from a position of advantage."[47]

Allied success on the Marne also led to the landmark creation of a separate American army. The issue had long been a sore spot between the Americans and their Allies, with Pershing pushing for a separate American First Army with its own dedicated sector of the western front. He had in fact sought to create two American armies, thus forming an army group. Critics of the plan cited American inexperience and the supply and leadership redundancies that would inevitably result from such a plan. Others thought that Pershing was aiming for the promotion to five-star rank that would accompany his expanded command authority.

Foch had been an early and enthusiastic supporter of creating an American army, but he did not wish to do so until he felt the time was right. On July 10, he noted that the Americans numbered more than one million men in France, and, with the American success at Le Hamel fresh in his mind, he made a dramatic statement to Pershing. "Today, when there are a million Americans in France, I am going to be still more American than any of you," he told Pershing. Then he announced, somewhat to Pershing's surprise, "The American Army must become an accomplished fact." The outbreak of the Second Battle of the Marne temporarily pushed those concerns to the back burner, but American performance during the battle had so impressed Foch that he agreed to the creation of the American First Army while this phase of the battle was still ongoing.[48]

With Foch's approval, on July 24, Pershing finally made the landmark announcement he had anticipated for so long. By bringing together two American corps, the United States would have the force structure necessary to form its own army. In his order of that day, written upon his return from Foch's headquarters, Pershing announced that the new American First Army would begin operations on August 10, although in reality the First Army was functioning by the end of July.[49]

Senior leaders on both sides of the Atlantic recognized the significance of the event. "History awaits you," wired Clemenceau to Pershing in his congratulatory telegram. "You will not fail it."[50]

It only remained to determine where the American First Army would make its presence felt first. Foch's memorandum envisioned the St. Mihiel salient near Verdun as the most promising area for the Americans to attack. Pershing accepted the challenge, and his staff began planning. The St. Mihiel offensive plan envisioned using four American divisions then fighting on the Marne, the 1st, 2nd, 3rd, and 42nd. The 1st and 2nd had already come off the line on the night of July 22–23. They did not return to the Marne; instead they formed the backbone of the new First Army's designs for the St. Mihiel operation. The 3rd Division left the Marne on July 27, replaced by the newly arrived 32nd Division (from Michigan and Wisconsin). The 42nd Division left on August 2, to be replaced eventually by New York City men in the 77th Division.

By the time Pershing had announced the creation of the American First Army, the Allies had advanced far enough to place the entire German line within range of accurate artillery fire. The crown prince and Ludendorff (who had belatedly realized the danger to the German position) decided that their rearguards had done their work. Concluding, "The enemy would renew his massed attacks. We had to make them very expensive for him," Ludendorff approved the decision to retreat.[51] On July 26 the Germans decided to withdraw most of their units to the north of the Ourcq and destroy all bridges over the river. Their rearguards had bought them the days they needed to organize new positions of resistance such as the Croix Rouge farm northeast of Epieds. The Germans had converted the farm, "a low, widespread group of stone farm buildings connected by walls and ditches" into a massive machine gun position, capable of all-around fire. The area around the farm was just as dangerous, as "almost every yard provided a new ambush position for the German rear guard" protecting the approaches to the Ourcq.[52]

Ludendorff hoped that these decisions might stabilize the immediate crisis on the Marne, but he was under no illusions as to the gravity of the overall German situation. Ludendorff, whom one senior German general said was "a physically and morally broken man" by this point of the war, ordered ten German infantry divisions broken up to create replacements for other divisions still fighting.[53] He also issued orders for Army Group Crown Prince Rupprecht to remain on the defensive in Flanders. Although Ludendorff could not bring himself to use the words, his orders effectively meant the cancellation of his offensive for Flanders.

The stage was thus set for the final phase of the Second Battle of the Marne. The Germans would try to conduct another fighting retreat, this time to the Aisne and Vesle rivers. Like the retreat to the Ourcq, this one would be covered by machine gun nests and centered around ambushes that took maximum advantage of the rugged terrain. Fortified towns such as Buzancy, Fère-en-Tardenois, and Sergy would form the backbone of this new German defensive network. The cancellation of Hagen, however, meant that this retreat would have little to no strategic purpose. It would, instead, be designed to save as many German soldiers as possible from encirclement.

The Allies, on the other hand, would seek to maintain the pressure on Army Group Crown Prince Wilhelm in order to prevent its men from reinforcing other sectors. Continued pressure would also keep German attention focused squarely on the Marne salient while the Allies prepared major attacks in other sectors, consistent with the aims of Foch's memorandum. The American attack at St. Mihiel was just one such attack. The British were also planning an attack of their own, based on the tactical ideas used by the British Fourth Army at Le Hamel, to free the Paris to Amiens railway. Allied intelligence suggested that the Germans did not suspect either offensive. Continuing the fight to the Vesle and the Aisne thus had important strategic and operational goals.

The fighting on the Marne since July 15 had been heavy and Allied losses high, but the Germans had been dislodged from their positions south of the Ourcq. The morale of Allied soldiers remained "excellent" and men still "full of fight," sensing as they did that the war was at its turning point.[54] Few men, however, were under any illusion about how difficult the road had been up to this point, and how much harder it would still be. The ground between the Ourcq and the Vesle featured the same thick woods and sharp ravines that had given Allied troops so much trouble thus far. The killing would thus continue, and the great Allied feats since July 15 would need to be repeated. If Sherman thought war was hell, wrote one American soldier, then he "should have seen this argument."[55]

EIGHT

THE FINAL PHASE, JULY 27 TO AUGUST 9

ON JULY 27, the normally cautious and meticulous French General Marie Émile Fayolle sent an uncharacteristic message to the senior officers of his *Groupe d'armées de Réserve* (GAR). Aware of the toll the Second Battle of the Marne had taken on the men of the GAR, Fayolle nevertheless hoped to inspire them and then push them on to further feats, including the rupture of the German defensive line in the Tardenois plain. "The moment has come," read the order, "to harvest the fruits of our counter-offensive, which has now lasted ten days: forward, whatever the fatigue of the men!"[1] The order demonstrates both that Fayolle had bought into the offensive mindset laid out by Foch on July 24 and that he understood the importance of continuing the offensive. The battle was not yet won, but perhaps a final push might create the decisive victory that he and Foch had been anticipating for several weeks.

Fayolle's atypical élan notwithstanding, the German positions in the Marne salient were still strong. At the time of his order, the German line along the western end of the salient still threatened large sections of the critical Soissons to Château-Thierry highway. The Allies had artillery and infantry close enough to the road to harass almost any German movement along it, but they could still not use the road themselves with safety. Thus Allied progress in the west had been negligible since July 19. On the other end of the salient, the slow British advance in the tough terrain of the Ardre River valley meant equally negligible progress in the east. In the center, the Allies had experienced more consistent progress, moving through stubborn German defensive positions in the Croix Rouge farm and placing forces within effective artillery range of the critical communications juncture of Fère-en-Tardenois.

Allied goals for this fourth major phase of the battle involved crossing the German defensive line in Tardenois and breaking the last main German line of resistance south of the Aisne. On July 28, advance elements of the French 52nd Division crossed the Marne and established a thin bridgehead by capturing Fère-en-Tardenois. The operation had been daring and aggressive; French units attacked with little immediate artillery support, catching the Germans off guard. They had in fact so surprised the Germans that they found more than one million German rations in depots in the town itself and an estimated $5 million worth of munitions in the supply dumps near the town. The loss of these supplies, especially the food, hurt the German supply situation, and the recovery of them provided needed succor to seriously overextended Allied troops.

In other liberated towns and villages near the Ourcq, the Germans had been much more thorough and had, according to contemporary reports, "destroyed everything they could and took away all food."[2] Wanton German destruction had now become a nearly universal feature of the German retreat, and it enraged Allied soldiers of all nations. Rudolf Binding described the German withdrawal from the perspective of German soldiers retreating from a French village:

"In the twinkling of an eye everything was turned upside-down, as if the looters were professionals. . . . The soldiers hacked whole beds to pieces for the sake of a length of sheeting the size of a towel. . . . There was not very much to be had, but in the end nearly everything was carried off."[3] Within a few months, the victorious Allies would call upon the vanquished Germans to pay for the damage that they had caused. More immediately, the Allied high commands wanted to maintain offensive pressure in order to deny the Germans the ability to destroy more French villages and towns.

On the operational level, the German withdrawal to the Ourcq allowed the Allies to reopen the full length of the Paris to Châlons railway, thus assuring an unfettered line of supply to eastern France. The opening of the railways proved especially important to the Americans, who now had access to a full rail network from the Atlantic ports to their new operational bases near St. Mihiel, Toul, and Nancy. With the

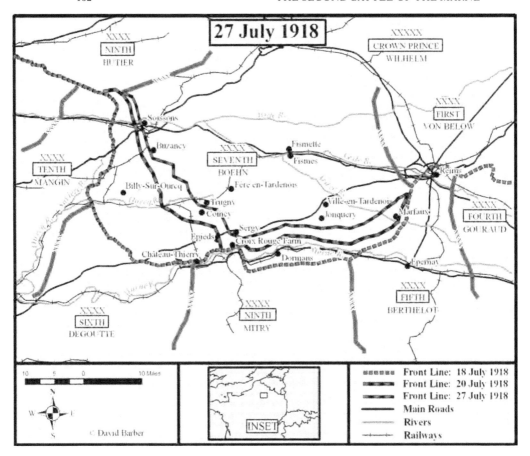

AEF's lines of supply now more secure, Foch urged Pershing to form his American First Army in Lorraine as quickly as possible in order to free up the relatively well-rested French divisions there to join French units further north. The French divisions in Lorraine were among France's last remaining units labeled as completely fresh; their entry into the line would give France more offensive power and give the units worn out from the Marne fighting some much needed reprieve.

To take even more pressure off the Marne sector, on July 28, Foch "invited" Douglas Haig to begin making final preparations for a major British offensive near Amiens on the Somme River. The offensive's goals were twofold. First, it would help to free up another major rail line for supplying Allied armies as they advanced. Second, a rupture near Amiens would impede German efforts to create another solid defensive line in front of the formidable Hindenburg Line.[4] As a show of faith to the British field marshal, Foch placed the French First Army to Haig's south under British operational command and promised to return the British XXII Corps (composed of the 51st and 62nd Divisions) from the Marne to Haig's direct control within forty-eight hours. Haig agreed to conduct the attack and wrote in his diary that he was "pleased that Foch should have entrusted me with the direction of these operations."[5] British Fourth Army officers had already begun planning the attack, which was to be conducted on the same general model as the Le Hamel offensive of July 4. It would rely heavily on surprise and be supported by armor instead of a rolling artillery barrage.

Fayolle saw early drafts of the plans for the Amiens offensive and noted that it was "an excellent project that can only provide the best results." But for the British attack to work, the Allies had to maintain pressure in the Marne sector. By doing so the Allies could keep German attention focused away from Amiens and keep alive the possibility of surprise. Continuing the Marne offensive thus remained important to the larger war effort, even if its exact role was evolving. To finish the Second Battle of the Marne, Fayolle still hoped to achieve simultaneous breakthroughs on the eastern and western edges of the salient, leading to an envelopment of German forces between the Ourcq and the Aisne rivers. Nevertheless, he saw how slowly Allied armies were progressing and, contrary to his July 27 order, wrote in his diary that "the retreat of the Boche is not going as quickly as we hoped. . . . Our progress is slow. We can only advance by heavy and strong blows [coups de force]. What is the Boche up to?"[6]

A slow and steady Allied advance played right into German plans. Knowing that they could not hold the Ourcq line for more than a few days, the Germans intended once more to retreat to a new line of resistance, this one along the heights of the Aisne and Vesle rivers. This position had stopped major Allied attacks several times before, most ominously in 1917 during the bloody fiasco of the Nivelle Offensive. The Germans knew the ground well and knew that it held excellent defensive positions, both natural and manmade. The Germans hoped to hold the Allies behind that line once again, but they needed a few days to get there in force; the Ourcq positions, they hoped, would buy that time.

Strong defensive lines were especially important to the Germans because their manpower situation had deteriorated terribly in the past ten days. On July 16 British intelligence estimated that Crown Prince Wilhelm's army group contained thirty-two fit divisions and sixty unfit divisions. On July 28, the British estimate showed just twenty fit divisions and eighty-seven unfit divisions.[7] Most of the divisions brought into the Marne sector came from Crown Prince Rupprecht's army group further to the north. The shift of German soldiers to the south was welcome news to British intelligence officers, meaning both that Rupprecht could not order an offensive in Flanders and that a strong British offensive near Amiens might catch the Germans unprepared. Nevertheless, the transfer of fifteen German divisions, however tired they were, also meant more powerful forces in the Marne sector to overcome.

The strength of German airpower weakened somewhat in late July, giving the Allies a few days of welcome parity in the air. German air units, having abandoned their bases south of the Ourcq, moved to hastily constructed airfields further north. The resulting temporary respite from German air assaults allowed Allied planes to harass the enemy by dropping bombs on German lines of retreat. One report cited the impressive figure of 284 tons of bombs dropped behind enemy lines by Allied aviators, mostly on enemy artillery batteries, supply centers, and areas of likely concentration of German troops.[8] But if Allied bombers were effective, Allied fighters seem to have continued to fly at a serious disadvantage. Allied soldiers continued to complain of the harassment caused by large numbers of German airplanes operating with impunity over their lines; one American regimental headquarters had to move three times in a single day because German airplanes repeatedly located and targeted it. Allied soldiers came to welcome the frequent periods of clouds and rain in late July, happy to exchange being wet and chilly for the relative safety from German airplanes that the bad weather provided.

News of how badly the Germans had been defeated on the Marne had finally reached the German home front, creating a morale crisis among civilians who had been told nothing but good news about the fate of the German offensive. Secrecy and censorship were getting harder to maintain, and evidence of a war beginning to go very badly was commonplace in German cities. Severe food shortages during the winter and spring had laid bare the failure of the German government to feed its people, and wounded German soldiers returned home with discouraging tales from the front. Allied intelligence officers had taken from prisoners of war copies of the Berlin *Tageblatt* and other documents that reported "scenes of unspeakable despair" in the German capital as news of the German defeat on the Marne had spread. The *Frankische Tageblatt* also reported "a dangerous nervousness on the part of the people."[9] Finally admitting to themselves that the "situation is terrible," German generals and civilians alike were beginning to see how the Second Battle of the Marne was revealing the essential bankruptcy of German strategy.[10]

In order to buy time and draw the Allies to a standstill that might have both moral and material advantages, the Germans once again set up lines of machine gun positions in the woods and ravines of the Marne sector. The first defensive position ran roughly along a line from the fortified towns of Hartennes to Sergy to Romigny. The Sergy position took advantage of a series of stone buildings in the village itself and was, in the judgment of the Americans opposite it, "particularly favorable for the enemy."[11] The second line ran from Billy sur Aisne to Mareuil en Dôle to Poilly. The Germans knew that these positions were far weaker than those along the Marne and the Ourcq had been because German units had fewer heavy weapons and less time to prepare new positions. Still, they did their job, with even Foch having to admit that by July 29 the battle in the Marne "had once more reached a deadlock."[12]

Breaking the deadlock would not be easy. Pétain informed Foch on July 31 that the Allied situation was not promising. He argued that until reinforcements arrived, the Tenth and Fifth Armies could not be expected to conduct major offensives. The Sixth Army, in the salient's southwest corner, would therefore have to take the lead. Pétain reported that the French armies in the Marne sector were short 120,000 men and that only 19,000 men were immediately available to be sent into the sector. French soldiers, he told Foch, "certainly have excellent morale, but fatigue is high. We are at the limits of our efforts."[13] The imminent departure of several American and British divisions from the sector added a further complication. Not only did the sheer numbers of Allied troops in the sector decline, but the departures came from men who had grown familiar with the terrain of the Marne sector and the methods developed for fighting inside it.

Pétain therefore still hoped to close the Marne pocket, but he was careful not to count too much on a complete rupture of German lines. He told Fayolle to limit his efforts to what could be supported with the resources on hand. He also warned Fayolle to take steps to avoid being drawn into a battle of attrition that the Allies did not have the resources to conduct. Fayolle even understood Pétain to be in favor of abandoning the operation in the Marne altogether. Foch, he thought, had overruled Pétain once again in the interests of keeping the Marne battle going for a few days longer, both to continue the quest for decisive victory and to give the Amiens offensive its best chance to succeed.[14] Pétain ordered a pause in operations on July 30 and July 31, but he informed Foch that it was temporary, designed to rest, regroup, and provision Allied troops for the next major push.

The terrain between the Ourcq and the Aisne posed a particularly frightening specter to Pétain. On this same ground just over a year before, French troops under Robert Nivelle had attacked well-sited German positions and had been slaughtered. Five days of attacks toward the Aisne had yielded no territorial gains worth the cost of 120,000 French casualties. All armies had experienced heavy losses for minimal territorial gain before, but the manifest incompetence and unrealistic expectations that surrounded this offensive had led to France's greatest morale crisis of the war. President Raymond Poincaré had taken the highly unusual step of personally intervening to stop the offensive and had also been instrumental in removing Nivelle from his command. Within a few weeks, the French government sent Nivelle to Algeria in order to get him far away from the western front.

Worst of all, the morale crisis of 1917 had led to what the French called "acts of collective indiscipline" as thousands of French soldiers refused orders to go back into the line. The French mutinies are a complex affair, best left to those who have studied it in detail; the key point here is that Pétain, charged in July 1918 with attacking toward the Aisne River sector, was the same man who had been brought in to quell the mutinies that occurred in this sector during April and May 1917.[15] Pétain had worked hard since the mutinies to rebuild trust between the army's men and its officers and to bring a measure of rationality to French military operations. He had also modernized the French army's weaponry and tactics and taken great pains to build up personal and professional links between the French and the Americans. It would have been only natural for him to have had unpleasant visions about operating in this area again with tired troops, and to have his doubts about placing everything he had worked for at risk along the difficult terrain of the Aisne River valley.

The physical appearance of the battlefield could not have done much to help Pétain's natural pessimism. American soldiers saw a region that "has all the appearances of having once been a very beautiful part of France, but it is certainly far from beautiful now." Smashed buildings, destroyed forests, and fields turned into moonscapes had rapidly made the Marne as badly damaged as any other part of the western front. The number of corpses, and their state of decay in the intense summer heat, also struck observers from all armies. One field artillerist moved through a village on the Ourcq that the Allies had taken and described the scene thus: "German dead were still lying about the street, some of them hanging out of windows, some of them with their feet upon the sidewalks and their heads in the gutters, others swelled up so that [they were cutting through] their clothes."[16]

Allied soldiers had also attended a number of funerals, turning them bitter and determined to see the battle to a successful conclusion. American soldiers in the 28th Division now had "many scores to settle. Every man felt he wanted to avenge the officers and comrades who had fallen in the earlier fighting, and it was a grimly-determined and relentless body of men that emerged" on the south bank of the Ourcq on July 29. The Americans had seen a number of false surrenders and even one incident where a German soldier threw his arms up in surrender, then activated his machine gun by means of a pedal. As a result, the men of the 28th Division had stopped taking prisoners.[17] Nor was this spirit of growing hatred only to be found among the newly arrived Americans. British Lieutenant Robert Lindsay Mackay spent his twenty-second birthday attending funerals of the men from his battalion. The experience had put him in a particularly sour and angry mood. "I hate the Hun," he wrote in his diary that night.[18]

Fighting to the Vesle

The new Allied attack plan focused on the center and the eastern half of the salient in order to give most of the units of the French Tenth Army some much-needed time to rest and refit. The plan for the center called for the American 4th and 32nd divisions to advance alongside the French 52nd and 68th divisions toward the town of Bazoches, while in the east French divisions that had relieved the British XXII Corps would continue to advance up the Ardre River. The attacks would advance like an upside-down V, trapping German units on the Tardenois plain before they could retreat to the Aisne and Vesle in force. The plan demanded a gargantuan effort from tired Allied units; the French 68th Division had

had no rest since July 18. At the other end of the spectrum, the American divisions were fresh, but at the same time terribly inexperienced. On the western edge, the Tenth Army had slightly more modest goals, with orders to put units on the Soissons to Château-Thierry highway and eliminate German strong points such as the Château de Buzancy.[19]

The British units on the eastern edge of the salient, the XXII Corps, had already been earmarked to leave the salient, but they had one more task to complete. They had been ordered to capture the Montagne de Bligny, a key piece of high ground on the north bank of the Ardre River. The task fell to the 62nd Division, which had already suffered heavy losses. As the division's history recounts, battalions had to reorganize before the attack, finding new leaders wherever they could: "Platoon sergeants had mostly to be drawn from young lance corporals who were quite strangers [to the men they were to lead], while the Lewis [light machine gun] teams could be given no more than two trained gunners. Amongst the reinforcements were many youngsters just out from England, who had never before been under fire."[20]

The 62nd also found itself on unfamiliar ground in "a sector rich in natural obstacles," which, according to the unit's war diary, "presented problems to all arms which had hitherto only been met in theory." Complicating matters further, the division did not receive its orders until 2:30 AM for an attack due to begin at 4:30 AM on July 28. A heavy rain, followed by a thick morning mist, made last-minute preparations difficult.[21] With no chance to scout or reconnoiter in the dark, locating machine gun nests among the natural obstacles of the Ardre Valley proved a tremendous challenge to the men of the 62nd Division. This unfamiliar, more mobile form of war also complicated adjoining units' efforts to maintain contact. The British learned to improvise a method of sending out patrols to scout and conduct reconnaissance by fire missions, essentially using some men of the unit as bait so that others could spot the flashes from hidden German machine gun nests.[22]

Limited in its objectives, the attack of the XXII Corps proved to be a moderate success. The 62nd captured the high ground around Bligny, with eight members of the West Yorkshire regiment receiving the French *Croix de Guerre* for their actions. South of the Ardre, the 51st completed an advance that had taken them four miles in eleven days, but it could not reach the main objective, the town of Ville-en-Tardenois. The corps had lost 120 officers and 3,918 other ranks to advance less than one mile. In all, the 51st Division's experience alone on the

Marne had cost it 175 officers and 3,390 other ranks.[23] Too exhausted to go any further, the XXII Corps came out of the line on July 29. The two divisions received some much-needed rest before fighting again at Arras, on the Hindenburg Line, and in battles on the Selle River. Both divisions also took part in the postwar occupation of Germany, but their bloody stay on the Marne was over.

As he was preparing to leave the Marne salient, XXII Corps commander General Sir Alexander Godley found much to praise: "The French have treated us very well, and though the difficulties of fighting in a language other than one's own, and of dealing with troops whose methods of fighting are so entirely different to our own, are great, still we have got on pretty well and I must say that they have helped us in every way." Godley also praised the Allied medical services, which reduced the number of British soldiers requiring hospitalization by half. He found the morale of Allied soldiers "excellent" and the men he saw "still full of fight" despite their fatigue. Losses in XXII Corps had been heavy, but "the general atmosphere since the counter-stroke is much more lively and one meets smiling faces everywhere."[24]

If he could report seeing smiling faces everywhere, then it seems unlikely that Godley passed through the British forces on the other end of the salient. The British 15th Division was one of the few Tenth Army units that attacked on July 28. The division had come into the line to replace the American 1st Division, and received orders to seize the Château de Buzancy and the high ground east of it. Eliminating the château would make possible the seizure of the northern part of the Soissons to Château-Thierry highway and possibly lead to a breakthrough into the relatively flat and featureless Buzancy plain, where the Allies could use their advantages in armor and mechanization. The task was a daunting one; the château had a high wall surrounding it and a wide park in front that offered the Germans excellent observation and clear fields of fire.

Given the challenges, the attack on Buzancy on July 28 received meticulous attention to detail from staff officers. Knowing from past experiences that the Germans sat down to lunch at 12:30 PM, they planned to attack then in hopes of catching the Germans off guard. The artillery barrage appeared without warning and was "of exceptional fury,"[25] with copious use of smoke to blind the German observers in the château. British forces then advanced into the town of Buzancy, moving from building to building. Having advanced quickly enough through the smoke screen, the British could use flamethrowers against any structure in which the Germans had hidden machine guns. British troops even got inside the château itself for a few hours. The 15th Division's initial advance had netted 200 German prisoners in just three hours.[26]

The surprise occasioned by attacking at midday also gave the Allies the added bonus of relatively unfettered (if temporary) command of the air. Good flying weather allowed the Allies to take maximum advantage of the opportunity. French airplanes flew over the Buzancy sector, taking careful note of German strongholds. Knowing that German fighters were likely to arrive in the sector as soon as word of the attack had reached their bases, the French observers did not stay around long. It also seems that they had run out of paper, as hurriedly scrambled messages from French pilots arrived at 15th Division headquarters on the back of photographs of "very charming" young ladies.[27] So far, so good, for the men of the 15th Division.

These methods proved sufficient to take Buzancy, but not sufficient to hold it. The Germans organized a counterattack that the British broke up with a deft defensive barrage. A second German attack, however, managed to put strong forces into the town. With German and British troops intermixed inside the town, British gunners were understandably reluctant to fire another defensive barrage, which might kill many of their countrymen. The Germans used the respite from British artillery to retake the château, giving them excellent observation over the town now that the smoke had cleared. By 4:35 PM, British officers at division headquarters began to see SOS flares coming from British soldiers in the southeastern corner of the town, but they could provide little help. Inside the town, the men of the 15th Division were out of ammunition and reduced to fighting with the German weapons they had seized during the hours they had held the château.

German after action reports on the fight for Buzancy indicate that the crisis had, from their perspective, passed as early as 2:45 PM. By then German battalions had recovered from the initial shock, regained contact with one another, and organized a counterattack on the town from three directions. The Germans were quick to praise the "brave defenders" of the town, especially the Scots, but by nightfall the Germans had retaken most of Buzancy. The British still commanded the roads into the town, but the inability of French units on the flanks to make significant advances forced the 15th to fall back. Yet again success had proved ephemeral. Despite the early success, the battle had once more failed to live up to expectations. The men of the 15th, one of the most experienced divisions in the British Army, called the attack on Buzancy its "most grueling" day of the entire war.[28] After the war, locals built a memorial at Buzancy that reads: "Ici fleurira toujours le glorieux chardon d'Ecosse parmi les roses de France" (Here a glorious Scottish heather will forever bloom among the roses of France).

The men of the 15th pulled back into nearby woods for safety, thereby giving up most of their gains from the day's hard fighting. The division then traded places with a French unit that went forward to take its place in the line opposite Buzancy. Given the heavy fighting there, the French were none too pleased to go into the sector; the French liaison officer to the men of the 1/8 Argyll Battalion welcomed them by pointing to key parts of the sector and giving them a curt "Liaison à gauche ici. Liaison à droite là. Mitrailleuses ici et ici. Les Boches là. Je vais" (Liaison on the left here. Liaison on the right there. Machine guns here and here. Germans there. I am leaving). The Argylls took shelter from German artillery and machine guns in a railway tunnel and amid champagne caves, but soon gave up these positions when the Germans began firing phosgene gas (heavier than air and thus capable of turning the shelters into death traps) at their positions.[29]

In the center of the salient, the Americans made their biggest effort yet. American intelligence had reported that the Germans hoped to hold the Tardenois line until August 1, by which time the new positions on the Aisne and Vesle would be ready. The Americans hoped to force their enemy's hand with a rush through the line between Fère-en-Tardenois and Sergy. For the first time in the war, most of the staff work to support the American 3rd, 28th, and 42nd divisions was American, and there were no French units interspersed among American ones. The attack the American staff planned for July 28 would be all American, and thus it had a particular sense of urgency about it.

The geography of the region once again provided a tremendous advantage to the defenders. The Ourcq river itself was small by American standards, and was fordable almost everywhere in the American sector. The problems were the heights on the north bank, which rose to as high as 200 meters, and the thick woods that provided excellent cover for German machine guns and snipers. "In every respect," noted one veteran, "the area was ideal for defensive purposes." Still, the Americans were determined to attack and break the German line of resistance.[30]

Unwilling to risk a complex night crossing, the Americans crossed the Ourcq during daylight, under full German observation. Thus the

Americans sacrificed any chance at surprise. The decision proved to be costly, yet another manifestation of American inexperience. Heavy German machine gun and artillery fire began as soon as the Americans put men in the river itself. American soldiers faced machine guns so well concealed that there "was no sign of the enemy in sight" despite the heavy fire they were facing. Elements of the 42nd Division managed to take the village of Sergy despite the heavy German resistance among what one veteran called the "slaughter pens" of the region.[31]

Once again, even minimal gains soon evaporated. The Germans organized a powerful counterattack on Sergy spearheaded by the elite 4th Prussian Guards Regiment. American units were dangerously exposed to a counterattack, and were "almost everywhere in inferior positions, dominated by German fields of fire."[32] The Prussians forced the Americans out of Sergy in another stage of the seesaw battle for the town, which changed hands eleven times in three days. American soldiers fought to regain the town, but battalions were "melting away" in the face of German machine gun fire. The Americans had to accept that their tactics were not working. As one veteran recalled, "rushing through the open up to the concealed German machine guns in the hope of frightening the gunners into surrender, or of catching them off guard, was sheer suicide. That was now certain."[33] American units began using leapfrog tactics learned from the French, wherein one unit covered the advance of another, then switched roles, and attacked under the cover of the unit that had just advanced.

The new American methods were not dashing, but they worked. They were also quite different from the "open warfare" ideals Pershing had tried to instill in his men during their training. Men learned to crawl instead of run, and officers learned to advance their units more slowly and deliberately. They also learned to remove the shiny metal insignia from their lapels to attract less attention from snipers. Still, the American advance stalled, leading division headquarters to send reinforcements for another attack on Sergy on July 29. Battalions of the 42nd got into the town, but found they could not hold it due to the power of German artillery, which turned the town into "an inferno of tossing masonry and flying steel."[34] Morale also became a problem, with some men questioning the wisdom of carrying on the attacks. One battalion commander even lodged a formal written complaint against orders to resume the attack on Sergy on July 30.

The American high command, however, was not yet ready to give up on Sergy. The American I Corps commander, Major General Hunter Liggett, dispatched still more men to the front of the 42nd and replaced one brigade commander who had "virtually collapsed under the strain of the fighting."[35] To replace the dismissed commander, Liggett sent newly promoted Brigadier General Douglas MacArthur. On July 30, MacArthur took over his new job and arrived at the command post of the 165th Regiment just in time to learn that the most famous member of 42nd, poet Joyce Kilmer, had just been killed near Seringes. The men of the 42nd were tired, low on food and water, and in need of being replaced. Still, MacArthur ordered new attacks. One of his first messages as commander of the 84th Brigade read:

> I am advancing my whole line with the utmost speed. If he [the enemy] has not already a prepared position in the Forêt de Nesles [northwest of Sergy], I intend to throw him into the Vesle. I am using small patrols acting with great speed and continually flanking him so that he can not form a line of resistance. I am handling the columns myself and my losses are extraordinarily light.[36]

MacArthur's bombast, however, could not overcome the challenges in front of the 42nd. Sergy traded hands several times on July 30, and it became increasingly obvious to American commanders that the Germans were using the combat at Sergy to cover a prepared retreat to the Aisne and Vesle. The Americans wanted to bring the fresh 32nd Division into the line in order to give the 3rd and 28th Divisions some rest, and also needed to prepare for the 4th Division to relieve the 42nd. Accordingly, orders for July 31 were far less aggressive in nature. On August 3, the 42nd finally left the line, having taken 8,000 casualties since July 14.

The bloody battles around Buzancy and Sergy underscored the central problem of breaking strong German defensive lines. The constant combat on the Marne had worn down Allied units, and the inability to overcome German air power had proved to be particularly problematic. German positions on the Aisne and the Vesle were their most obstinate yet; breaking them would require an effort beyond the capabilities of Allied units unless they received reinforcements and rest. These realizations led to a brief pause while Allied commanders made the decisions that would determine the battle's final outcome.

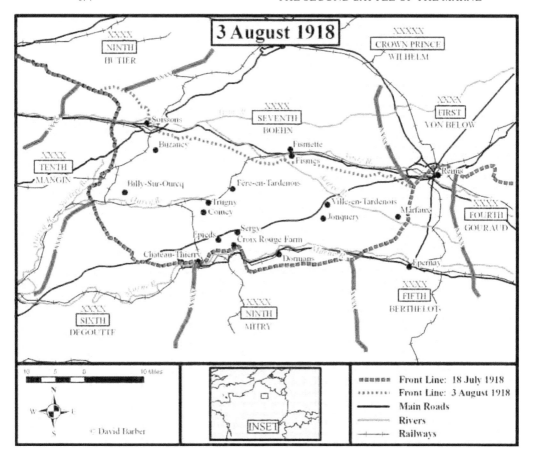

The Final Phase of the Second Battle of the Marne

As July came to an end, the Allies took a short pause to rest and to reassess their position. The Marne pocket remained formidable, measuring 10 miles deep by 23 miles long, with strong German positions resisting Allied advances on both the eastern and western edges. The machine gun nests that formed the backbone of German defenses remained difficult to locate and even more difficult to destroy. Perhaps most disturbingly, Allied failure to break enemy lines allowed the Germans to begin an orderly withdrawal to even stronger positions on the Vesle and the Aisne. German airplanes became a problem once again, with men especially complaining of Allied inability to stop German pilots from marking their positions with flares in order to aid German heavy artillery batteries.

Allied units were tired and needed at least two days to bring in rein-forcements. Pétain informed Foch on July 31 that he had no fresh units available to send to the Tenth Army. All units reported high casualties and low levels of critical supplies. Pétain might therefore be forgiven for some of his pessimism about the prospects for further offensive action in the Marne, especially after he learned that the British offensive at Amiens had been set for August 8. With that offensive would inevitably come a major shift in Allied strategic direction, making the Marne a clearly secondary theater.

Most Allied units rested on July 30 and 31, taking the time to refit and reestablish contact with neighboring units. Allied units received orders on August 1 to prepare to resume the offensive the next day. Fay-olle told the armies under his command to proceed, but to "proportion efforts to means." Tenth Army commander General Charles Mangin was more aggressive in passing his orders down the chain of command, telling the divisions under him to reach the Vesle and the Aisne by nightfall on August 2.

For their part, the Germans used the pause of July 30 and 31 to complete yet another staged withdrawal. Their stubborn defense on the Ourcq bought enough time to conduct an orderly retreat to new positions. A withdrawal this massive could not be kept secret; signs of a German retreat to the Aisne were everywhere. Allied aerial recon-naissance spotted enormous fires near German supply centers such as Fismes and Soissons, a sure sign that the Germans were destroying equipment that they could not take with them north of the Aisne. Allied patrols also reported the disappearance of German rearguards north of the Ourcq.[37]

On August 1, Allied units resumed their advances, only to find that most German units opposite them had melted away. Allied command-ers reacted cautiously, knowing how well the Germans had used the terrain of this part of France over the past few weeks. Advance patrols confirmed that there were few Germans in the woods and ravines im-mediately north of the Ourcq, although the Germans continued to target roads and concentration points with both high explosives and gas shells.

Fayolle reacted with optimism, but remained cautious. He noted in his diary on August 2, the fourth anniversary of Germany's invasion of Luxembourg and Belgium, "So now we have had four years of war come full circle. The year that now begins [the fifth of the war] must surely be the last."[38] That night he issued orders for an attack "without respite, but with order." The next day he told Mangin to attack with the Tenth Army in the direction of the Vesle, but to moderate his goals and to "remove from the battlefield those units that have suffered the most." He urged Mangin to reconstitute his reserves and make sure to advance methodically. Fayolle also told his army commanders that no attacks were to be made without sufficient artillery support. "This method," he wrote, "is still the surest way to advance quickly and deeply."[39]

Allied units thus moved forward deliberately and in unison, reaching the Aisne and Vesle Rivers on August 2 and August 3. They had to move slowly, because of both the ever-present danger of German rearguards and the damage the Germans had caused to the terrain as they retreated north. One soldier described Fère-en-Tardenois as his unit moved through it on August 3 thus:

> [We] could go no farther as the place was in complete ruins from the shell fire and we could not get through. Buildings had fallen right across the streets, all of them were still burning, explosions were still going on where the Germans had mined the place before they left, and we were looking anytime to have the street on which we were pulling the heavy pieces [off the roads] to go up into the air.

Once through the town, the men found that the Germans had felled trees across the roads leading north, in an effort to slow Allied pursuit. The stench of death in the region was so bad that men walked with one hand holding a handkerchief over their noses and mouths. Most men, though hungry, found the stench too overpowering to even think about eating.[40]

As part of the general retreat, the Germans had finally withdrawn from Soissons, although their artillery still made Allied occupation of the town's eastern half precarious. The capture of the town's western end meant that the Allies now had full control of both the Soissons to Château-Thierry and the Soissons to Fère-en-Tardenois highways. After two weeks of fighting, however, the roads and railways were in terrible shape, and they would need several weeks of intensive attention from engineers to make them passable. As one American remarked on seeing the state of the roads and railways, "Inwardly, we swelled with pride at our [artillery's] accuracy, but outwardly we swore at it for causing us so much trouble now." If engineers could quickly rebuild the roads they could give the Allies a critical logistical advantage that the Germans would not be able to match, but in the immediate future supply would continue to be a serious limiting factor to any offensive actions. One American field artillery regiment subsisted for two days on rations taken from dead comrades until food reached them on August 3. Their horses were so tired and weak from hunger that they lacked the strength to move guns into position.[41]

Once again, the rivers themselves presented less resistance than the heights around them. The Vesle especially struck most Americans as little more than a brook, being no more than 15 yards wide in most places. As on the Marne and Ourcq, however, the woods and ravines on the far side concealed powerful defensive positions laced with enemy machine guns. The Americans soon found more to fear in the Vesle than they had expected, as the Germans had dammed parts of it in order to create swift currents and even a few eddies. They had also placed barbed wire on both of the Vesle's marshy banks, making any rapid movement impossible.[42]

Even the weather added to Allied misery. Torrential downpours increased the speed of the current in the Vesle and complicated Allied attempts to move heavy equipment over muddy roads. In part because of the rain and mud, the supply situation had become especially critical. At night the Germans used star flares to illuminate Allied lines so they could keep up a steady and accurate artillery bombardment at all hours of the day and night. In between periods of heavy rain, the Germans remained in command of the air, meaning that little reconnaissance of the depth of German positions was possible. The Vesle and the Aisne promised more of the same bloody, hard fighting, but the Allies were determined to keep the battle going, both to continue the pressure and to keep the Germans busy in order to maintain surprise for the planned offensive near Amiens.

Attacks by elements of the American 4th Division on August 4 and 5 soon revealed the strength of German positions. Americans who crossed the Vesle came under "tornado like" fire "microscopic in accuracy" almost immediately from the direction of the village of Bazoches and the appropriately named Château du Diable. Those few Americans (approximately 1,000) who made it across the river soon found themselves in a dangerously exposed and untenable position. Around 5:00 PM on August 5, the Americans retreated to the south bank of the Vesle, having accomplished little other than proving that the Germans were in force north of the river.

Determined to cross the river despite heavy German opposition, the Americans and French worked together on a new plan. French gunners promised a four-hour barrage designed to "wipe the towns of Bazoches and Haute Maison . . . off the map," with the hope of eliminating German ability to use the towns as small fortifications. The gunners would then fire a barrage aimed at the north shore, mixing high explosive with smoke to cover a river crossing to be made with hastily assembled pontoon bridges. The bridges would permit Allied soldiers to cross with heavy equipment such as machine guns in order to support their operations on the north side of the Vesle.

The operation began as designed on the afternoon of August 6. A French barrage hit the German lines, then elements of the French 62nd Division and American 4th Division crossed the river as scheduled. They spent a very uncomfortable night on the north bank, hoping that their efforts would lead in the morning to the creation of an Allied bridgehead across the Vesle. The next day, however, the Germans began an aggressive counterattack, with artillery targeting the pontoon bridges and the ubiquitous German airplanes correcting the accuracy of the German gunners. The Germans fired on Allied soldiers with heavy doses of gas, causing many unexpected casualties. Allied soldiers found that many of their gas masks failed to function properly because they had gotten wet during the crossing. To make matters even worse, with the pontoon bridges destroyed, wounded men could not be evacuated and the Americans on the other side of the river could not be supplied. In all, the Germans fired seven thousand shells in two days, destroying the Allied attack on Bazoches.[43]

German air attacks continued, with airplanes flying far enough behind Allied lines to report the location of Allied heavy artillery batteries to German gunners. The Allies nevertheless tried again, crossing the Vesle on August 8, and approaching Bazoches from three sides. On August 9, Allied soldiers captured the town, only to find, yet again, that they could not hold it. The German counterattack against Bazoches featured heavy doses of airpower, against which the Allies had no answer. "Nothing is so demoralizing to men on the ground," noted one veteran, "as an attack from the air." Americans in Bazoches were helpless against German bombers. "When that plane hovers overhead [the soldier] is as helpless as the field mouse in the shadow of the hawk's wings. Of this helplessness is born a terror which makes him furious."[44] Unable to stop a German counterattack so forcefully supported, the

Americans had to give up Bazoches, which remained in German hands until September 3.

There were no easy answers to the dilemma of Allied air inferiority. Beginning on August 8, the Americans started to receive better airplanes, but the planes alone would not make much difference. As untested technologies, they presented challenges to both the pilots who had to fly them and the mechanics who had to repair them. The Germans, moreover, had destroyed the airbases they had evacuated, rendering them unusable to Allied pilots until they could be repaired. The closest Allied airbases were so far away that Allied pilots had to stop at Coincy (a former German airbase whose runways were rudimentarily repaired) to refuel just to have two hours of flying time over the front line.[45]

The inability of the Allies to force their way through the Vesle and the Aisne river lines demonstrated to many Allied commanders that the battle had run its course. American commanders concluded that to force the Germans out of their solid defenses "would take a major offensive operation following carefully matured plans and the massing of great artillery concentration."[46] These resources were not available, having been moved north to support the Amiens offensive or east to help the Americans prepare for their St. Mihiel offensive. Influenza also became a greater concern among Allied units in the sector, sending many men into hospitals.[47] The Second Battle of the Marne had accomplished all it could. The focus of operations now moved to other sectors of the western front.

On August 8, the British Fourth Army launched its massive attack near Amiens. The Germans had been once again caught badly unawares, just as they had been on July 18. Like the Second Battle of the Marne, Amiens was a fully international battle. The British Fourth Army had overall control of the battle, but the plan relied heavily on the soldiers of the French First Army and the American 33rd Division, as well as the Australians and Canadians who became so critical to the final battles of the war. The German defeat at Amiens had been grave enough to lead Ludendorff to call it "the black day" of the German army. The Germans had indeed suffered a decisive defeat; their losses included six miles of territory and 28,000 men on the first day alone. German forces began to retreat to the prepared defensive line known as the Hindenburg Line, and German diplomats began looking for neutral third parties that might help them attain a compromise peace.

The German retreat from Amiens did not stop the fighting on the banks of the Aisne and Vesle. One French unit history reports that German resistance on the Aisne and the Vesle in fact grew stronger on August 9, probably as part of an attempt to cover the German retreat from Amiens.[48] The departure of so many American units from the region led to fears that the Germans might resume their own attacks, although these fears were certainly exaggerated. Still, a French Zouaves unit received orders to prepare defenses along the Aisne because of fears that heightened German activity in the region portended an enemy counterattack in force.[49]

On August 10, the Germans did in fact cross the Vesle, although it was not part of a larger strategic offensive. The Americans had made another attempt to capture the Château du Diable and the town of Fismette. Once again they had been unsuccessful, and left themselves exposed to a vigorous German counterattack, again supported by large numbers of airplanes, which were still "much in evidence" in the region.[50] The Germans pursued the Americans across the Vesle, but seem to have quickly realized the foolishness of their actions, and they retreated back to the north bank.

To provide fresh troops and new vigor to the region, the Americans brought in a new division, the 77th, from New York. Seeing their first battlefield, the New Yorkers concluded that "this promised to be no gentleman's war," only "strain and drudgery."[51] The soldiers of the 77th had missed the worst of the fighting, but they still had to deal with same learning curve as their predecessors. Their attacks on Bazoches suffered from the same problems of communication and artillery support as had attacks by previous American divisions in the region.

The Americans also brought in newer and more powerful artillery batteries in an attempt to support their inexperienced replacements to the maximum extent possible. The French Tenth Army reinforced as well, and attacked northeast of Soissons on August 19. That attack yielded only minimal gains, as did repeated American attempts on the Château du Diable. The only success the Allies had in late August was the temporary capture of Fismette after bitter house-to-house fighting on August 22, but the Germans retook it on August 27. The battle had reached a standstill. Elsewhere on the western front, the Germans had retreated behind the Hindenburg Line, and the American operation at St. Mihiel, just two weeks away, was still in its planning stages. The Second Battle of the Marne was beginning to lose its *raison d'être*.

By late August, the German position on the Aisne and Vesle had become untenable. British capture of the critical German supply center of Albert placed all German units west of the Hindenburg Line in great jeopardy. On September 3, Allied soldiers on the Aisne and Vesle awoke to a strange silence; German artillery had stopped firing. Cautious patrols soon confirmed that the Germans had indeed abandoned the Vesle and Aisne river positions for a new line of resistance nearer the Hindenburg Line. A relative calm descended over the Aisne-Marne region, and within just over two months the war would be over. The Allied counterstroke on the Marne had made possible something few on the Allied side had even dared to dream in early July: the end of the war in 1918.

CONCLUSION: HONORING FOCH

MEN ON BOTH sides of the lines immediately knew how important the Second Battle of the Marne had been. On August 6, Foch received a handwritten letter from Prime Minister Georges Clemenceau addressed to "my dear general and dear friend." Clemenceau, an anti-clerical politician who distrusted generals, and Foch, a devoutly Catholic general who loathed politicians, had a long and tortured relationship. The two had first met in 1907, shortly after Foch had been told that he would not become commander of the prestigious *École Supérieur de Guerre* (ESG) in Paris because of rumors that he had awarded higher grades to Catholic students during his years as a professor there. On the advice of a friend, Foch went personally to talk to Clemenceau, then serving his first term as French prime minister. During the meeting, Clemenceau repeated the allegations, adding a new one from a personnel file that charged that Foch had anti-republican political tendencies. Foch defended himself, but seemingly to no avail. After the meeting, Foch sent Clemenceau copies of books he had written, based on the lectures he had given when he was a professor at the ESG. The books advocated aggressive offensive action and preached the moral superiority of French soldiers to Germans. Clemenceau was impressed enough with the books to recall Foch to his office and give him the job of commandant of the ESG.

Since that meeting Foch and Clemenceau had both come a long way. They had both learned how to fight a modern, industrial, total war whose meanings and solutions defied easy pontifications such as the ones in Foch's books. Together these two very different men had formed the civilian-military team that had seen France to its recent triumphs. Clemenceau had supported Foch's appointment to command of the Allied armies in March when things looked bleak, telling a group "at least [with Foch in charge] we'll die with a rifle in our hands."[1] Since then, the war had seen ups and downs, but Clemenceau and Foch had done much more than just go down fighting; they had changed the momentum of the war and placed victory within France's grasp. The relationship between the two men was not always friendly, and after the war it degraded to intense hostility and bitter diatribe. But as long as the war went on, each man knew that he needed the other.

Clemenceau's letter informed Foch that he was to be awarded the rank of marshal of France, the highest military honor France could give. The French Third Republic had actually banned the rank, out of fear of generals acquiring too much power and prestige, but the war's need for heroes had forced a reconsideration. The government had revived the rank in 1916 as a way to cushion the blow of forcing General Joseph Joffre to give up his command of the French army. Thus the French government could sell Joffre's forced retirement to the French people and the Allies as a promotion and a richly deserved honor for the man who had saved France in 1914. The government could then send Joffre on a triumphant speaking tour of the United States as a decorated hero rather than a humiliated failure.

Unlike Joffre's promotion, given to cover a defeat, Foch's was awarded for his tremendous victory on the Marne. Clemenceau's letter spelled out the connection directly, if somewhat verbosely:

> At the hour when the enemy, by virtue of a powerful offensive on a front of 100 kilometers, counted on forcing a decision and imposing on us a German peace that would mean the servitude of the world, General Foch and his soldiers vanquished him.
>
> Paris freed, Soissons and Château-Thierry reconquered after fierce strug-gle, more than 200 villages delivered from the enemy, 35,000 enemy prisoners and 700 guns captured . . . , the glorious armies of the Allies, buoyed by a single élan, victorious from the banks of the Marne to the banks of the Aisne, such are the results of a maneuver so well conceived by the high command and so superbly executed by the incomparable commanders.

The honor would have been inconceivable a month earlier, when German forces were still advancing and doubts about Foch's abilities pervaded French government circles. Now, with the Second Battle of the Marne won, Foch could receive France's highest military honor. Unlike Joffre's, Foch's honor was not only for past services, but for, in Clemenceau's words, "the authority of the great man of war called to conduct the Entente armies to the final victory" that almost everyone on both sides now expected.[2]

The final tally, as recorded in the French official history of the war, gives a sense of the toll the Second Battle of the Marne took on the Germans. The Allies captured 609 German officers and 26,413 enlisted men. Of that number, British forces were responsible for capturing 1,600 soldiers and the Americans responsible for capturing 8,000. These figures mean that French soldiers must have captured approximately 17,000 Germans, an indication of the central role played by French soldiers in this battle. The Allies also captured 612 enemy artillery pieces, 221 *Minenwerfer*, and 3,330 machine guns. They also recaptured 181 Allied artillery pieces and 393 Allied machine guns taken by the Germans in the course of their 1918 offensives.

The battle left the Germans in a precarious, and ultimately indefensible, state. French intelligence estimated that seventy-five separate German divisions fought on the Marne against fifty-nine Allied divisions (forty-five French, eight American, four British, and two Italian), although it should be noted that American divisions were twice the size of European divisions and that the German army probably had the smallest divisions on the western front in July 1918. As a result of this wearing out of the German army, the number of divisions in the German reserve fell during the course of the battle from sixty-two to forty-two. The vast majority of those divisions were classified as unfit, meaning that they could, at best, be depended upon for defensive operations only. To complete the picture, French intelligence reported that the Germans had just 243,000 men of uneven quality immediately available as replacements and potentially another 300,000 men from the conscription class of 1920. By contrast, the Americans were landing more than 300,000 men in France per month.[3]

The morale consequences of the Second Battle of the Marne might have been even more damaging to the Germans than the material ones. German soldier Rudolf Binding noted from his position along the Aisne in August that "carelessness and callousness are spreading like plagues" among the men, many of whom spoke openly of giving Alsace and Lorraine back to France if it might mean an end to the war. But among officers he found "endless self-delusion" and an inability to recognize how fundamentally the Second Battle of the Marne had changed Germany's situation. On August 12, Binding prophetically wrote in his diary that "I dreamed I saw the Kaiser entering what seemed to be the gateway of a camp, bareheaded and on foot, forced by his people to give himself up to their mercy."[4] With three months of Binding's dream, the kaiser had indeed abdicated and fled into exile in Holland, where, despite international calls to put him on trial, he never did have to answer for his culpability in the war.

Ludendorff had been no less certain than Clemenceau that the Second Battle of the Marne had been the critical turning point of the war. "This was the first great setback for Germany," he later wrote. "There now developed the very situation which I had endeavored to prevent. The initiative passed to the enemy. Germany's position was extremely serious. It was no longer possible to win the war in a military sense."[5] Because Germany knew no other way to use military power in 1918 except for its own sake, Ludendorff's postmortem essentially meant that he knew the war was over when the Allied counterstroke of July 18 succeeded.

Conclusion: *De Quoi S'Agit-Il?*

Ferdinand Foch, the man who more than any other sits at the center of the Second Battle of the Marne, often pointedly asked of officers briefing him, "De quoi s'agit-il?" Roughly translated, the phrase means "What is it really about?" In the spirit of Marshal Foch, I will end this book by turning that same question upon myself. What is this book really about? What has it contributed to our understanding beyond merely bringing to life a battle that appears in virtually all general histories of the war, but lacks a scholarly history of its own? *De quoi s'agit-il?*

My first set of analytic conclusions begins with Foch himself. The Second Battle of the Marne was a vindication of his command style, symbolized by his elevation to the rank of marshal of France. Foch understood from the moment he became generalissimo in March that the Allied war effort had to be directed as a single entity. The Americans, the British, and not least the French would all have their roles to play, with

Foch himself acting as the conductor of the symphony. Most of the significant decisions of this battle were his, including convincing Douglas Haig to place four British divisions into the theater, naming Mangin the head of the Tenth Army, and on several important occasions overruling Pétain's almost preternatural caution and pessimism.

I do not mean to make Foch out to be a genius, although his decisions (and, perhaps more importantly, his decision-making process) stand up better than those of his peers. Above all, he had a clear sense of what he expected military force to accomplish and how far he could reasonably push the men under his command. He proved adept at deciphering contradictory evidence and developing a keen sense of what the Germans opposite him were trying to accomplish. He proved even more adept at overseeing a method to stop them from accomplishing their goals, then turning a defensive battle into an offensive battle that changed the entire tenor of the war and made victory in 1918 possible.

By contrast, German commanders never did understand the ultimate purpose of military force, a supreme irony given that their fellow countryman was Carl von Clausewitz. My second fundamental set of arguments, therefore, reinforces the conclusions drawn by Isabel Hull in her brilliant book *Absolute Destruction*.[6] By 1918, the German high command had reached the point that it could accept no victory short of total victory in the west, yet at the same time it had no clear definition of what total victory might mean. Unwilling to compromise and unchecked by any meaningful civilian authorities, the German high command launched its offensive on the Marne with no real sense of what it might accomplish.

Worse still, the Germans should have known that the arrival of hundreds of thousands of Americans made a total victory impossible. Yet they fought on toward the absolute destruction that Professor Hull so eloquently analyzes. The grand strategy of Ludendorff and his subordinates thus became nothing more than a means for killing American, British, French, and German soldiers to no real purpose. A German victory on the Marne would simply have led to a German offensive in Flanders, then another German offensive after that, until at last the Germans had worn themselves out as fully as they had worn out their enemies.

The contrast with the Allies could not have been more stark. A mere three months after the German attack on the Marne, Foch had overseen Herculean efforts by the Allied armies to drive the Germans out of France and Belgium. In October, at the request of the French government, Foch drew up the conditions he believed were necessary before the Allies could agree to any armistice the Germans might seek. He demanded German evacuation of all French and Belgian territory the Germans had occupied since 1870 (thus including Alsace and Lorraine), the German surrender of thousands of weapons and railway cars, and the creation of three bridgeheads across the Rhine River. He believed that these conditions could stop the Germans from using an armistice to gather strength and continue to fight in 1919.

Some Allied officers (most notably Pershing) argued for a full-scale invasion of Germany in 1919, but Foch disagreed, telling President Woodrow Wilson's representative in France, Edward House, that "I am not waging war for the sake of waging war. If I obtain through the armistice the conditions that we wish to impose on Germany, I am satisfied. Once this object is attained, nobody has the right to shed one more drop of blood."[7] Foch, unlike Ludendorff, understood that the point of the war was to end it on favorable political terms, not to perpetuate it, even long after it had lost any larger meaning.

Third, this book supports the recent conclusions of scholars who have begun to reexamine the role of the French army in 1918. Robert Bruce, Robert Doughty, Michel Goya, and others have all tackled this problem from different angles, and thus this book does not claim to be breaking entirely new ground on this score.[8] Despite the work of these and other scholars, the image of a France bled to death at Verdun and broken in spirit on the Chemin des Dames remains forceful. It must be discarded. The men of the French army in 1918 were certainly tired, at the limits of their efforts, and deeply desirous of peace. But in these respects the French army was little different from any other army except perhaps the American. What is significant, however, and deserving of much more historical research, is the ability of the French army (and France more generally) to recover, adapt, and make major contributions to Allied victory.

The image of a worn-out, tired French army does not appear in any accounts from the Second Battle of the Marne. The impressions of the French army as recorded by the British and American soldiers who fought alongside them were almost universally full of praise and admiration.[9] After World War I the reputation of the French military remained uniformly high. Winston Churchill described the inter-war French army as "incomparably the strongest military force in Europe," and many German generals agreed until June 1940.[10] Lord Halifax also agreed, noting in his diary on 25 May 1940 that the French army was "the one firm rock on which everybody had been willing to build."[11] That the French military of 1940 was not as strong as most believed it to be, and that the society it was serving suffered from deep-seated and fundamental crises, does not detract from the larger point: Europeans from 1918 to 1940 did not think of Verdun or the Chemin des Dames when they saw the French army. Instead they saw in their mind's eye a triumphal force that had surely lost heavily from 1914 to 1918, but had still emerged as a (perhaps *the*) senior partner in the Allied victory. Our notion of the Hundred Days to Victory should begin with the joint triumph at the Second Marne, not the British triumph at Amiens.

Simplistic and unsophisticated images of the French army as "all wine and no spine" are thus products of 1940, not 1918. France's ignominious collapse and descent into the home-grown fascism of Pétain and Pierre Laval's National Revolution revealed the vaunted French army to be a paper tiger, protecting a system that lacked the will or the ability to fight another world war. Although it would take much more research to confirm, one could safely advance the argument that the negative images (or simple absence) of the French army in histories of 1918, which have become so commonplace in Anglo-American renderings of the war today, are an anachronistic and backward misreading of later events.

Nor of course did victory in 1945 erase the horrible stigma of 1940. Instead France had to face the humiliation of Dien Bien Phu, the ineffectiveness of Suez, and, finally and most importantly, the even more divisive war in Algeria. Thus it should come as no surprise that the "generation of '68" turned against the military and came to see France's martial past as a lie. Anglo-American historians and popular writers have also built a veritable cottage industry undermining French efforts in the world wars, in some cases to highlight by contrast the contributions of their own armies.

The Second Battle of the Marne proves without a doubt the abiding strength of the French army in 1918. The plans were French, the army and corps commanders (with one exception) were French, and most of the weaponry was French. It should go without saying that this argument does not in any way degrade or belittle the accomplishments of the American and British soldiers on the Marne. They were themselves almost universal in their praise of French determination, skill, and efforts at inter-Allied cooperation. It would thus be unfair and inaccurate to claim that the Second Battle of the Marne was a French battle, but it would be equally unfair and inaccurate to treat the battle (indeed all of 1918) without the French as some scholars and amateurs have done.

The role of the Americans in the war's final year has been the subject of much debate. But to date there has been only one scholarly book on the American role at the Second Battle of the Marne, Douglas V. Johnson and Rolfe L. Hillman's *Soissons, 1918*.[12] The critical role of this battle in shaping the doctrine and methods of the American Expeditionary Forces (AEF) has thus gone largely unnoticed, although Mark Grotelueschen's *The AEF Way of War* should do much to correct the oversimplifications and generalizations that surround the AEF.[13] Most histories of the AEF, moreover, treat St. Mihiel as the first large-scale American offensive of the war. To the extent that such authors are concerned with an American command structure and American leadership at all levels, they are correct, but the sheer number of American divisions at the Second Battle of the Marne makes it a critical event in American military history, and it must be recognized as such. As Grotelueschen clearly shows, the lessons of the Second Marne were critical to forming the American army that fought at St. Mihiel, the Meuse-Argonne, and elsewhere.

Finally, this book has shown the diversity and complexity of the First World War. The trench experience has rightly claimed the lion's share of study of the western front, but scholars and students alike are well served to remember that the war was more than trenches. The Second Battle of the Marne proved that fluid, open warfare also existed. In large part, this relative fluidity was a function of the decisions of the senior leaders of the German army not to dig in on the Marne. But the return of limited movement to the battlefield also owed much to new technologies, new learning curves, and new methods of fighting. This study does not attempt to make systematic comparisons between July 1918 and May 1940, but perhaps there are more connections than historians have heretofore recognized. In many ways, the Second Battle of the Marne resembles the opening campaigns of World War II much more than the opening campaigns of World War I. Perhaps the armies of the inter-war years took more positive lessons out of the war and its final years than scholars allow. In any event, scholars must recognize that the war by mid-1918 was far different from the war of 1916, 1917, or even March 1918.

There is a value in bringing the Second Battle of the Marne out of the regrettable obscurity to which it has somehow been condemned. There are other major campaigns for which we still lack good histories, including the French Battles of the Frontiers, the 1915 Champagne offensive, and the crucial Brusilov Offensive on the eastern front in 1916. Other major battles such as Verdun, the Chemin des Dames, and the First Battle of the Marne are overdue for new treatments. Still, the Second Marne's near anonymity in the literature is especially unfortunate because it marks the point when the fortunes of the war turned for good in favor of the Allies.

I hope that this book has been able to make contributions beyond merely analyzing the events near the *joli fleuve* that Joffre described. Those events are certainly important in and of themselves, but they also can help inform larger questions and debates about the First World War. For all that the war did to shape the modern world and for all of the importance that scholars ascribe to it, the war remains badly understood and curiously understudied, especially in the United States. The research that is underway by scholars on both sides of the Atlantic (as well as in Australia and New Zealand) is excellent, but we need still more work, and we need it to speak to many large, still unresolved issues.

In conclusion, this book is not, I hope, the final word on any of these subjects. Rather, I hope to have advanced arguments in order to contribute in some small way to an increasingly healthy and vibrant debate between scholars of this critically important war. I also hope that in its own limited way it can help to spur more work, because for all that has been written on World War I, there is still much, much more to learn.

NOTES

INTRODUCTION

Epigraph: Gary Sheffield and John Bourne, eds., *Douglas Haig: War Diaries and Letters, 1914–1918* (London: Weidenfeld and Nicolson, 2005), p. 430.

1. Andrew Wiest, *Haig: Evolution of a Commander* (Dulles, Va.: Potomac Books, 2005), p. 19.

2. Oral History of Jesse Marion Hughes, F341.5 .M57x vol. 237, University of Southern Mississippi Oral History Program, McCain Library and Archives. My thanks to my colleague and friend Stephen Sloan for finding this oral history interview for me.

3. The city of Rheims is sometimes spelled Reims, and other place names also have variant spellings. Spellings in quotations remain as in the original, and may vary from the text spellings.

4. Wilhelm, Crown Prince of Germany, *My War Experiences* (New York: Robert McBride, 1923), p. 333.

5. The latter rumor reached American General Hunter Liggett. He took it seriously enough to recall it in his memoir, *AEF: Ten Years Ago in France* (New York: Dodd, Mead, 1928), p. 88.

1. JERUSALEM IN THE MARNE VALLEY

1. Facsimile copy of Michelin Company, Ltd., *Illustrated Michelin Guides to the Battle-fields (1914–1918): The Battlefields of the Marne (1914)* (Easingwold, York: G. H. Smith, 1919), p. 16.

2. *Le Six-Six à la Guerre, 1914–1918* (n.p.: Barrot et Gallon, 1919), entry for July 1918.

3. Richard Foot, "Once a Gunner" (1964), Imperial War Museum, London, 86/57/1, p. 91. Unfortunately for Foot and his comrades they were sent off on an errand and found their foie gras "well raided" before their return.

4. Foot, "Once a Gunner," p. 92. Foot was writing about the Ardre River valley.

5. Joseph J. Gleason, *A Soldier's Story: A Daily Account of World War I, January, 1918 to March, 1919 by Sergeant Joseph J. Gleason*, ed. Mark Gleason (Oakmont, Pa.:

Privately published, 1999), located at the University of Pittsburgh Hillman Library Special Collections section, D640.G625.

6. Christian Bach, *The Fourth Division: Its Services and Achievements in the Great War* (n.p., 1920), p. 97.

7. *History of the Seventy-Seventh Division, August 25th, 1917 to November 11, 1918* (New York: Wynkoop Hallenbeck Crawford, 1919), p. 40.

8. "Attaques de la 48ème Division d'Infanterie les 18 et 19 Juillet 1918, Violane, Villers-Helon" available at http://batmarn2.club.fr/48eme_di.htm. Accessed on June 6, 2006.

9. James Harbord, *Leaves from a War Diary* (New York: Dodd, Mead, 1925), p. 323.

10. Donald Smythe, *Pershing: General of the Armies* (Bloomington: Indiana University Press, 1986), p. 154.

11. General Sir W. P. Braithwaite to Sir James Edmonds, 13 September 1933, Letters to Brig. Gen. Sir James Edmonds, CAB 45/126, National Archives, Kew Gardens.

12. Sir Alexander Godley to Clive Wigram, military secretary to King George V, 27 July 1918, in Godley Papers 1/5–29, Liddell Hart Centre for Military Archives, King's College, London (microfilm), p. 86.

13. John Pershing, *My Experiences in the World War*, vol. 2 (New York: Frederick Stokes, 1931), p. 159.

14. Everard Wyrall, *The West Yorkshire Regiment in the War, 1914–1918*, vol. 2 (London: John Lane, n.d.), p. 297.

15. Jean-Norton Cru, *War Books* (San Diego: San Diego State University Press, 1976), p. 4. The book was originally published as *Temoins* in 1931.

16. Leonard V. Smith, Stéphane Audoin-Rouzeau, and Annette Becker, *France and the Great War* (Cambridge: Cambridge University Press, 2003), p. 45.

17. Georges Blond, *The Marne: The Battle That Saved Paris and Changed the Course of the First World War* (London: Prion, 2002), p. 16. Originally published in 1962.

18. Michel Goya, *La Chair et L'Acier: L'invention de la Guerre Moderne, 1914–1918* (Paris: Tallandier, 2004), p. 160.

19. Cru, *War Books*, pp. 83–84.

20. "Offensive to the Utmost."

21. Douglas Porch, *The March to the Marne: The French Army 1871–1914* (Cambridge: Cambridge University Press, 1981), p. 177, reports that in 1903 the average age of French generals was 61, compared to 54 in Germany. As late as 1910 a report showed that an amazing 30 generals and 20 colonels were physically unfit for campaign. Consequently, the critical autumn maneuvers became more of an elaborate retirement ceremony than a serious field test of men, equipment, and ideas.

22. French Chief of Staff General Joseph Joffre noted in 1913: "The spirits (of corps commanders) were too often paralyzed by routine and often strategic education was left entirely to chance." Goya, *La Chair et L'Acier*, p. 118.

23. Foch's path was not, however, linear. He spent much of the early part of 1917 in a series of relatively meaningless assignments as part of a high command shakeup before assuming command of the French army in May of that year. Michael S. Neiberg, *Foch: Supreme Allied Commander in the Great War* (Dulles, Va.: Potomac Books, 2003).

24. Émil Wanty quoted in Goya, *La Chair et L'Acier*, p. 178.

25. Goya, *La Chair et L'Acier*, pp. 179–182, quotation from p. 182.

26. *Les armées françaises dans la grande guerre*, tome 8, vol. 1 (Paris: Imprimerie nationale, 1936), pp. 21–23.

27. Robert Doughty, *Pyrrhic Victory: French Strategy and Operations in the Great War* (Cambridge, Mass.: Harvard University Press, 2005), p. 514.

28. Ibid., p. 509.

29. Smith, Audoin-Rouzeau, and Becker, *France and the Great War*, pp. 121–122. See also Smith's terrific study, *Between Mutiny and Obedience: The Case of the French Fifth Infantry Division during World War I* (Princeton: Princeton University Press, 1994).

30. Smith, Audoin-Rouzeau, and Becker, *France and the Great War*, p. 126.

31. Ibid., p. 108.

32. Doughty, *Pyrrhic Victory*, p. 510.

33. Robert Lindsay Mackay, "Personal Diary of Lt. Mackay While Serving in France with the 11th Battalion, later the 1st/8th Battalion Argyll and Seaforth Highlanders, September, 1916 to January, 1919," Imperial War Museum, London, P374, pp. 66–67.

34. John Clarke MacDermott, *An Enriching Life* (privately published, 1979), p. 108, located at Liddell Hart Centre for Military Archives, King's College, London. Mac-Dermott also recorded his impression that French soldiers preferred the Scots to the English, even though the language barrier was even more of a problem.

35. F. W. Brewsher, *The History of the 51st (Highland) Division* (Edinburgh: William Blackwood, 1921), p. 332.

36. J. Stewart and John Buchan, *The Fifteenth (Scottish) Division* (Edinburgh: William Blackwood and Sons, 1926), p. 254.

37. To cite just a few examples, Tim Travers's *How the War Was Won* (London: Routledge, 1992), while admittedly focused on the British, has just fourteen citations on the French army in the entire book. Martin Middlebrook's *The Kaiser's Battle* (London: Allen Lane, 1978) has just four references to the French army, but four *pages* of references to British military units. Perhaps the guiltiest party is Rod Paschall, *The Defeat of Imperial Germany* (Chapel Hill: Algonquin Books of Chapel Hill, 1989), which has almost seventy references to American units, but just four references to French units. John Mosier, *The Myth of the Great War* (New York: Harper Perennial, 2002) is another example. Mosier's book has rightly been panned by serious scholars of the war, but the attention it has received is another example of this mindset.

38. Situation of Allied and Enemy Forces 10/VII–6/VIII (Marne II), WO 153/89, National Archives, Kew Gardens.

39. *Historique du 74me Régiment d'Infanterie, 1914–1918* (n.p.: Imprimerie L. Wolf, n. d.), p. 27.

40. Smith, Audoin-Rouzeau, and Becker, *France and the Great War*, p. 57.

41. Ibid., pp. 154–155.

42. Lt. I. R. S. Hamilton, "Mainly About Myself from January, 1917 to April, 1919" (1925), Imperial War Museum, London, P323, pp. 42–43.

43. MacDermott, *An Enriching Life*, pp. 99 and 104.

44. Everitte St. John Chaffee, *The Egotistical Account of an Enjoyable War* (n.p.: Adams, 1951), p. 41.

45. Harry A. Benwell, *History of the Yankee Division* (Boston: Cornhill, 1919), p. 37.

46. Smith, Audoin-Rouzeau, and Becker, *France and the Great War*, p. 57.

47. Gary Sheffield, *Leadership in the Trenches: Officer-Man Relations, Morale, and Discipline in the British Army in the Era of the First World War* (New York: St. Martin's, 2000), chapter 1.

48. Peter Simkins, "The Four Armies, 1914–1918," in *The Oxford Illustrated History of the British Army*, ed. David Chandler and Ian Beckett (Oxford: Oxford University Press, 1994), pp. 241–262, quotation from p. 242.

49. An excellent place to begin research on the New Armies is Peter Simkins, *Kitchener's Army: The Raising of the New Armies, 1914–1916* (Manchester: Manchester University Press, 1988).

50. The famous "Jock on a Rock" monument at Beaumont-Hamel is a memorial to the men of the 51st (Highland) on the Somme.

51. There were also exemptions for the unfit, approved conscientious objectors, and sole supporters of dependents.

52. Foot, "Once a Gunner," p. 89.

53. Sheffield, *Leadership in the Trenches*, pp. 35–38.

54. Frederic Manning, *Her Privates We* (London: Hogarth, 1986), p. 80. Originally published in 1929 under the title *The Middle Parts of Fortune*, the book remains one of the single best novel/memoirs to come out of the war.

55. See John Terraine, *To Win A War: 1918, the Year of Victory* (London: Cassell, 2003), pp. 79–80.

56. Simkins, "The Four Armies," pp. 261–262.

57. Foot, "Once a Gunner," p. 89.

58. John Shakespear, *The Thirty-Fourth Division, 1915–1919* (London: Witherby, 1921), p. 254.

59. Terraine, *To Win a War*, p. 89.

60. Gary Sheffield and John Bourne, eds., *Douglas Haig: War Diaries and Letters, 1914–1918* (London: Weidenfeld and Nicolson, 2005), pp. 430–431. Emphasis in original.

61. Ferdinand Foch, *The Memoirs of Marshal Foch* (Garden City, N.Y.: Doubleday, 1931), p. 359. For the sake of clarity and simplicity, hereafter I will drop the appellations in the British divisions and refer to them only by their numbers.

2. MARCHING TOWARD THE MARNE

1. For more, see Holger Herwig, *The First World War: Germany and Austria-Hungary* (London: Edward Arnold, 1997).

2. See Dennis Showalter, *Tannenberg: Clash of Empires*, rev. ed. (Dulles, Va.: Potomac Books, 2003), for more on both the battle itself and the events leading up to it.

3. Peter Gatrell, *Russia's First World War: A Social and Economic History* (London: Longman, 2005), pp. 22–23.

4. On Falkenhayn, see Roger Chickering, *Imperial Germany and the Great War, 1914–1918*, 2nd ed. (Cambridge: Cambridge University Press, 2005), pp. 52–53.

5. See Michael S. Neiberg, *Fighting the Great War: A Global History* (Cambridge, Mass.: Harvard University Press, 2005), p. 77ff.

6. Haig to Kitchener, 29 September 1915, reproduced in Sheffield and Bourne, *Douglas Haig*, p. 160.

7. Quoted in Goya, *La Chair et L'Acier*, p. 256.

8. Doughty, *Pyrrhic Victory*, p. 140. French General Fernand de Langle de Cary quoted on p. 143. Despite the failure in Champagne, de Langle was promoted to army group commander, an indication that the French blamed neither the men nor the leadership for the bloody failures of 1915. He was among those held responsible for the shoddy state of Verdun's defenses in 1916 and was removed from command in 1917.

9. Gary Sheffield, *The Somme* (London: Cassell, 2003), pp. 35–36.

10. An officer of the 56th Division quoted in Sheffield, *The Somme*, p. 37.

11. Sheffield and Bourne, *Douglas Haig*, p. 307.

12. Goya, *La Chair et L'Acier*, p. 262. Goya sees these shifts in more paradigmatic terms than I do, although I agree with the general tenor of his arguments.

13. *Les armées françaises dans la grande guerre*, pp. 24–27.

14. David French, "The Meaning of Attrition, 1914–1916," *English Historical Review* 103 (1988): 385–405.

15. See Robert T. Foley, *German Strategy and the Path to Verdun: Erich von Falkenhayn and the Development of Attrition, 1870–1916* (Cambridge: Cambridge University Press, 2005).

16. Although it is now more than 40 years old and has some flaws, Alistair Horne, *The Price of Glory: Verdun, 1916* (London: Penguin, 1962) remains a frequently cited source. It should be noted that the memorandum which Falkenhayn cited in his memoirs, and upon which Horne bases his estimates of German intentions, has never been found, leading some historians to conclude that Falkenhayn had intended to break through at Verdun and only invented his attrition rationale after that plan failed. Still, there is enough evidence from German actions to infer that Horne had the general picture more or less right.

17. French, "The Meaning of Attrition," pp. 390–391.

18. Wiest, *Haig*, pp. 42–43.

19. Haig took the report seriously, writing in his diary, "This clearly shows how regular and persistent is the pressure by the British." Sheffield and Bourne, *Douglas Haig*, p. 221.

20. David Zabecki, *The German 1918 Offensives: A Case Study in the Operational Level of War* (London: Routledge, 2006), p. 67.

21. Sheffield and Bourne, *Douglas Haig*, p. 265.

22. Holger Herwig, "The German Victories, 1917–1918" in *The Oxford Illustrated History of the First World War*, ed. Hew Strachan (Oxford: Oxford University Press, 1998), pp. 253–264, quotation at 254.

23. I have borrowed the image of incarceration from Smith, *Between Mutiny and Obedience*.

24. Quoted in Edward M. Coffman, *The War to End All Wars: The American Military Experience in World War I* (Lexington: University Press of Kentucky, 1968; 1998), p. 20.

25. Ibid., p. 55.

26. Quotation from ibid., p. 20. On the corruption, especially in the aviation industry, see Linda Robertson, *The Dream of Civilized Warfare: World War I Flying Aces and the American Imagination* (Minneapolis: University of Minnesota Press, 2003), chapter 2.

27. Coffman, *War to End All Wars*, p. 151.

28. Center of Military History, United States Army, *American Armies and Battlefields in Europe* (Washington: U. S. Government Printing Office, 1938), p. 17.

29. See Robert Bruce, *A Fraternity of Arms: America and France in the Great War* (Lawrence: University Press of Kansas, 2003). The Americans did get along very well with the Australians, who shared many of the same suspicions about the British. See Dale Blair, "Diggers and Doughboys: Australian and American Troop Interaction on the Western Front, 1918," *Journal of the Australian War Memorial* 35 (Dec. 2001). http://www.awm.gov.au/journal/j35/blair.htm

30. Quoted in Benwell, *History of the Yankee Division*, p. 40. The nickname "Dutchmen" for Germans comes from the German *Deutsch* and *Deutschland* and had a long history in the United States, as evidenced by the Pennsylvania "Dutch" community and baseball star Honus "the Flying Dutchman" Wagner, both German.

31. Pershing quoted in David Kennedy, *Over Here: The First World War and American Society* (Oxford: Oxford University Press, 1980), p. 173.

32. Benwell, *History of the Yankee Division*, p. 38.

33. James J. Cooke, *The Rainbow Division in the Great War, 1917–1919* (Westport, Conn.: Praeger, 1994), p. 93; Walter B. Wolf, *A Brief Story of the Rainbow Division* (New York: Rand, McNally, 1919).

34. Benwell, *History of the Yankee Division*, p. ix.

35. Joseph Dickman, *The Great Crusade: A Narrative of the Great War* (New York: D. Appleton, 1927), p. 38. Dickman was the 3rd Division's commander.

36. Benwell, *History of the Yankee Division*, p. 33.

37. Coffman, *War to End All Wars*, pp. 66–67.

38. Bach, *The Fourth Division*, p. 59.

39. Bullard quoted in Jennifer D. Keene, *The United States and the First World War* (London: Longman, 2000), p. 56. Emphasis in original.

3. GERMAN DESIGNS ON THE MARNE

1. In May, 1914, Italy made an offer to send two corps and three cavalry divisions to Alsace in the event of war. The kaiser and Chancellor Theobald von Bethmann Hollweg took the offer seriously as a token of Italian commitment to the Triple Alliance, but, notably, the German general staff did not include these troops in its mobilization planning. When the July crisis began, Italy concluded, correctly, that the Triple Alliance was defensive in nature and that, as the Italians saw Austria-Hungary as the aggressor, they were under no obligation to honor their alliance commitments. See Annika Mombauer, *Helmuth von Moltke and the Origins of the First World War* (Cambridge: Cambridge University Press, 2001), p. 169.

2. Quoted in Mombauer, *Helmuth von Moltke*, p. 145, emphases in original.

3. Quoted in Holger Herwig, "Disjointed Allies: Coalition Warfare in Berlin and Vienna, 1914," *Journal of Military History* 54 (July 1990): 265–280, quotation from p. 275.

4. Many German generals, including Alfred von Schlieffen, insisted on the need to invade Holland as well in order to create more strategic space for the outflanking of French defenses. Moltke disagreed, arguing that a neutral Holland could serve as a conduit through which Germany could trade with the outside world, an indication that he expected a long war. He also presumed that if Germany did not invade Holland, then Britain would not do so either. Moltke thus seems to have feared being outflanked by a British amphibious operation. The diplomatic problem for Germany, of course, was that Britain had treaty obligations to Belgium, not to Holland.

5. The two Morocco crises would have placed Britain and France on mobilization much more quickly because British and French security interests were directly threatened. The July crisis, by contrast, affected British and French leaders so indirectly that few bothered to cancel summer vacation plans.

6. Chickering, *Imperial Germany and the Great War*, p. 13.

7. Barbara Tuchman, *The Guns of August* (New York: Random House, 1962), p. 133.

8. Quoted in Herwig, *The First World War*, p. 75. See also Evelyn Blücher, *An English Wife in Berlin* (New York: E. P. Dutton, 1920).

9. The phrase belongs to Trevor Dupuy, *A Genius for War: The German Army and General Staff, 1807–1945* (Upper Saddle River, N.J.: Prentice-Hall, 1977).

10. Captain von Hentig quoted in Sheffield, *The Somme*, p. 155.

11. Jack Sheldon, "The Other Learning Curve," paper delivered at "The Somme: 90 Years On," School of History, University of Kent, Canterbury, United Kingdom, 18 July 2006. See also Sheldon's *The German Army on the Somme, 1914–1916* (London: Pen and Sword, 2005).

12. It is critical to note that the French took heavy casualties on the Somme as well, with most estimates putting French losses just over 200,000. See Sheffield, *The Somme*, pp. 151–152.

13. German casualty figures remain a hotly debated topic. For more, see James McRandle and James Quirk, "The Blood Test Revisited: A New Look at German Casualty Counts in World War I," *Journal of Military History* 70 (July 2006): 667–702. I am grateful to William Philpott for taking the time to discuss this issue with me. His own forthcoming book on the Somme will help to situate this battle as a contest between three armies.

14. Herwig, *The First World War*, pp. 332–333.

15. See Xu Guoqi, *China and the Great War: China's Pursuit of a New National Identity and Internationalization* (Cambridge: Cambridge University Press, 2005), chapter 4.

16. Herwig, *The First World War*, pp. 315 and 320. Hindenburg seems to have been closer to the kaiser's opinions, claiming, "I don't give a damn about America," and stating that America's impact on the war would be "minimal, in any case not decisive." Still, his support of great efforts to win the war in the spring of 1918 shows he may have had more concerns than he expressed in front of the kaiser and his own staff. Quotation from Herwig, *The First World War*, p. 315.

17. Hew Strachan, *European Armies and the Conduct of War* (London: Routledge, 1983), p. 99.

18. See Mario Morselli, *Caporetto 1917: Victory or Defeat?* (London: Frank Cass, 2001).

19. See Bruce Gudmundsson, *Storm Troop Tactics: Innovation in the German Army, 1914–1918* (Westport, Conn.: Praeger, 1995) and Martin Samuels, *Doctrine and Dogma: German and British Infantry Tactics in the First World War* (Westport, Conn.: Praeger, 1992).

20. Even if one accepts the argument that Haig expected a German attack further north in Flanders, it is still baffling to understand the granting of so much leave.

21. Ernst Jünger, *Storm of Steel*, trans. Michael Hoffman (London: Penguin, 2003), pp. 228–229, originally published in 1920.

22. Zabecki, *The German 1918 Offensives*, p. 85.

23. Quoted in Basil Henry Liddell Hart, *Foch: The Man of Orléans* (Boston: Little, Brown, 1932), p. 258.

24. To be sure, there were plenty of problems, but given the level of stress and the differences of nationality, the degree to which Haig, Pershing, Pétain, and Foch resolved differences amicably is notable. Pershing and Pétain become close friends. Haig noted in a letter to Lord Esher that the senior members of the British government "never thought that I and Foch would get on as well as we do." See Sheffield and Bourne, *Douglas Haig*, p. 428. Foch and Haig met 60 times between April and November 1918.

25. Zabecki, *The German 1918 Offensives*, p. 207.

26. Doughty, *Pyrrhic Victory*,pp. 449–450.

27. Zabecki, *The German 1918 Offensives*, p. 215.

28. Ibid., p. 222.

29. Mangin had achieved spectacular results at Verdun, but his units had taken enormous casualties at the Chemin des Dames, and General Robert Nivelle removed him from command. Mangin's blithe dismissal of the human costs of war ("Whatever you do, you lose a lot of men") had made him unpopular with politicians, but Foch admired his aggressive streak and his seemingly endless supply of energy.

30. Quoted in Doughty, *Pyrrhic Victory*, p. 455.

31. Coffman, *The War to End All Wars*, p. 213; Foch, *Memoirs*, p. 321.

32. There remains some controversy about German casualty figures. I have used figures from Strachan, *European Armies and the Conduct of War*, p. 146, and McRandle and Quirk, "The Blood Test Revisited."

33. Jünger, *Storm of Steel*, p. 243.

34. *The Two Battles of the Marne: The Stories of Marshal Joffre, General von Ludendorff, Marshal Foch, and Crown Prince Wilhelm* (New York: Cosmopolitan Books, 1927).

35. *Les armées françaises dans la grande guerre*, pp. 25–27.

36. Charles Mangin, *Comment Finit la Guerre* (Paris: Plon, 1920), p. 194. A separate GQG report concluded that by the end of June, the Germans had just 31 "fresh" divisions. See *Pourquoi l'Allemagne a Capitulé le 11 Novembre 1918: Étude Faite sur Documents du G. Q. G. Français* (Paris: État-Major des Armées, 1919).

37. "German Offensive, 1918: The Battles of the Aisne and Marne," German Order of Battle I-V-1918 to 4-VIII-1918, WO 153/308, National Archives, Kew Gardens.

38. Wilhelm, *My War Experiences*, p. 330.

39. *The Two Battles of the Marne*, pp. 219–220.

40. Coffman, *The War to End All Wars*, p. 222.

41. Sgt. Harry Lankert, quoted in J. Stuart Richards, ed. *Pennsylvania Voices of the Great War* (Jefferson, N.C.: McFarland, 2002), p. 83.

42. Jünger, *Storm of Steel*, p. 255. It should be noted that Jünger did not fight on the Marne.

43. Herwig, *The First World War*, pp. 395–396.

44. In many places, the Germans were advancing over territory they had devastated during their withdrawal to the Hindenburg Line. Thus the terrain was denuded of needed resources by their own hands.

45. Again I have chosen to use the Sanitats data from McRandle and Quirk, "The Blood Test Revisited," p. 683. These data argue for a reduction in German casualty estimates from those put forth by the United States War Department and Winston Churchill in his *World Crisis* (London: Macmillan, 1926).

46. Herwig, *The First World War*, p. 416.

47. James Edmonds, *Military Operations in France and Belgium, 1918* (London: Imperial War Museum, 1939), pp. 215–216.

48. Harry G. Proctor, *The Iron Division in the World War* (Philadelphia: John C. Winston Co., 1919), p. 53.

49. Francis Whiting Halsey, *The Literary Digest History of the World War*, vol. 5 (New York: Funk and Wagnalls, 1919), p. 224.

50. Jünger, *Storm of Steel*, p. 266.

4. THE PEACE OFFENSIVE

1. Liggett, *AEF*, p. 77.

2. See Belinda Davis, *Home Fires Burning: Food, Politics, and Everyday Life in Berlin* (Chapel Hill: University of North Carolina Press, 2000) and Keith Allen, "Sharing Scarcity: Bread Rationing and the First World War in Berlin, 1914–1923," *Journal of Social History* 32, no. 2 (1998): 371–393.

3. Terraine, *To Win a War*, p. 75.

4. Zabecki, *The German 1918 Offensives*, p. 316.

5. Haig diary entry for 28 June quoted in Sheffield and Bourne, *Douglas Haig*, p. 424.

6. In 1914 and 1915, Foch was commander of *Groupe d'armées du nord*, a joint French, British, and Belgian formation that fought the First Battle of Ypres and the Battle of the Yser in 1914. I have argued elsewhere that the experience was critical for Foch in learning how to manage multi-national coalitions, especially when the commanders technically under his authority were in fact senior to him in rank. See Neiberg, *Foch*, chapter 3.

7. Sheffield and Bourne, *Douglas Haig*, p. 424.

8. Marie Émile Fayolle, *Cahiers Secrets de la Grande Guerre* (Paris: Plon, 1964), p. 282.

9. *Les armées françaises dans la grande guerre*, p. 3.

10. *The Two Battles of the Marne*, p. 175.

11. Mangin, *Comment Finit La Guerre*, pp. 193–194.

12. Foch, *Memoirs*, chapter 7.

13. Foch once said of his opponent, "Je me demande si Ludendorff connaît son métier" (I wonder if Ludendorff knows his craft). General Sir Charles Grant, "Some Notes Made at Marshal Foch's Headquarters, August to November, 1918," Grant papers 3/2, p. 5, Liddell Hart Centre for Military Archives, King's College, London.

14. Quoted in James Harbord, *The American Army in France, 1917–1919* (Boston: Little, Brown, 1936), p. xiv.

15. Zabecki, *The German 1918 Offensives*, p. 27.

16. I am grateful to David Zabecki for his willingness to share his unparalleled insight and knowledge of the German source records on this subject.

17. Center of Military History, United States Army, "Annex to Aisne-Marne Operation, Disposition of German Armies for Marne Operations," June 14, 1918, in *The United States Army in the World War, 1917–1919*, vol. 5 (Washington: Government Printing Office, 1948), p. 663.

18. Wilhelm, *My War Experiences*, p. 327.

19. Zabecki, *The German 1918 Offensives*, p. 251.

20. Wilhelm, *My War Experiences*, pp. 330 and 328.

21. Erich von Ludendorff, *Ludendorff's Own Story* (New York: Harper and Bros., 1919), p. 306.

22. Wilhelm, *My War Experiences*, p. 330.

23. *The Two Battles of the Marne*, p. 221.

24. General Service Schools, *The German Offensive of July 15, 1918 (Marne Source Book)* (Ft. Leavenworth, Kans.: General Service Schools Press, 1923), document number 300, p. 385.

25. Ludendorff, *Ludendorff's Own Story*, p. 307.

26. For more on Wilhelm, see Isabel V. Hull, *The Entourage of Kaiser Wilhelm II, 1898–1918* (Cambridge: Cambridge University Press, 1982).

27. Wilhelm, *My War Experiences*, p. 332.

28. Ludendorff, *Ludendorff's Own Story*, p. 308.

29. Ibid., p. 309.

30. Liggett, *AEF*, p. 90.

31. Edmonds, *Military Operations*, pp. 221–223.

32. "Movement of Troops for Champagne-Marne Operation," 5 July 1918, in *The United States Army in the World War*, vol. 5, p. 3.

33. Fayolle, *Cahiers Secrets de la Grande Guerre*, p. 285.

34. *Being the Narrative of Battery A of the 101st Field Artillery [Regiment]* (Cambridge, Mass.: Brattle Press, 1919), pp. 114–117.

35. Bach, *The Fourth Division*, p. 63. The officers also returned to find that the holsters they had recently been issued were too small to hold their pistols.

36. Benwell, *History of the Yankee Division*, p. 91.

37. Harbord, *The American Army in France*, p. 306. Harbord was then a brigade commander in the 2nd Division. He assumed command of the division on July 15.

38. Foch, *Memoirs*, p. 352.

39. Fayolle, *Cahiers Secrets de la Grande Guerre*, pp. 285–286.

40. Quoted in Wolf, *A Brief Story of the Rainbow Division*, pp. 22–23. Gouraud had a rough start with the Rainbows, who were placed under his command. Gouraud's driver accidentally ran over the first member of the division he met. The incident did not permanently sour their relations, as Gouraud became the honorary president of the Rainbow Veterans Association and maintained close links with the group until his death in 1946.

41. Foch, *Memoirs*, p. 356.

42. Private Charles Sayler to his "folks," July 17, 1918, quoted in Richards, *Pennsylvania Voices of the Great War*, p. 74.

43. Pershing, *My Experiences in the World War*, pp. 145–151.

44. Sheffield and Bourne, *Douglas Haig*, p. 428.

45. Lt. Colonel L. M. Dyson to James Edmonds, 26 November 1933, Letters to Brig. Gen. Sir James Edmonds, CAB 45/126, National Archives, Kew Gardens, London.

46. Braithwaite to Edmonds, 13 September 1933.

47. War Diary of General Staff, 62nd (West Riding) Division, July 1918, WO 95/3070, National Archives, Kew Gardens, London; Everard Wyrall, *The History of the 62nd (West Riding) Division, 1914–1918* (London: John Lane, 1924), pp. 169–173.

48. Harbord, *Leaves from a War Diary*, pp. 314–319.

49. "Personal Diary of Lt. Robert Lindsay Mackay," p. 65, emphasis in original. Mackay noted that the confusion "shows up the staff in a very bad light," but the stresses under which the staffs operated must be appreciated.

50. *Narrative of Battery A*, p. 113.

5. TURNING THE TIDE OF THE WAR

1. The Germans converted all areas of France and Belgium under their control to German time; thus a German soldier's one o'clock in the morning would be midnight to a French soldier just across the trenches.

2. Quotations here and in following paragraph from General Service Schools, *The German Offensive of July 15, 1918*, document number 463, Kurt Hesse, "The Drama of the Marne 15 July 1918," pp. 668–670.

3. Rudolph Binding, *A Fatalist at War* trans. F. D. Morrow (London: Allen and Unwin, 1928), p. 233.

4. Proctor, *The Iron Division in the World War*, p. 55. The Iron Division was one the nicknames of the 28th U.S. Division, more commonly known as the Keystone Division.

5. Halsey, *The Literary Digest History of the World War*, p. 215.

6. Edmonds, *Military Operations*, p. 229; Wilhelm, *My War Experiences*, p. 333.

7. Sunrise on July 15, 1918 came at approximately 4:30 AM. All times in French time, unless otherwise noted.

8. Dickman, *The Great Crusade*, pp. 81–84. Dickman was the commander of the United States 3rd Division.

9. Liggett, *AEF*, pp. 103–104. The young assistant secretary of the navy, Franklin Roosevelt, was one of the first distinguished visitors to see the gun emplacement after the Americans captured it.

10. Proctor, *Iron Division*, p. 57.

11. Quoted in Halsey, *The Literary Digest History of the World War*, p. 241. All five of Roosevelt's children served the Allied cause. His daughter Ethel was a volunteer nurse in Paris; his son Kermit was an officer with the British Army in the Middle East, then an artillery officer with the Americans; son Archibald won the French Croix de Guerre; and son Theodore Roosevelt Jr. won the Distinguished Service Cross for his performance at Soissons and in the Meuse-Argonne. He later became the only American general to land with the first wave on D-Day, June 6, 1944, despite arthritis and a limp so bad he needed a cane to walk. He died in his sleep from a heart attack on July 12, 1944, and was posthumously awarded a medal of honor.

12. Elmer F. Straub, *A Sergeant's Diary in the World War* (Indianapolis: Indiana Historical Commission, 1922), p. 125.

13. Dale van Every, *The AEF in Battle* (New York: D. Appleton, 1928), pp. 96 and 113.

14. Halsey, *The Literary Digest History of the World War*, p. 225.

15. Van Every, *The AEF in Battle*, pp. 102–103.

16. Major J. Corbabon, quoted in Bruce, *A Fraternity of Arms*, p. 233.

17. The rumor that German soldiers were wearing Allied uniforms appeared in several memoirs and letters, but not in any official histories or intelligence reports. It thus seems to be more a product of fear and confusion than reality.

18. Chaffee, *The Egotistical Account of an Enjoyable War*, p. 41. Emphasis mine. His understanding of the first phase as the "defensive" shows that even enlisted men not privy to the deliberations at higher headquarters saw the battle as having two phases.

19. Edmonds, *Military Operations*, p. 229n2.

20. Binding, *A Fatalist at War*, p. 236.

21. Goya, *La Chair et L'Acier*, p. 247.

22. MacArthur, *Reminiscences*, p. 57.

23. James Harbord, quoted in Bruce, *A Fraternity of Arms*, p. 228.

24. See Goya, *La Chair et L'Acier*, pp. 376–377.

25. Dickman, *The Great Crusade*, p. 81.

26. Quoted in Bruce, *A Fraternity of Arms*, p. 230.

27. Quoted in Smythe, *Pershing*, p. 151.

28. Fayolle, *Cahiers Secrets de la Grande Guerre*, p. 288; Halsey, *The Literary Digest History of the World War*, p. 217.

29. Display at the museum of the Fort de la Pompelle, outside Rheims.

30. *Historique du 70e Régiment d'Infanterie* (Rennes: Imprimeries Oberthur, 1920), p. 7.

31. *Historique du 74e Régiment d'Infanterie, 1914–1918* (Lyon: Imprimerie L. Wolf, n.d.), p. 27.

32. Edmonds, *Military Operations*, p. 231.

33. General Service Schools, *The German Offensive of July 15, 1918*, document number 371, Diary of the 6th Grenadier Regiment, July 15, 1918, p. 516.

34. Quoted in Coffman, *The War to End All Wars*, p. 226.

35. An American staff exercise done after the war concluded that Butts had made the correct decision. See ibid., p. 225.

36. McAlexander was not in fact sleeping on duty, but spending the night at a forward command post, a leadership technique he often employed. That a colonel found sleeping at the front line would be presumed to be a slacker speaks volumes about the nature of senior leadership in trench warfare.

37. Van Every, *The AEF in Battle*, p. 111.

38. General Service Schools, *The German Offensive of July 15, 1918*, document number 462, Report of the 6th Grenadier Regiment [on the events of July 15], July 17, 1918, p. 662; also Kurt Hesse, "Drama of the Marne," p. 672.

39. Dickman, *The Great Crusade*, p. 115.

40. Fayolle, *Cahiers Secrets de la Grande Guerre*, p. 289.

41. Edmonds, *Military Operations*, p. 227.

42. Wilhelm, *My War Experiences*, pp. 333–334.

43. Binding, *A Fatalist at War*, pp. 234–236.

44. General Service Schools, *The German Offensive of July 15, 1918*, Kurt Hesse, "Drama of the Marne," p. 672.

45. Ibid.

46. Wilhelm, *My War Experiences*, p. 334.

47. Wolf, *A Brief Story of the Rainbow Division*, p. 28.

48. Erich von Ludendorff, *Ludendorff's Own Story* (New York: Harper and Bros., 1919), p. 310.

49. Wyrall, *The History of the 62nd (West Riding) Division*, p. 175.

50. Brewsher, *The History of the 51st (Highland) Division*, p. 328.

51. Godley to Wigram, 27 July 1918, p. 84.

52. Liggett, *AEF*, pp. 99–102.

53. Alexander Johnson, *The Aisne-Marne Offensive*, M.A. thesis, Georgetown University, 1929, Lauringer Library, Georgetown University, LAU Thesis 591; see also *La guerre racontée par nos généraux par Fayolle et Dubail* (Paris: Librairie Schwartz, 1921).

54. Foch, *Memoirs*, p. 359;

6. THE ALLIES STRIKE, JULY 18–21

1. Gleason, *A Soldier's Story*, p. 33.

2. Emerson G. Taylor, *New England in France, 1917–1919: A History of the Twenty-Sixth Division, USA* (Boston: Houghton-Mifflin, 1920), p. 171.

3. Van Every, *The AEF in Battle*, p. 117.

4. MacDermott, *An Enriching Life*, pp. 101–102.

5. Bach, *The Fourth Division*, p. 75.

6. Mark Ethan Grotelueschen, *The AEF Way of War: The American Army and Combat in World War I* (Cambridge: Cambridge University Press, 2007), p. 89.

7. "Report Concerning the French Attack of July 18, 1918," Headquarters of the

XIII (Royal Wurttemburg) Corps, August 6, 1918, quoted in Douglas Johnson and Rolfe Hillman, *Soissons, 1918* (College Station: Texas A and M Press, 1999), p. 18.

8. Van Every, *The AEF in Battle*, pp. 120–121.

9. Mangin quoted in Goya, *La Chair et L'Acier*, p. 398.

10. These figures and equivalent figures for the other French armies come from *Les armées françaises dans la grande guerre*, pp. 59–66.

11. Quoted in Johnson and Hillman, *Soissons*, p. 39.

12. *Les armées françaises dans la grande guerre*, pp. 23.

13. *Les armées françaises dans la grande guerre*, p. 52. According to Mangin, *Comment Finit la Guerre*, p. 195, only 321 of those tanks saw action on July 18.

14. "Attaques de la 48ème Division d'Infanterie les 18 et 19 Juillet 1918."

15. Proctor, *The Iron Division in the World War*, pp. 87–88.

16. *Cahiers Secrets de la Grande Guerre*, p. 289.

17. Isabel V. Hull, *Absolute Destruction: Military Culture and the Practices of War in Imperial Germany* (Ithaca: Cornell University Press, 2005), p. 303.

18. *Les armées françaises dans la grande guerre*, p. 50.

19. German Order of Battle for July 17, 1918 from United States Army Center of Military History, *The United States Army in the World War, 1917–1919* (Washington: Government Printing Office, 1948), vol. 5, p. 664.

20. *Les armées françaises dans la grande guerre*, p. 68.

21. Philip Gibbs, *Open Warfare: The Way to Victory* (London: William Heinemann, 1919), pp. 351 and 353.

22. "Glorious day! The dawn of the final victory": *Historique du 31me Régiment d'Infanterie Territoriale, 1914–1918* (Saint-Cloud: A. Felix, n.d.), p. 9.

23. *Les armées françaises dans la grande guerre*, p. 77.

24. *Being the Narrative of Battery A*, p. 124.

25. *Historique du 74e Régiment d'Infanterie*, p. 27.

26. Edith Wharton, from "A Backward Glance," in Jennifer Lee, ed., *Paris in Mind* (New York: Vintage, 2003), p. 11.

27. Halsey, *The Literary Digest History of the World War*, p. 237.

28. Van Every, *The AEF in Battle*, p. 123.

29. Frank B. Sibley, *With the Yankee Division in France* (Boston: Little, Brown, 1919), p. 211.

30. Quoted in Smythe, *Pershing*, p. 157.

31. Braithwaite to Edmonds, 13 September 1933.

32. "Attaques de la 48ème Division d'Infanterie les 18 et 19 Juillet 1918."

33. Chaffee, *The Egotistical Account of an Enjoyable War*, pp. 48–49.

34. *Historique du 31me Régiment d'Infanterie Territoriale, 1914–1918*, p. 9.

35. Mangin, *Comment Finit la Guerre*, p. 196.

36. Foch, *Memoirs*, p. 364.

37. Mangin, *Comment Finit la Guerre*, p. 198.

38. General Sir Alexander Godley to Lady Godley, 18 July 1918, in "First World War, France and Belgium, 1916–1918. Letters from General Sir Alexander Godley to Lady Godley," volume 2, Godley papers 4/2, Liddell Hart Centre for Military Archives, King's College, London.

39. Mangin, *Comment Finit la Guerre*, p. 196.

40. Liggett, *AEF*, p. 119.

41. William J. Astore and Dennis E. Showalter, *Hindenburg: Icon of German Militarism* (Dulles, Va.: Potomac Books, 2005), p. 66.

42. Ludendorff, *Ludendorff's Own Story*, p. 314.

43. General Service Schools, *The German Offensive of July 15, 1918*, document number 441, VII Army War Diary, 18 July 1918, pp. 611–612.

44. Binding, *A Fatalist at War*, p. 237.

45. Paul von Hindenburg, *Out of My Life*, vol. 2 (New York: Harper and Bros., 1920), p. 208.

46. Quoted in Harbord, *The American Army in France*, p. xiv.

47. Wilhelm, *My War Experiences*, pp. 336–338.

48. General Service Schools, *The German Offensive of July 15, 1918*, document number 456, 20 July Estimate of Divisions, pp. 649–650.

49. Edmonds, *Military Operations*, p. 242. Regrettably, not much information exists on the Italians except for the generally low impressions most Allied officers held of them. They were quickly relieved of their place in the line and transferred away.

50. Ibid., p. 248.

51. Grotelueschen, *The AEF Way of War*, p. 92n80.

52. Ibid., p. 97.

53. Ludendorff, *Ludendorff's Own Story*, p. 316.

54. Smythe, *Pershing*, p. 157. Presumably, Smythe's comment comes from Pershing's own impressions. Pershing had little respect for the Air Service. He had written in an earlier draft of his memoirs that "there was, perhaps, no branch of the service that gave us more trouble than aviation." He later deleted it in line with his policy of "not giving offense." Smythe, *Pershing*, p. 143.

55. *Historique du 4me Régiment de Zouaves, 1914–1918* (n.p.: Imp. Française, n.d.). http://batmarn2.club.fr/RZ-004.htm. Accessed on 6 June 2006.

56. Frederick Maurice, *The Last Four Months: How the War Was Won* (Boston: Little, Brown, 1919), p. 97; *Les armées françaises dans la grande guerre*, p. 85.

57. Dickman, *The Great Crusade,*p. 120.

58. *Les armées françaises dans la grande guerre*, p. 90.

59. *Being the Narrative of Battery A*, p. 127.

60. Godley to Wigram, 27 July 1918.

61. Wyrall, *The West Yorkshire Regiment in the War*, pp. 297–298.

62. Lt. I. R. S. Harrison, "Mainly About Myself from January 1917 to April 1919" (1925), Imperial War Museum, London, P323, p. 44.

63. War Diary of General Staff, 62nd (West Riding) Division. The 62nd's war diary notes that its rolling barrage preceded at the same rate as that of the 51st. The staffs of the two divisions were even housed together to facilitate liaison between them and corps headquarters.

64. War Diary of the 1/6th Battalion, Black Watch (Royal Highlanders), July 1918, National Archives, WO 95/2876, Kew Gardens, London.

65. Godley to Wigram, 27 July 1918.

66. Benwell, *History of the Yankee Division*, p. 104.

67. Gleason, *A Soldier's Story*, p. 34.

68. Sgt. Harry Lankert to his brother, 21 July 1918 in Richards , *Pennsylvania Voices of the Great War*, p. 84.

69. Dickman, *Great Crusade*, p. 122.

70. Fayolle, *Cahiers Secrets*, p. 290.

71. Taylor, *New England in France*, p. 187.

72. Sheffield and Bourne, *Douglas Haig*, p. 433.

73. Taylor, *New England in France*, p. 189.

7. THE BATTLE OF TARDENOIS, JULY 22–26

1. J. B. Milne, incomplete manuscript, Imperial War Museum, London, 87/51/1, p. 30.

2. Benwell, *History of the Yankee Division*, p. 129.

3. Eddie V. Rickenbacker, *Fighting the Flying Circus: The Greatest True Adventure to Come Out of World War I* (Garden City, N.Y.: Doubleday, 1965), p. 152.

4. Admiral Georg Alexander von Müller (chief of the naval cabinet), quoted in Bruce, *A Fraternity of Arms*, p. 247.

5. Wilhelm, *My War Experiences*, pp. 339–341.

6. Edmonds, *Military Operations*, pp. 260–261.

7. Tenth Army had just 225 of its tanks arrive on the battlefield as planned on July 18. Of these, the Germans put 102 out of action. On July 19, the Germans put 50 of 109 tanks out of action. Casualty rates among tank personnel approached 25%. See Johnson and Hillman, *Soissons*, p. 95.

8. Colonel A. R. Bain to James Edmonds, 14 October 1933, Letters to Brig. Gen. Sir James Edmonds, CAB 45/126, National Archives, Kew Gardens, London.

9. Straub, *A Sergeant's Diary*, p. 132.

10. Edmonds, *Military Operations*, p. 259.

11. *Historique du 36ème RAC [Régiment d'Artillerie de Campagne]* (n.p.: Chevillat et Roussillon, n. d.), p. 15.

12. Fayolle, *Cahiers Secrets de la Grande Guerre*, p. 290.

13. Sgt. John Duffy to his father, 24 July 1918, quoted in Richards, *Pennsylvania Voices of the Great War*, pp. 92–93.

14. Proctor, *The Iron Division in the World War*, p. 91.

15. Wyrall, *The West Yorkshire Regiment in the War, 1914–1918*, p. 300.

16. MacDermott, *An Enriching Life*, p. 103.

17. War Diary of 1/8 BTN Argyll and Seaforth Highlanders Headquarters, entries for 23 July.

18. *Historique du 53e—253e Régiment d'Artillerie de Campagne Pendant la Guerre 1914–1918* (n.p.: de Bussac, 1923), p. 40.

19. Braithwaite to Edmonds, 13 September 1933.

20. Major General C. W. Glynn to James Edmonds, no date, Letters to Brig. Gen. Sir James Edmonds, CAB 45/126, National Archives, Kew Gardens, London.

21. Dyson to Edmonds, 26 November 1933.

22. Major General C. R. Newman to James Edmonds, 9 September 1933, Letters to Brig. Gen. Sir James Edmonds, CAB 45/126, National Archives, Kew Gardens, London.

23. Godley to Wigram, 27 July 1918.

24. 7th (Fife) Battalion, The Black Watch (Royal Highlanders), Narrative of Operations South West of Reims from 20th to 31st July 1918, War Diary of 1/6th Battalion BLACK WATCH (Royal Highlanders) July 1918, WO 95/2876, National Archives, Kew Gardens, London, entry for July 20.

25. *Historique du 23ème Régiment d'Infanterie Coloniale* (Paris: Imp. Berger-Levrault, n. d.), p. 15.

26. *Historique du 74e Régiment d'Infanterie*, p. 28.

27. Wyrall, *The History of the 62nd (West Riding) Division*, pp. 194–195.

28. Milne, incomplete manuscript, 28.

29. Godley to Clive Wigram, 27 July 1918.

30. Wyrall, *The History of the 62nd (West Riding) Division*, p. 194.

31. Ibid., pp. 193 and 197.

32. Ibid., p. 202.

33. War Diary of General Staff, 62nd (West Riding) Division.

34. Stewart and Buchan, *The Fifteenth (Scottish) Division*, p. 232.

35. Marc Bloch, *Strange Defeat: A Statement of Evidence Written in 1940* (New York: Norton, 1968), p. 35.

36. Stewart and Buchan, *The Fifteenth (Scottish) Division*, pp. 232–236.

37. *Being the Narrative of Battery A*, p. 132.

38. Taylor, *New England in France*, pp. 192 and 195.

39. Proctor, *The Iron Division in the World War*, p. 91.

40. Sibley, *With the Yankee Division in France*, pp. 223–224.

41. Ibid., p. 221.

42. Dickman, *The Great Crusade*, p. 122.

43. Bach, *The Fourth Division*, pp. 89–90. For more scholarly treatments, see Bruce, *A Fraternity of Arms*, and Grotelueschen, *The AEF Way of War*.

44. Straub, *A Sergeant's Diary*, pp. 132–134. It is worth noting that few French or British letters and diaries pay sustained attention to these matters, probably because they had become so much less novel.

45. *Les armées françaises dans la grande guerre*, pp. 107–110.

46. Foch, *Memoirs*,. 370. The original French that Foch used is even more stirring than the translation by T. Bentley Mott in Foch's memoirs. It reads "Les armées alliées arrivent donc au tournant de la route: en plein bataille elles viennent de reprendre l'initiative des opérations. . . . Le moment est venu de quitter l'attitude générale défensive imposé par l'infériorité numérique et de passer à l'offensive." The original wording can be found in *Les armées françaises dans la grande guerre*, p. 112.

47. Godley to Lady Godley, p. 392. Interestingly, Haig wrote to Sir Henry Wilson that "nothing startling happened at the meeting at Foch's HQ today." As Wilson and Foch were close friends (and certainly closer to one another than either was to Haig), it is likely that Wilson already knew about the memorandum. Haig might thus have been telling Wilson that nothing startling happened *in addition to* the memorandum. Haig to Wilson, quoted in Sheffield and Bourne, *Douglas Haig*, p. 434.

48. Quoted in Coffman, *The War to End All Wars*, p. 263.

49. Pershing, *My Experiences in the World War*, p. 171.

50. Quoted in Coffman, *The War to End All Wars*, p. 263.

51. Ludendorff, *Ludendorff's Own Story*, p. 318.

52. Van Every, *The AEF in Battle*, pp. 147 and 152.

53. Herwig, *The First World War*, p. 419.

54. Godley to Clive Wigram, 27 July 1918.

55. Gleason, *A Soldier's Story*, p. 35.

8. THE FINAL PHASE, JULY 27–AUGUST 9

1. *Les armées françaises dans la grande guerre*, p. 121.

2. Halsey, *The Literary Digest History of the World War*, pp. 267 and 285.

3. Binding, *A Fatalist at War*, pp. 238–239.

4. *Les armées françaises dans la grande guerre*, p. 127.

5. Sheffield and Bourne, *Douglas Haig*, p. 435.

6. Fayolle diary entries for July 28, July 29, and July 30 in Fayolle, *Cahiers Secrets de la Grande Guerre*, pp. 291–292.

7. "German Offensive, 1918: The Battles of the Aisne and Marne."

8. Halsey, *The Literary Digest History of the World War*, p. 269.

9. Ibid., p. 286.

10. General Oskar von Hutier, quoted in Herwig, *The First World War*, p. 419.

11. Bach, *The Fourth Division*, p. 95.

12. Foch, *Memoirs*, p. 367.

13. *Les armées françaises dans la grande guerre*, p. 132.

14. Ibid., pp. 132 and 141; Fayolle, *Cahiers Secrets de la Grande Guerre*, p. 292.

15. See Smith, *Between Mutiny and Obedience*, and Bruce, *Pétain: Verdun to Vichy*.

16. Straub, *A Sergeant's Diary*, pp. 137–138.

17. Proctor, *The Iron Division in the World War*, pp. 131–132.

18. "Personal Diary of Lt. Robert Lindsay Mackay," p. 72.

19. *Les armées françaises dans la grande guerre*, pp. 122–127.

20. Wyrall, *The West Yorkshire Regiment in the War*, p. 304.

21. Wyrall, *The History of the 62nd (West Riding) Division*, pp. 206–207.

22. War Diary of General Staff, 62nd (West Riding) Division.

23. Fred A. Farrell, *The 51st (Highland) Division War Sketches* (Edinburgh: T. C. and E. C. Jack, 1920), p. 28.

24. Godley to Wigram, 27 July and 1 August 1918.

25. Stewart and Buchan, *The Fifteenth (Scottish) Division*, p. 240.

26. War Diary of 1/8 BTN Argyll and Seaforth Highlanders Headquarters, entries for 28 July.

27. Stewart and Buchan, *The Fifteenth (Scottish) Division*, p. 241n1.

28. Edmonds, *Military Operations*, pp. 275–277.

29. War Diary of 1/8 BTN Argyll and Seaforth Highlanders Headquarters, entries for 29 July.

30. Van Every, *The AEF in Battle*, p. 156.

31. Cooke, *The Rainbow Division*, p. 118.

32. Van Every, *The AEF in Battle*, p. 163.

33. Quoted in Cooke, *The Rainbow Division*, p. 126.

34. Van Every, *The AEF in Battle*, p. 167.

35. Coffman, *The War to End All Wars*, p. 255.

36. Quoted in Cooke, *The Rainbow Division*, p. 132.

37. *Les armées françaises dans la grande guerre*, p. 142.

38. Fayolle diary entry for August 2 in Fayolle, *Cahiers Secrets*, p. 292.

39. *Les armées françaises dans la grande guerre*, p. 144, annexes 440 and 456.

40. Straub, *A Sergeant's Diary*, pp. 144–146.

41. *Being the Narrative of Battery A*, p. 139.

42. Van Every, *The AEF in Battle*, p. 185.

43. Bach, *The Fourth Division*, pp. 121–122.

44. Van Every, *The AEF in Battle*, pp. 195 and 197.

45. Rickenbacker, *Fighting the Flying Circus*, p. 166.

46. Van Every, *The AEF in Battle*, p. 198.

47. *Historique du 11ème RACP [Régiment d'Artillerie de Campagne]* (Paris: L. Fournier, n.d.), p. 11.

48. *Historique du 42° Régiment d'Artillerie de Campagne du 31 juillet 1914 au 11 novembre 1918* (n. p.: Berger-Levrault, 1919), p. 95.

49. *Historique du 4ème Régiment de Zouaves* (Paris: Imp. Française, n. d.), section II, "Les rives de l'Aisne."

50. *History of the Seventy-Seventh Division*, p. 45.

51. Ibid., pp. 41 and 45.

CONCLUSION

1. Quoted in Smith, Audoin-Rouzeau, and Becker, *France and the Great War*, p. 150. On the other hand, after the Doullens agreement establishing the supreme command had been signed, Clemenceau turned to Foch and said, "Well, you've got it at last, your high command." Foch shot back, "It's a fine present you have made me; you give me a lost battle and tell me to win it." Quoted in Liddell Hart, *Foch*, p. 278.

2. Quoted in Maxime Weygand, *Foch* (Paris: Flammarion, 1947), p. 226.

3. *Les armées françaises dans la grande guerre*, pp. 160–163.

4. Binding, *A Fatalist at War*, pp. 240–242.

5. *The Two Battles of the Marne*, p. 224.

6. Hull, *Absolute Destruction*.

7. Foch, *Memoirs*, p. 463.

8. Bruce, *A Fraternity of Arms*; Doughty, *Pyrrhic Victory*; Goya, *La Chair et L'Acier*.

9. It may be worth noting that the only anti-French sentiment I found from British or American veterans of the Second Battle of the Marne came from a letter to James Edmonds from General Sir W. P. Braithwaite written in 1933, when postwar feelings undoubtedly influenced Braithwaite's recollections of the war years. See Braithwaite to Edmonds, 13 September 1933.

10. Winston Churchill, *The Gathering Storm* (London: Folio Society, 2000), p. 14.

11. Quoted in David Reynolds, *In Command of History: Churchill Fighting and Writing the Second World War* (New York: Random House, 2005), p. 165.

12. Douglas V. Johnson and Rolfe L. Hillman, *Soissons, 1918* (College Station: Texas A and M Press, 1999).

13. Mark Ethan Grotelueschen, *The AEF Way of War: The American Army and Combat in World War I* (Cambridge: Cambridge University Press, 2007).

BIBLIOGRAPHY

PRIMARY SOURCES

Bach, Christian. *The Fourth Division: Its Services and Achievements in the Great War.* N.p., 1920.

Being the Narrative of Battery A of the 101st Field Artillery [Regiment]. Cambridge, Mass.: Brattle Press, 1919.

Benwell, Harry A. *History of the Yankee Division.* Boston: Cornhill, 1919.

Binding, Rudolph. *A Fatalist at War,* trans. F. D. Morrow. London: Allen and Unwin, 1928.

Bloch, Marc. *Strange Defeat: A Statement of Evidence Written in 1940.* New York: Norton, 1968.

Blücher, Evelyn. *An English Wife in Berlin.* New York: E. P. Dutton, 1920.

Brewsher, F. W. *The History of the 51st (Highland) Division.* Edinburgh: William Blackwood, 1921.

Center of Military History, United States Army. *American Armies and Battlefields in Europe.* Washington: U.S. Government Printing Office, 1938.

———. *The United States Army in the World War, 1917–1919.* Washington: Government Printing Office, 1948.

Chaffee, Everitte St. John. *The Egotistical Account of an Enjoyable War.* N.p.: Adams, 1951.

Churchill, Winston. *The Gathering Storm.* London: Folio Society, 2000.

———. *World Crisis.* London: Macmillan, 1926.

Dickman, Joseph. *The Great Crusade: A Narrative of the Great War.* New York: D. Appleton, 1927.

Edmonds, James. *Military Operations in France and Belgium, 1918.* London: Imperial War Museum, 1939.

Farrell, Fred A. *The 51st (Highland) Division War Sketches.* Edinburgh: T. C. and E. C. Jack, 1920.

Fayolle, Marie Émile. *Cahiers Secrets de la Grande Guerre.* Paris: Plon, 1964.

Foch, Ferdinand. *The Memoirs of Marshal Foch.* Garden City, N.Y.: Doubleday, 1931.

Foot, Richard. "Once a Gunner." 1964. Imperial War Museum, London.

General Service Schools. *The German Offensive of July 15, 1918 (Marne Source Book).* Ft. Leavenworth, Kans.: General Service Schools Press, 1923.

"German Offensive, 1918: The Battles of the Aisne and Marne." German Order of
    Battle I-V-1918 to 4-VIII-1918. National Archives, Kew Gardens.
Gibbs, Philip. *Open Warfare: The Way to Victory*. London: William Heinemann, 1919.
Gleason, Joseph J. *A Soldier's Story: A Daily Account of World War I, January, 1918
    to March, 1919 by Sergeant Joseph J. Gleason*. Ed. Mark Gleason. Oakmont,
    Pa.: Privately published, 1999. (Located at the University of Pittsburgh Hillman
    Library Special Collections section, D640.G625.)
Godley Papers. Liddell Hart Centre for Military Archives. King's College, London
Grant papers. Liddell Hart Centre for Military Archives. King's College, London.
Halsey, Francis Whiting. *The Literary Digest History of the World War*. Vol. 5. New York:
    Funk and Wagnalls, 1919.
Hamilton, I. R. S.. "Mainly about Myself from January, 1917 to April, 1919." 1925.
    Imperial War Museum, London.
Harbord, James. *Leaves from a War Diary*. New York: Dodd, Mead, 1925.
———. *The American Army in France, 1917–1919*. Boston: Little, Brown, 1936.
Hindenburg, Paul von. *Out of My Life*. Vol. 2. New York: Harper and Brothers, 1920.
History of the Seventy-Seventh Division, August 25th, 1917 to November 11, 1918. New
    York: Wynkoop Hallenbeck Crawford, 1919.
Hughes, Jesse Marion. Oral history. University of Southern Mississippi Oral History
    Program. McCain Library and Archives.
Jünger, Ernst. *Storm of Steel*. Trans. Michael Hoffman. London: Penguin, 2003.
La guerre racontée par nos généraux par Fayolle et Dubail. Paris: Librairie Schwartz,
    1921.
Les armées françaises dans la grande guerre. Tome 8. Vol. 1. Paris: Imprimerie nationale,
    1922–1937.
Letters to Brig. Gen. Sir James Edmonds. National Archives, Kew Gardens.
Liggett, Hunter. *AEF: Ten Years Ago in France*. New York: Dodd, Mead, 1928.
Ludendorff, Erich. *Ludendorff's Own Story*. New York: Harper and Bros., 1919.
MacArthur, Douglas. *Reminiscences*. New York: McGraw-Hill, 1964.
MacDermott, John Clarke. *An Enriching Life*. Privately published, 1979. (Located at
    Liddell Hart Centre for Military Archives, King's College, London.)
Mackay, Robert Lindsay. Personal Diary. Imperial War Museum, London.
Mangin, Charles. *Comment Finit la Guerre*. Paris: Plon, 1920.
Manning, Frederic. *Her Privates We*. London: Hogarth, 1986.
Maurice, Frederick. *The Last Four Months: How the War Was Won*. Boston: Little,
    Brown, 1919.
Michelin Company, Ltd. *Illustrated Michelin Guides to the Battle-fields (1914–1918):
    The Battlefields of the Marne (1914)*. Easingwold, York: G. H. Smith, 1919.
Milne, J. B. Incomplete manuscript. Imperial War Museum.
Pershing, John. *My Experiences in the World War*. Vol. 2. New York: Frederick Stokes,
    1931.
*Pourquoi l'Allemagne a Capitulé le 11 Novembre 1918: Étude Faite sur Documents du
    G. Q. G. Français*. Paris: État-Major des Armées, 1919.
Proctor, Harry G. *The Iron Division in the World War*. Philadelphia: John C. Winston,
    1919.
Rickenbacker, Eddie V. *Fighting the Flying Circus: The Greatest True Adventure to
    Come Out of World War I*. Garden City, N.Y.: Doubleday, 1965.
Shakespear, John. *The Thirty-Fourth Division, 1915–1919*. London: Witherby, 1921.
Sibley, Frank B. *With the Yankee Division in France*. Boston: Little, Brown, 1919.

"Situation of Allied and Enemy Forces 10/VII - 6/VIII." National Archives, Kew Gardens.

Stewart, J., and John Buchan. *The Fifteenth (Scottish) Division.* Edinburgh: William Blackwood and Sons, 1926.

Straub, Elmer F. *A Sergeant's Diary in the World War.* Indianapolis: Indiana Historical Commission, 1922.

Taylor, Emerson G. *New England in France, 1917–1919: A History of the Twenty-Sixth Division, USA.* Boston: Houghton-Mifflin, 1920.

The Two Battles of the Marne: The Stories of Marshal Joffre, General von Ludendorff, Marshal Foch, and Crown Prince Wilhelm. New York: Cosmopolitan Books, 1927.

Van Every, Dale. *The AEF in Battle.* New York: D. Appleton, 1928.

War Diary of 1/6th Battalion Black Watch (Royal Highlanders), July 1918. National Archives, Kew Gardens.

War Diary of 1/8th Battalion Argyl and Sutherland Highlanders, March 1918–November 1919. National Archives, Kew Gardens.

War Diary of General Staff, 62nd (West Riding) Division, July 1918. National Archives, Kew Gardens.

Wilhelm, Crown Prince of Germany. *My War Experiences.* New York: Robert McBride, 1923.

Wolf, Walter B. *A Brief Story of the Rainbow Division.* New York: Rand, McNally, 1919.

Wyrall, Everard. *The History of the 62nd (West Riding) Division, 1914–1918.* London: John Lane, 1924.

———. *The West Yorkshire Regiment in the War, 1914–1918.* Vol. 2. London: John Lane, n.d.

UNPUBLISHED SOURCES

French Unit Histories, accessible through http://batmarn2.club.fr.

"Attaques de la 48ème Division d'Infanterie les 18 et 19 Juillet 1918, Violane, Villers-Helon."

Historique du 4me Régiment de Zouaves, 1914–1918. N.p.: Imp. Française, n.d.

Historique du 11ème RACP [Régiment d'Artillerie de Campagne]. Paris: L. Fournier, n.d.

Historique du 23ème Régiment d'Infanterie Coloniale. Paris: Imp. Berger-Levrault, n.d.

Historique du 31me Régiment d'Infanterie Territoriale, 1914–1918. Saint-Cloud: A. Felix, n.d.

Historique du 36ème RAC [Régiment d'Artillerie de Campagne]. N.p.: Chevillat et Roussillon, n.d.

Historique du 42° Régiment d'Artillerie de Campagne du 31 juillet 1914 au 11 novembre 1918. N.p.: Berger-Levrault, 1919.

Historique du 53e—253e Régiment d'Artillerie de Campagne Pendant la Guerre 1914–1918. N.p.: de Bussac, 1923.

Historique du 70e Régiment d'Infanterie. Rennes: Imprimeries Oberthur, 1920.

Historique du 74me Régiment d'Infanterie, 1914–1918. N.p.: Imprimerie L. Wolf, n.d.

Le Six-Six à la Guerre, 1914–1918. N.p.: Barrot et Gallon, 1919.

United States Army Heritage and Education Center, Carlisle, Pennsylvania.

Allen J. Stevens Collection.
Clarence Anderson Collection.
Francis Contino Collection.
Robert H. Peck Papers.
Roy Coles Collection.
Veteran's Interviews, 26th Division.
Veteran's Interviews, 28th Division.

SECONDARY SOURCES

14–18: Mourir pour la Patrie, Paris: Editions du Seuil, 1992
Allen, Keith. "Sharing Scarcity: Bread Rationing and the First World War in Berlin, 1914–1923." *Journal of Social History* 32, no. 2, 1998.
Astore, William J., and Dennis E. Showalter. *Hindenburg: Icon of German Militarism.* Dulles, Va.: Potomac Books, 2005.
Audoin-Rouzeau, Stéphane, and Annette Becker. *14–18: Retrouver la Guerre.* Paris: Editions Gallimard, 2000.
Blond, Georges. *The Marne: The Battle That Saved Paris and Changed the Course of the First World War.* London: Prion, 2002.
Bruce, Robert. *A Fraternity of Arms: America and France in the Great War.* Lawrence: University Press of Kansas, 2003.
———. *Pétain: Verdun to Vichy.* Dulles, Va.: Potomac Books, 2007.
Chickering, Roger. *Imperial Germany and the Great War, 1914–1918.* 2nd ed. Cambridge: Cambridge University Press, 2005.
Chickering, Roger, and Stig Förster, eds. *Great War, Total War: Combat and Mobilization on the Western Front, 1914–1918.* Cambridge: Cambridge University Press, 2006.
Coffman, Edward M. *The War to End All Wars: The American Military Experience in World War I.* Lexington: University Press of Kentucky, 1968; 1998.
Cooke, James J. *The Rainbow Division in the Great War, 1917–1919.* Westport, Conn.: Praeger, 1994.
Cru, Jean-Norton. *War Books.* San Diego: San Diego State University Press, 1976.
Davis, Belinda. *Home Fires Burning: Food, Politics, and Everyday Life in Berlin.* Chapel Hill: University of North Carolina Press, 2000.
Doughty, Robert. *Pyrrhic Victory: French Strategy and Operations in the Great War.* Cambridge, Mass.: Harvard University Press, 2005.
Foley, Robert T. *German Strategy and the Path to Verdun: Erich von Falkenhayn and the Development of Attrition, 1870–1916.* Cambridge: Cambridge University Press, 2005.
French, David. "The Meaning of Attrition, 1914–1916." *English Historical Review* 103, 1988.
Gatrell, Peter. *Russia's First World War: A Social and Economic History.* London: Longman, 2005.
Goya, Michel. *La Chair et L'Acier: L'invention de la Guerre Moderne, 1914–1918.* Paris: Tallandier, 2004.
Greenwood, Paul. *The Second Battle of the Marne, 1918.* Shrewsbury : Airlife Books, 1998.

Grotelueschen, Mark Ethan. *The AEF Way of War: The American Army and Combat in World War I.* Cambridge: Cambridge University Press, 2007.

Gudmundsson, Bruce. *Storm Troop Tactics: Innovation in the German Army, 1914–1918.* Westport, Conn.: Praeger, 1995.

Herwig, Holger. "Disjointed Allies: Coalition Warfare in Berlin and Vienna, 1914." *Journal of Military History* 54 (July 1990): 265–280.

———. *The First World War: Germany and Austria-Hungary.* London: Edward Arnold, 1997.

———. "The German Victories, 1917–1918." In *The Oxford Illustrated History of the First World War,* ed. Hew Strachan. Oxford: Oxford University Press, 1998.

Hull, Isabel V. *Absolute Destruction: Military Culture and the Practices of War in Imperial Germany.* Ithaca: Cornell University Press, 2005.

———. *The Entourage of Kaiser Wilhelm II, 1898–1918.* Cambridge: Cambridge University Press, 1982.

Johnson, Alexander. *The Aisne-Marne Offensive.* M.A. thesis, Georgetown University, 1929. Lauringer Library, Georgetown University, LAU Thesis 591.

Johnson, Douglas, and Rolfe Hillman. *Soissons, 1918.* College Station: Texas A&M Press, 1999.

Keene, Jennifer D. *The United States and the First World War.* London: Longman, 2000.

Kennedy, David. *Over Here: The First World War and American Society.* Oxford: Oxford University Press, 1980.

Liddell Hart, Basil Henry. *Foch: The Man of Orléans.* Boston: Little, Brown, 1932.

McRandle, James, and James Quirk. "The Blood Test Revisited: A New Look at German Casualty Counts in World War I." *Journal of Military History* 70 (July 2006).

Middlebrook, Martin. *The Kaiser's Battle.* London: Allen Lane, 1978.

Miquel, Pierre. *Les Poilus: La France Sacrifiée.* Paris: Plon, 2000.

Mombauer, Annika. *Helmuth von Moltke and the Origins of the First World War.* Cambridge: Cambridge University Press, 2001.

Neiberg, Michael S. *Fighting the Great War: A Global History.* Cambridge, Mass.: Harvard University Press, 2005.

———. *Foch : Supreme Allied Commander in the Great War.* Dulles, Va.: Potomac Books, 2003.

Paschall, Rod *The Defeat of Imperial Germany.* Chapel Hill: Algonquin Books of Chapel Hill, 1989.

Porch, Douglas. *The March to the Marne: The French Army 1871–1914.* Cambridge: Cambridge University Press, 1981.

Reynolds, David. *In Command of History: Churchill Fighting and Writing the Second World War.* New York: Random House, 2005.

Richards, J. Stuart, ed. *Pennsylvania Voices of the Great War.* Jefferson, N.C.: McFarland, 2002.

Samuels, Martin. *Doctrine and Dogma: German and British Infantry Tactics in the First World War.* Westport, Conn.: Praeger, 1992.

Sheffield, Gary. *Leadership in the Trenches: Officer-Man Relations, Morale, and Discipline in the British Army in the Era of the First World War.* New York: St. Martin's, 2000.

———. *The Somme.* London: Cassell, 2003.

Sheffield, Gary, and John Bourne, eds. *Douglas Haig: War Diaries and Letters, 1914–1918.* London: Weidenfeld and Nicolson, 2005.

Showalter, Dennis. *Tannenberg: Clash of Empires*. Rev. ed. Dulles, Va.: Potomac Books, 2003.

Simkins, Peter. "The Four Armies, 1914–1918." In *The Oxford Illustrated History of the British Army*, ed. David Chandler and Ian Beckett. Oxford: Oxford University Press, 1994.

———. *Kitchener's Army: The Raising of the New Armies, 1914–1916*. Manchester: Manchester University Press, 1988.

Smith, Leonard V. *Between Mutiny and Obedience: The Case of the French Fifth Infantry Division during World War I*. Princeton: Princeton University Press, 1994.

Smith, Leonard V., Stéphane Audoin-Rouzeau, and Annette Becker. *France and the Great War*. Cambridge: Cambridge University Press, 2003.

Smythe, Donald. *Pershing: General of the Armies*. Bloomington: Indiana University Press, 1986.

Strachan, Hew. *European Armies and the Conduct of War*. London: Routledge, 1983.

Stevenson, David. *Cataclysm: The First World War as Political Tragedy*. New York: Basic Books, 2004.

Terraine, John. *To Win A War: 1918, the Year of Victory*. London: Cassell, 2003.

Travers, Tim. *How the War Was Won*. London: Routledge, 1992.

Tuchman, Barbara. *The Guns of August*. New York: Random House, 1962.

Weygand, Maxime. *Foch*. Paris: Flammarion, 1947.

Wiest, Andrew. *Haig: Evolution of a Commander*. Dulles, Va.: Potomac Books, 2005.

Zabecki, David. *The German 1918 Offensives: A Case Study in the Operational Level of War*. London: Routledge, 2006.

INDEX

MICHAEL S. NEIBERG is Professor of History at the University of Southern Mississippi. He is author of *Fighting the Great War: A Global History*; *Warfare and Society in Europe, 1898–Present*; *Foch: Supreme Allied Commander in the Great War*; and other books.

*The story of the battle that stopped the final
German advance on Paris during World War I*

"There is very little on the French in the July offensive in any language:
how they fought, what they had learned, or not learned, from the past
four years. This is an original contribution. I'm only sorry I didn't get
the idea first."
—Dennis Showalter, author of *Tannenberg: Clash of Empires, 1914*

INDIANA
University Press
Bloomington & Indianapolis

http://iupress.indiana.edu
1-800-842-6796

ISBN 978-0-253-35146-3

52795

9 780253 351463

www.ingramcontent.com/pod-product-compliance
Ingram Content Group UK Ltd.
Pitfield, Milton Keynes, MK11 3LW, UK
UKHW030606220125
453889UK00005B/131